FRIGHTMARES

FRIGHTMARES
A HISTORY OF BRITISH HORROR CINEMA
BY
IAN COOPER

ACKNOWLEDGEMENTS

I'd like to thank John Atkinson at Auteur for saying yes to this project (appropriately enough on a Halloween). His suggestions, advice and patience are very much appreciated. Without him, this book wouldn't have happened. I also want to thank Garry Johnson and Gav Whitaker, aka Gav Crimson, who provided me with some useful material. I'm grateful to everybody who helped me out with ideas and thoughts, either in (ahem) real life or through social media. I do owe a particular debt to the following: Brecht Andersch, Dan Berlinka, Scott Bradley, Robert Chandler, Hugh Kenneth David, Jackie Downs, J. Marie Gregoire, Jeanie Laub, Neil Mitchell, Joseph Marr and the late Dan Tunstall.

First published in 2016 by
Auteur
24 Hartwell Crescent, Leighton Buzzard LU7 1NP
www.auteur.co.uk

Copyright © Auteur Publishing 2015
Designed and set by Nikki Hamlett at Cassels Design
Printed and bound in the UK
Cover: *The Abominable Dr Phibes* (1971) © American International Pictures, courtesy Stephen Jones (www.monstersfromhell.co.uk)

British Library Cataloguing-in-Publication Data
A catalogue record for this book is available from the British Library

ISBN: paperback 978-0-9930717-3-7
ISBN: ebook 978-0-9930717-4-4

CONTENTS

INTRODUCTION

London is a city which has never been slow to exploit its violent and lurid history. There are no longer severed heads mounted on London Bridge or public executions at Tyburn but the capital city retains its dark glamour. One can visit the Chamber of Horrors at Madame Tussaud's wax museum off Baker Street and encounter infamous killers such as Dr. Crippen (played on screen by Donald Pleasence) and John Christie (Richard Attenborough). There are also facsimilies of letters purportedly from Jack the Ripper on display, written (of course) in red ink. In the London Dungeon, as well as interactive exhibits illustrating torture and bubonic plague, the Jack the Ripper experience offers an animated restaging of one of Saucy Jack's crimes. Until the attraction was extensively overhauled, there were graphic autopsy photos of mutilated women on display. Want more Jack? You can also take a Ripper Tour along the back alleys of Whitechapel, passing close to The Blind Beggar pub on Whitechapel Road where the gangster Ronnie Kray shot George Cornell through the eye. (Rumour has it the bullet passed through the unfortunate Cornell's head and hit the jukebox, which started playing 'The Sun Ain't Gonna Shine Anymore' by The Walker Brothers.) Whitechapel Road is also the location of the London Hospital where John Merrick, The Elephant Man who inspired the gothic David Lynch film, lived for the last four years of his life and it was also where an enterprising waxwork show depicting the Ripper murders was set up in 1888, unable even to wait until the murder cycle had finished before capitalising on it. In Bram Stoker's novel *Dracula* (1897), one of the Count's London addresses is in Whitechapel. The Ripper walking tours – they've proved so popular there are a number of competing firms providing them – traditionally end in The Ten Bells pub, which contains various items of Ripperabilia, including a handsome, wall-mounted Victim Board. Indeed, from 1976 until 1988 the pub was actually called The Jack the Ripper, until protests by feminist groups led to it reverting to The Ten Bells.

Across town in Kensington, one can go to see Hitchcock's old house, marked with a blue plaque. From there it's just a short walk to The Goat tavern, where John George Haigh, the acid bath killer, met a wealthy fairground owner who he would go on to batter to death before drinking a cup of his blood. Until a few years ago, Haigh was name-checked on a plaque inside the pub. Upon his arrest, he was keen to exploit his new-found notoriety and became an enthusiastic participant in the ghoulish fascination his crimes aroused. He played the role of the urbane English murderer, always appearing impeccably dressed and referring to his arrest as 'this little pickle'. It's surely a measure of how skillfully Haigh played the archetypal English cad that when he was immortalised on film it wasn't by the sinister likes of Pleasence or Attenborough but by the comic actor Martin Clunes (in the TV movie *A is for Acid* [2002]). Haigh's legal defence was paid for by the *News of the World*, in return for the exclusive rights to his story. Sentenced to death for six murders, he bequeathed his best suit to Madame Tussaud's. His likeness can still be seen there, alongside that of Dennis Nilsen, who killed 15 young men between 1978 and

1983.[1] Nilsen picked up one of his victims in Piccadilly Circus, a one-time hangout for rent boys and close to another of Count Dracula's houses. It's in Piccadilly where the Count achieves his desire:

> ...to go through the crowded streets of your mighty London, to be in the midst of the whirl and rush of humanity, to share its life, its change, its death and all that makes it what it is. (Stoker 1897: 31)

Nilsen picked up most of his victims in the Golden Lion pub on Dean Street in Soho, 5 minutes walk from Piccadilly Circus. Soho, of course, has long been associated with the film industry and its seedy sibling, the porn business. The Golden Lion was the local of US grindhouse auteur Andy Milligan during his London sojourn in the early 1970s, when he came up with the likes of *The Bloodthirsty Butchers* (1970) and *The Rats Are Coming, The Werewolves Are Here* (1972). Further up Dean Street, the actor Charles Laughton used to live in a flat – in what had been the house of Karl Marx – along with his wife, Elsa Lanchester, who played the twin roles of Mary Shelley and the shock-haired, hissing monster's mate in *Bride of Frankenstein* (1935).

On Wardour Street, the imposing art deco building standing at 113–117 is Hammer House, formerly the head office for the best-known makers of British horror, and if you walk towards Oxford Street, you'll end up in Soho Square, the location of the offices of the British Board of Film Classification (BBFC). Jon Finch makes a telephone call from the square in Hitchcock's *Frenzy* (1972). Murder, sex and film are all brought together in Michael Powell's once-loathed, now-celebrated film *Peeping Tom*. It's on the fringes of Soho that we first meet the sympathetic cameraman/killer Mark Lewis as he picks up a victim in Newman Passage, filming her as he does so. Powell shot some of the film in the suburb of Cricklewood, once the location of a film studio and just around the corner from the flat in Melrose Avenue where Nilsen killed a dozen of his victims before dismembering them and boiling, burning or burying them under the floorboards in his living room…

BOUND FOR THE LOST CONTINENT

Until very recently, British horror cinema has been ignored and maligned, hidden away like the eponymous feral brother in the *The Beast in the Cellar* (1970). Even when it was celebrated, neglect was not far behind: David Pirie's seminal study *A Heritage of Horror* (1973) was out of print for decades. What studies there were, even those which were avowedly encyclopaedic, have concentrated largely on the output of Hammer, the best-known producers of British horror. But recent years have seen a number of books of this once-despised tradition (see Boot 1996; Rigby 2000; Chibnall and Petley 2002) as well as a long overdue update of the Pirie book. The extremely influential central thesis of the latter is still relevant:

It certainly seems to be arguable on commercial, historical and artistic grounds that the horror genre, as it has been developed in this country by Hammer and its rivals, remains the only staple cinematic myth which Britain can properly claim its own, and which relates to it in the same way as the western relates to America. (2007 [1973]: xv)

Julian Petley's 1986 essay, 'The Lost Continent' (which takes its title and central metaphor from one of Hammer's wackier efffforts) reinforces Pirie's argument, describing a neglected tradition of fantastic, horrific and sensational cinema which formed:

An other, repressed side of British cinema, a dark disdained thread weaving the length and breadth of that cinema, crossing authorial and generic boundaries, sometimes almost entirely invisible, sometimes erupting explosively, always received critically with fear and disapproval. (1986: 98)

This refusal to acknowledge this 'other, repressed side' is compounded by the dominance of certain forms of cinema which represent the 'real', the everyday, the naturalistic. For Petley, this:

Vaunting and valorising of certain British films on account of their 'realism' entails, as its corollary… the dismissal and denigration of those films deemed un- or non-realist. (ibid.)

This tendency to reject the kind of cinema which dwells in this Lost Continent, when combined with a very British kind of island mentality, has also led to the horrific and the sensational being not just sidelined but actively suppressed. It's not for nothing that Mark Kermode has written of the 'hundred-year terror' that the British Board of Film Classification (nee Censors) has visited upon the horror genre (Kermode 2002: 22). Given this deep-seated and abiding suspicion of the popular and the fantastic, it comes as no surprise that both Pirie and Petley seek to locate Hammer et al in an illustrious literary tradition. For the former, the fact that so many British horror films 'are derived… from literary sources' (2007: xv) is highly significant:

The literary basis of the films is so striking that I make no apology for the literary orientation of this book; the film medium is not an extension of literature (or of anything else) but in this instance literary comparison becomes not only illuminating but essential. (ibid.)

Petley, meanwhile, when observing the lengthy period it took for the genre to establish itself in the medium of film draws on that same literary tradition, noting how:

For the country which produced Mary Shelley, Lord Byron, Bram Stoker, Anne Radcliffe, Charles Maturin, Matthew Lewis, M.R. James, Algernon Blackwood, William Hope Hodgson and William Beckford, Britain was peculiarly slow in developing the horror film and the whole area of fantasy cinema. (1986: 113)

3

But the likes of Radcliffe and Byron are only part of the story, albeit perhaps the most palatable part, the part most likely to convince the unconverted of the merits of the genre. The truth is that British horror cinema is a curious form spawned by twin, seemingly-incompatible traditions: a celebrated literary history exemplified in the works of Mary Shelley, Bram Stoker and Robert Louis Stevenson and an abiding lurid fascination with the dark side of life as seen in end-of-the-pier Chamber of Horrors attractions, murder melodramas, Penny Dreadfuls, Jack the Ripper tours and sensational tabloid newspaper accounts of infamous murders. As the artist Walter Sickert put it in 1935, 'It is said that we are a great literary nation but we really don't care about literature, we like films and we like a good murder' (in Tickner 2012). The horror film reveals as much, if not more, about the British national psyche as the heritage film or the social realist drama. Indeed, as Jean-Paul Török wrote at the height of the horror boom in the early 1960s:

> There is a great deal of talk about Free Cinema. But through its power of suggestion, its frenetic pace, its invitation to travel to the world of dark and wondrous things and imaginary eroticism, is not English horror cinema the real Free Cinema? (2002 [1961]: 71)

While the literary antecedents are well-documented, the enduring fascination with the morbid and macabre in what can only be termed low-culture is also an important influence which merits some consideration. The British horror film has (appropriately enough) a dark(er) side, a fascination with the seamy, the sensational and the sometimes staggeringly tasteless. It is a tradition which has indelibly marked the genre just as much as the carny, the freak show and the comic book helped shape the American horror film. The horror genre has been the site of numerous spectacular collisions between respectable cultural traditions and marginalised pulp. It's where the theatrical knight Sir Ralph Richardson can play the Cryptkeeper in an EC comic adaptation, The Bible and Shakespeare can inspire a string of flamboyantly gruesome murders and genre veteran Roman Polanski can mount a blood-soaked Macbeth financed by Playboy. Both traditions are embodied in Hitchcock, the vulgar showman fond of tabloid murder stories, practical jokes and sleaze and the modernist innovator behind some of the most acclaimed films ever made. More than any other genre, the British horror film is the site where high- and low-culture converge.

This book is not an encylopaedic guide but rather an examination of the most important strands in home-grown horror. I want to consider those oft-sidelined low-culture roots of the genre and the long-running fascination with the macabre of which horror films are merely the most recent manifestation of a tradition which includes murder sightseeing and Penny Bloods, true crime melodrama and even ornamental pottery inspired by infamous killings. As far as the content goes, I'm keen to reclaim Hitchcock for the British horror tradition, which is where at least a proportion of his output belongs. There's a slant towards the films Hammer produced in its latter years, 1970-5, in part because of my feeling that they have been critically sidelined in favour of those from the company's early and 'mature' periods. For much the same reason, I'm keen to highlight the frequently overlooked work of Tod Slaughter, Robert Hartford-Davis and Jose Larraz.

I want to consider the sheer range of the home-grown horror film, from costume gothics to starry literary adaptations, art films to slasher movies, black comedies to outright parodies. It's a tradition that encompasses not only British but American and European talent and which involves celebrated auteurs such as Hitchcock and Polanski, as well as a series of opportunistic, often-unashamed hacks (indeed, Pete Walker manages to be in both categories at the same time, hailed as 'the greatest British exploitation film-maker' by Steve Chibnall [1998] while screenwriter David McGillivray has described him 'as having the sensibilities of a used-car salesman'[in Hunt 1998: 153]). It's also a tradition which veers wildly from innovative art cinema to bargain basement rip-offs, icily restrained auteur works to amateurish bloodbaths. To focus on the prestigious likes of *Dead of Night* (1945) and *Peeping Tom* (1960) while ignoring the dubious pleasures of *The Monster Club* (1980) and *Don't Open 'Til Christmas* (1984) would present a very skewed, if not completely false view of British horror history. I offer a number of in-depth analyses of specific home-grown horror titles, with each chapter anchored by a close study of at least two key films. Although the approach is broadly chronological, with the book broken down into decades, there are a number of digressions and asides. So Chapter 2, which is largely devoted to Hammer, not only looks at the output of their imitators (Baker and Berman, Anglo Amalgamated) but also a group of films which reacted against the new explicitiness initiated by the company. There is also an attempt to connect things, however tenuously, whether thematically – as in the way a study of the Ealing film *Dead of Night* is followed by a consideration of Amicus, the production company who made a series of anthologies inspired by the earlier film – or more generally – so a consideration of the enormous contribution made by Tony Tenser and his company Tigon in Chapter 5 (Bloody Foreigners) is included as a consequence of their work with Roman Polanski.

There are omissions, of course. I've written in-depth elsewhere on Michael Reeves, one of the most important figures in British horror (see Cooper 2011). His best-known film is the remarkable *Witchfinder General* (1968) but his regrettably brief filmography – cut short by his death aged only 25 – merits further attention. Indeed, one review of my *Witchfinder General* monograph dismissed both of the director's previous features – *Revenge of the Bloodbeast* (1965) and *The Sorcerers* (1967) – as 'not very good' (Steel 2011), an overly harsh judgement on these rough-hewn but fascinating films. That book also contains some consideration of other films which explore similar themes – *Blood on Satan's Claw* (1971), a remarkably stylish and erotic witch-cult film directed by Piers Haggard for Tigon, as well as the much less interesting *The Cry of the Banshee* (1970) – so there is little about those films in here. There is also little on *The Wicker Man* (1973), a fascinating and important film, which has nevertheless been done to death in the last few years.

I've not paid too much attention to generic purity, partly for fear of tying myself into the kind of knots that the editors of the Aurum Encyclopedia (1984) got themselves into, regarding David Cronenberg's earlier films such as *Shivers* (1976) as 'sci-fi' and a whole host of Frankenstein adaptations as 'horror'. Kim Newman's term 'nightmare movies' (1988) is a useful way into the wider reaches of the horror genre and brings in a lot of outlying figures and films which are certainly horrific if not strictly speaking horror. So the grim and nasty likes of *10 Rillington Place* (1971) and *The Offence* (1972) are in here alongside films about vampires, mummies and ghosts. In recent years the serial killer and the sex murderer have taken their place in the pantheon of horrors and one of the ideas examined in this book is the process by which such flesh-and-blood criminals become semi-mythic archetypes, something which is not by any means new.

THE ART OF MURDER

Real-life horror has always been easily transformed into generic fantasy. The English fascination with murder is one enduring example of the way horror can be repackaged as entertainment. As Judith Flanders puts it:

> Crime, especially murder, is very pleasant to think about in the abstract. It is like hearing blustery rain on the window pane while sitting indoors. It reinforces a sense of safety – even of pleasure – to know that murder is possible. Just not here. (2011)

Thomas De Quincey's satirical essay from 1827, 'On Murder Considered as One of the Fine Arts' is an important text here. It purports to be the transcript of a lecture delivered at a meeting of the (entirely fictional) Society for the Encouragement of Murder, composed of those who:

> Profess to be curious in homicide, amateurs and dilettanti in the various modes of carnage and in short, Murder-Fanciers. Every fresh atrocity of that class which the police annals of Europe bring up, they meet and criticise as they would a picture, a statue or other work of art. (De Quincey 1827)

The lecturer begins by acknowledging the growing fascination with violent crime, a fascination which appears to grow in inverse proportion to the murder rate. The safer we feel, the greater our interest in murder. Delivering a lecture on the growth of murder

> ...might have been easy enough three or four centuries ago when the art was little understood and few great models had been exhibited, but in this age, when masterpieces of excellence have been executed by professional men, it must be evident that in the style of criticism applied to them the public will look for something of a corresponding improvement... People begin to see that something more goes into the composition of a fine murder than two blockheads to kill and to be killed, a knife, a purse and a dark lane. Design, gentlemen, grouping, light and shade, poetry, sentiment, are now deemed indispensable to attempts of this nature. (ibid.)

De Quincey's influence can be seen in George Orwell's essay 'The Decline of the English Murder', published in 1944, a consideration of what makes some killings more memorable than others. The opening is a lyrical evocation of an England long gone:

It is Sunday afternoon, preferably before the war. The wife is already asleep in the armchair, and the children have been sent out for a nice long walk. You put your feet up on the sofa, settle your spectacles on your nose, and open the *News of the World*. Roast beef and Yorkshire, or roast pork and apple sauce, followed up by suet pudding and driven home, as it were, by a cup of mahogany-brown tea, have put you in just the right mood. Your pipe is drawing sweetly, the sofa cushions are soft underneath you, the fire is well alight, the air is warm and stagnant. In these blissful circumstances, what is it that you want to read about? Naturally, about a murder. (Orwell 1944)

For Orwell, the 'perfect' murder should be domestic, committed by a 'little man of the professional class', preferably involving poison. He notes how certain murders – he singles out nine cases, including those of Dr. Crippen and Joseph Smith, the 'Brides in the Bath' murderer – acquire infamy. While putting the Ripper case to one side ('in a class of its own'), he notes that at least four of the nine cases

…have had successful novels based on them, one has been made into a popular melodrama, and the amount of literature surrounding them, in the form of newspaper write-ups, criminological treatises and reminiscences by lawyers and police officers, would make a considerable library. (ibid.)

He goes on to decry the recent 'Cleft-Chin Murder', the shooting of a taxi driver by an AWOL GI and his would-be moll on a crime spree, as there 'was no depth of feeling in it' (ibid.). Ironically, given Orwell's suggestion that the case wouldn't be remembered, it would eventually become the subject of a film, *Chicago Joe and the Showgirl* (1990). Orwell's depiction of murder as an almost-civilised, primarily domestic affair is one familiar from the novels of Agatha Christie and can still be found in such cosy, attractively-shot prime-time comfort TV as *Midsomer Murders* (1997 – present). Hitchcock's remark that his preferred murders were 'like blood on a daisy' (in Goodman 1995: 4) fits comfortably into this tradition, as does his oft-quoted 'With the help of television, murder should be brought into the home where it rightly belongs' (Hitchcock 1974: 34) and the related observation that 'Some of our most exquisite murders have been domestic, performed with tenderness in simple, homey places like the kitchen table. Nothing is more revolting to my sense of decency than the underworld thug who is able to murder anyone – even people to whom he has not been properly introduced' (ibid.). Both quotes appear in a speech the director gave in New York to the Film Society of Lincoln Center, a speech which he ended with a quote from De Quincey's essay:

If once a man indulges himself in murder, very soon he comes to think little of robbing, and from robbing he comes next to drinking and Sabbath-breaking, and from that to incivility and procrastination. Once begun on this downward path you never know where you are to stop. Many a man dates his ruin from some murder or other that perhaps he thought little of at the time. (De Quincey 1827)

Which is where we came in…

GOTHIC LITERATURE TO BLOODS, DREADFULS, AWFULS

David Pirie has written of the importance of the gothic novel of the late eighteenth century, a kind of anti-Enlightenment vision of the spooky, visceral and decadent, and also identified the way that so much of its imagery and stock characters would be echoed in British horror cinema. *The Castle of Otranto* (1764), subtitled 'A Gothic Story', a novel reportedly – and fittingly – inspired by a dream, had a considerable impact. The poet Thomas Gray was not alone when he wrote that Walpole's story left him 'afraid to go to bed o'nights' (in *In Our Time: Gothic*, BBC Radio 4 2012). Walpole's novel would prove extremely influential, inspiring gothic romances such as Ann Radcliffe's very successful *The Mysteries of Udolpho* (1794) and Matthew Lewis's startlingly sadistic horror tale *The Monk* (1796).

The publishing history of Walpole's novel is also significant, in that it at first purported to be a genuine medieval tale, written by an Italian monk in the 12th century. The subsequent revelation that it was nothing of the sort earned the author a certain amount of critical disdain but it has also proved remarkably prescient. Walpole's brand of 'phony authenticity' can be seen not only in Stoker's *Dracula*, which uses diary entries, letters and the like to create a vividly realised late-Victorian milieu but it is also present in the 'found footage' genre which has proliferated in the wake of *The Blair Witch Project* (1999), the majority of which have been horror or sci-fi.

Julian Petley has observed how the shock and outrage aimed at the gothic novels mirrored that aimed at British horror films in the 1950s and 60s (see Petley 2002). The perceived excesses of the gothic were all the more worrying to some as literacy increased and the demand grew for exciting and accessible fiction. As Maggie Kilgour put it:

> To many early concerned critics, gothic novels were the unlicensed indulgence of an amoral imagination that was a socially subversive force… The escapist imagination was denounced as corruptive of family values, as, when uncontrolled by reason, it rendered the vulnerable proverbial 'young person' unfit for real life… It was feared that readers of fictions, seduced by the enticing charms of an illusory world, would lose their grip on or their taste for reality. (Kilgour in Petley 2002)

But just as with the Eastmancolor excesses of Hammer nearly 200 years later, such critical disapproval didn't stop the gothic from becoming extremely popular. By 1821, the essayist Leigh Hunt couldn't help but observe that contemporary fiction abounded with:

Haunting Old Women and Knocking Ghosts, and Solitary Lean Hands, and Empusas on one leg and Ladies Growing Longer and Longer, and Horrid Eyes meeting us through Keyholes and Plaintive Heads and Shrieking Statues and Shocking Anomalies of Shape and Things which, when seen, drove people mad. (Hunt in Haining 1976: 13)

There is a clear line of influence from the gothic novel to the cheap mass-market publications which sprang up in their wake offering abridged, plagiarised versions of well-known books as well as true crime stories. These publications included the Sixpenny Shocker, Shilling Shockers and Penny Bloods, also known as Penny Dreadfuls or Penny Awfuls. Indeed, the Bloods and their ilk can be seen as the dissolute, even more disreputable offspring of the likes of Walpole and Radcliffe.

The Bloods were a popular form of Victorian fiction printed on cheap paper and featuring serialised stories which shared themes and imagery from their literary predecessors – highwaymen and bandits, gothic castles and evil deeds. A consideration of the Bloods is particularly fascinating, not just for the way that it underlines that an interest in sensational and lurid stories of horror and crime predates the cinema, but also that this interest has long been frowned on.

Some of the stories therein were simply rewrites of popular thrillers such as Walpole's *Otranto* while others were original, such as *Varney the Vampyre* or *The Feast of Blood*. A sprawling epic more than likely written by James Malcom Rymer, this was the tale of the villainous Sir Francis Varney and his nefarious designs on the Bannerworth family, told over 2 years (1845–7) and clocking in at a daunting 667,000 words. The episodic nature leads to frequent lapses and inconsistencies – characters vanish without explanation and the period setting is very wobbly – while Varney's motives are subject to change; sometimes he is a literal vampire seeking blood, sometimes he is motivated by money (a similar play on the term 'bloodsucker' would reappear in Hammer's *The Satanic Rites of Dracula* [1973]). But the appeal of *Varney* lay in its lurid descriptions of gruesome deeds:

The glassy, horrible eyes of the figure ran over that angelic form with a hideous satisfaction – horrible profanation. He drags her head to the bed's edge. He forces it back by the long hair still entwined in his grasp. With a plunge he seizes her neck in his fang-like teeth – a gush of blood and a hideous sucking noise follows. The girl has swooned, and the vampire is at his horrid repast. (qtd. in Deighan 2011)

While Varney displays many of the familiar attributes of vampirism – he has fangs and bites his victims on the neck – he is also impervious to the effects of daylight, garlic and crosses. He can be wounded or even killed but is always revived by moonlight. At one point, he is even brought back to life by a medical student using galvanisation, a nod to Shelley's *Frankenstein*. Varney is ultimately a tragic figure, a sympathetic victim of the curse of vampirism who eventually throws himself into Mount Vesuvius. The serial nature of stories like *Varney* anticipate the multi-part Frankenstein and Dracula stories popularised by Universal and later exploited with even more success by Hammer. The series of origin stories which appear in Varney have close parallels in the latter's Dracula series, the Count being variously thawed out of ice, given life by a passing bat and conjured up by black magic ritual. The lesser-known *Wagner the Were-Wolf* is another Blood monster, created in 1847 by George Reynolds. In one episode, the titular beast meets Faust, a familiar figure from Goethe, Marlowe and numerous stage adaptations, surely one of the earliest instances of the 'monster mash ups' (*Frankenstein Meets the Wolfman* [1943], *Freddy Vs. Jason* [2003], etc.). The best-known Penny Blood tale is undoubtedly *The String of Pearls: A Romance* (1846–7), which introduced the character of Sweeney Todd. This story of the 'demon barber' who slits the throats of his customers before turning them into meat pies was also written by Rymer and has proved remarkably enduring: it would become a staple in the repetoire of Tod Slaughter, must surely be the only story to inspire both an Andy Milligan film (*Bloodthirsty Butchers*) and a Stephen Sondheim musical (*Sweeney Todd: The Demon Barber of Fleet Street* [1979]), later filmed by Tim Burton while also being adapted as a video game, *Penny Dreadfuls: Sweeney Todd*.

The theatrical equivalents of the Bloods were the penny gaffs, rowdy live performances of short dramatic pieces which dealt with similar subjects – highwaymen, cut-throats and criminals. It is very significant that the word 'gaff' was originally the term used for a cockfighting pit.

The concern that exposure to lurid tales of violence, whether in print or performed would inflame the lower orders, particularly young men, may still be with us (a 2012 BBFC report declared that their policy toward sexual violence would be changed for fear of the effect such material may have on just this group), as are campaigns to censure material perceived to be aimed at a predominantly working class male readership (see the various recent attempts to restrict the sales of 'lad's mags' such as *Nuts* and *Zoo*). But these very same concerns have been around for a long time. In 1844, the chaplain at Brixton House of Corrections declared that:

> ...almost all of the boys there had been led astray by visits to penny gaffs or fairs where they had watched depictions of crimes calculated to inflame the passions. (Flanders 2011)

Similarly, one visitor to a penny gaff opined that if the police:

> ...be roused to increased vigilance in the suppression, as well as the arrest of criminality, it would be as well if those in authority directed their especial attention to these penny theatres. As they at present exist, they are nothing better than hot-beds of vice in its vilest forms. (Rosen 2007)

GA Sarler, a Blood writer who went on to become a journalist, vividly described the world they created:

> ...a world of dormant peerages, of murderous baronets and ladies of title addicted to the studies of toxicology, of gypsies and brigand chiefs, men with masks and women

with daggers, of stolen children, withered hags, heartless gamesters, nefarious roués, foreign princesses, Jesuit fathers, gravediggers, resurrection men, lunatics and ghosts. (Flanders 2011)

Most, if not all, of these characters recur time and again in British horror cinema. As well as the obvious generic staples of men with masks and gravediggers, lunatics and ghosts, one can find in the output of Hammer alone, decadent aristos such as Dracula and Baron Frankenstein, foreign princesses such as Ayesha, She Who Must Be Obeyed in *She* (1965), bands of bloodthirsty brigands (from *The Stranglers of Bombay* [1959] to *The Pirates of Blood River* [1962]) and a veritable gaggle of withered hags, whether it's the faded stars in a series of thrillers made in the wake of *Whatever Happened to Baby Jane?* (1962) – Bette Davis in *The Nanny* (1965) and *The Aniversary* (1968), Tallulah Bankhead in *Fanatic* (1965), Margarette Scott in *Crescendo* (1968) – or the various creepy crones from *The Brides of Dracula* (1960), *The Mummy's Shroud* (1967) or *Countess Dracula* (1970). In much the same way, the highwayman, romantic anti-hero of so many of the Bloods would turn up in another 'disreputable' romp, the Gainsborough melodrama *The Wicked Lady* (1945). Similarly, a lot of the imagery found in the Bloods would find echoes in British genre films. As well as the vampires, werewolves and serial killers, there were lurid tales of torture in faraway lands – Turks roasted over a fire, Russian pirates hung on meathooks – which resemble the exotic sadism of *The Terror of the Tongs* (1961). *Red Ralph, or the Daughter of the Night*, a 'romance of the road in the days of Dick Turpin' by Percival Wolfe featured episodes such as 'Torturing a Witch', accompanied by an image of a topless woman appearing to pray as a mob watches her burn which looks forward to *Witchfinder General* and its imitators. Sometimes this imagery would have an almost eerie prescience such as another episode from the Wolfe story, 'The Boy Savages' illustrated with a drawing of the titular street gang waylaying a man in a tunnel, beating him with a stick more than a century before Alex and his Droogs would do likewise in *A Clockwork Orange* (1971).

Peter Haining has pointed out how the Blood titles 'were kept deliberately low-key' (1976: 26) in an attempt to avoid the opprobrium of the authorities, whilst relying on their startling illustrations to arouse the viewer's interest. So the fairly innocuous-sounding Curiosity and Wonder, a Weekly Miscellany of the Surprising, Remarkable and Astonishing offered an Extraordinary Account of a Woman with a Pig's Face, The Ghost featured The Dead Devoured by the Living (with a graphic image of said devouring) and Tales of All Nations: Popular Legends and Romances dealt with 'madness, incest and suicide' (ibid.).

The popular Newgate Calendar, given the supremely evocative sub-title of The Malefactor's Bloody Register, was published alongside the Bloods and, while its appeal was much the same, it offered to be 'improving'. One telling illustration showed a mother handing a copy of the Journal to her young son while also pointing out of the window at a gibbeted corpse. To this end, it combined real crime reports – tales of Jonathan Wild, Dick Turpin *et al* – that were supposed to serve as cautionary tales alongside editorials attacking those perceived as threatening the nation, e.g. Catholics, the French and those who drink to excess or gamble. Significantly, this kind of phony moralising, trading in the thrill of crime while condemning social transgression, will be familiar to anyone who reads a contemporary tabloid newspaper.

An example of this breathless reportage is from a story about Sawney Beane, the mythical Scots cannibal whose story would be referenced in a number of important horror films:

> An incredible Monster who, with his Wife, lived by Murder and Cannibalism in a Cave. Executed at Leith with his whole Family in the Reign of James I. The following account, though as well attested as any historical fact can be, is almost incredible; for the monstrous and unparalleled barbarities that it relates; there being nothing that we ever heard of, with the same degree of certainty, that may be compared with it, or that shews [sic.] how far a brutal temper, untamed by education, may carry a man in such glaring and horrible colours. (anon. a)

One of the stories in the Calendar was that of William York:

> 'The Boy Murderer', convicted of the Murder of another Child in the Poorhouse of Eyke, in Suffolk, May, 1748. THIS [sic.] sinner was but just turned ten years of age when he committed the dreadful crime. He was a pauper in the poorhouse belonging to the parish of Eyke, in Suffolk, and was committed, on the coroner's inquest, to Ipswich Jail for the murder of Susan Mahew, another child, of five years of age, who had been his bedfellow… This 'boy murder' [sic.] was found guilty, and sentence of death pronounced against him; but he was respited from time to time, and on account of his tender years, was at length pardoned. (anon. b)

Unlike the Beane tale, this detailed a real crime, one which has queasy echoes of a couple of other notorious crimes which we'll come to later. The influence of this low-brow popular literature can be seen most obviously in the pulp fiction and horror comics which would cause a moral panic of their own in the 1950s. But there are more than a few connections to the tabloid press, not only in the appeal to the working class but also thematic concerns: scandal, violence, murder, often treated in a sensational, extremely intemperate manner. The best example of this tendency was the *News of the World*, the recently-defunct Sunday tabloid which specialised in the lurid treatment of various forms of bad behaviour, from extra-marital affairs to cocaine use, rape to murder. Kim Newman has remarked of the typical British film psycho, whose

> …misdeeds (raped schoolgirls, throttled tarts, squandered inheritances) are the stuff of the *News of the World* end of the newspaper market. (2002: 80)

The same newspaper was, of course, singled out by Orwell in his aforementioned essay and it was also reportedly Hitchcock's favourite newspaper (see Spoto 1983: 33).

In 1961, Jean-Paul Török, writing about the new wave of British horror films for Positif suggested that:

The character of the sex maniac of which Jack the Ripper is the most famous historical manifestation haunts the quiet streets of small villages in the English counties to this day. A mother would never for anything in the world leave her children at home out of fear that a lecher might enter, a fear reinforced by reading the news columns in the gutter press. Great Britain has always held the record for sexual assaults and crime. (Török 2002 [1961]: 70-1)

While he is guilty of a number of exaggerated claims, Török's statement underlines the mixture of fear and fascination engendered in part by the popular press. For the painter Walter Sickert, too it was a cultural obsession:

If there is not a murder about every day they [the press] put one in. They have put in every murder which has occurred during the past ten years again, even the Camden Town murder. Not that I am against that because I once painted a whole series about the Camden Town murder, and after all murder is as good a subject as any other. (Tickner 2012)

Sickert's comments are doubly ironic today after the American crime writer Patricia Cornwell suggested the artist's interest in murder went beyond the merely theoretical. In her somewhat optimistically-titled book *Portrait of a Killer: Jack the Ripper—Case Closed* (2002), she declares Sickert *was* the Ripper, a theory which is perhaps a trifle flawed when one considers the artist was in France when four of the five murders were committed. But speaking of Saucy Jack…

RIPPEROLOGY

Reality and fiction can bleed into each other over time. There have been claims over the years that Sweeney Todd may have been real (see Haining 1979; 1993) while historical accounts of werewolf trials when examined today seem to be clear-cut (pardon the pun) cases of serial murder. One example of this is the case of the German farmer and alleged werewolf Peter Stumpp. Stumpp, who lived in a village near Cologne, was arrested in 1859 and under torture confessed to being the owner of a satanic belt which gave him the power to transform into a wolf. In this bestial guise, he had killed and eaten 14 children – including one of his own sons – two pregnant women and a large number of farm animals. He was executed by being broken on a wheel, having his flesh torn off with red-hot pincers and decapitated before his body was burned on a pyre. His wife and daughter were flayed, raped and strangled before being burned alive with his corpse. The ghastly executions took place, appropriately enough, on Halloween. Stumpp is perhaps the best-known werewolf in medieval Europe but he was no means unique. In reality, he may have been a fantasist, he may certainly have been a serial killer but there was no supernatural basis to his crimes.

This enduring confusion between brutal reality and mythic horror is best exemplified by the first modern serial killer, Jack the Ripper, whose crimes – or at least the crimes attributed to him – ushered in what Jane Caputi refers to as the Age of Sex Crime (see Caputi 1988), bringing us, as one newspaper put it at the time 'face to face with some mysterious and awful product of modern civilisation' (in Tickner 2012). The term 'Ripperology' has been coined to describe the small industry that has sprung up around Jack and for the sake of clarity – and a certain amount of thematic consistency – I'm going to consider the Ripper murders as five – those of Mary Ann Nichols, Annie Chapman, Elizabeth Stride, Catherine Eddowes and Mary Jane Kelly – committed by one man in Whitechapel between 31st August and the 9th November 1888. (There may have been many more murders – one of the more fanciful suggestions, for example, has the Whitechapel murderer killing a seven year-old boy in Bradford at the end of 1888 while others claim he struck at least once in New York.)

It may be the case that the murders were committed by different people and grouped together to sell more newspapers and/or to draw attention to the terrible living conditions in the East End of the richest city in the world. But this is really something best left to the Ripperologists. Jack the Ripper aka the Whitechapel Murderer aka Saucy Jack aka Leather Apron swiftly transcended the sordid yet banal reality – of desperately poor women hacked to death and mutilated by a sociopathic sex murderer – and became a semi-mythic character, kin to Dr. Mabuse or even Satan himself, a personification of evil hidden behind a façade. This façade has slowly mutated over time, from the first drawings in the likes of The Illustrated London News of an everyday man with a secret life through to the image we still have today, of a respectable Victorian gentlemen, right down to the top hat and cloak.

This dual identity, man and monster, is right out of Robert Louis Stevenson's *The Strange Case of Dr. Jekyll and Mr. Hyde*, first published in 1886. Stevenson was no stranger to the process of turning true crime into art. In 1884, he published the short story 'The Body Snatcher' based on the antics of Burke and Hare. The duo's crime spree in Edinburgh in 1828, when they 'progressed' from bodysnatching to murder, killing 16 people in all, would be replayed a number of times in the British cinema of the next century. Stevenson also based the character of Henry Jekyll on the outwardly respectable cabinet maker and city councillor turned gambler and prolific burglar, Deacon Brodie.

The real Ripper, if indeed there ever was one killer, has acquired over time the characteristics of a number of fictional characters and consequently casts a remarkable shadow over the British horror cinema, as well as a few oddball items from farther afield (Anthony Perkins played a strung-out, coked-up Jekyll and Hyde who also moonlights as the Ripper in *Edge of Sanity* [1989] and the character even turns up in an episode of *Star Trek* written by Robert Bloch. *Wolf in the Fold* [1967] has the Ripper as Redjac, one of the manifestations of a woman-hating alien entity).

It's remarkable how quickly these ideas around the Ripper as semi-fictional, pseudo-mythical character took hold. Jonathan Rigby rightly describes the Jekyll/Hyde/Ripper connection as 'almost as old as Stevenson's original novel' (2000: 283). On the 4th August, 1888 a stage production of *The Strange Case of Dr. Jekyll and Mr. Hyde* opened at the Lyceum with the bombastic American actor Richard Mansfield in the dual role. Fresh from successful runs in Boston and New York, the play caused a significant stir with its crowd-pleasing on-stage transformation which employed a gauze screen and lighting effects alongside Mansfield's very dramatic performance. *The Times* said of the actor's Hyde:

> He plays with a rough vigour or power which, allied to his hideous aspect, thrills the house, producing a sensation composed in equal measure of the morbidly fascinating and the downright disagreeable. (Sharp 2004)

After the murder of Mary Ann Nichols at the end of the month, it took just over a week for a Hyde/Ripper connection to be made. In the Irish Times of the 7th September, one writer noted (fairly breathlessly) how:

> The Whitechapel murderer has taken a turn of most ghastly romance. Those whose sensations were not handicapped while they read it by a haunting idea that 'the strange case of Dr. Jekyll and Mr. Hyde' was a performance at least as grotesque as it was grim will remember how the horrible Mr. Hyde in one of his transformations butcher-ed [sic.] a woman just for the fun of the thing. That is an effective passage in the book, and those whom it thrilled with a pleasing terror will snatch fearful joy from the story of 'Leather Apron'. (ibid.)

The fact that Hyde actually does no such thing in the novel didn't stop these connections being made in a number of stories that followed including pieces in Freeman's Journal, September 10th ('These atrocities and apparently cause-less murders show that there is abroad at the present time in the East End a human monster even more terrible than Hyde' [ibid.]) and in a letter to The Star three days later ('you and every one of the papers have missed the obvious solution of the Whitechapel mystery. The murderer is a Mr Hyde who seeks in the repose and comparative respectability of Dr Jekyll security from the crimes he commits in his baser form' [ibid.]).

A letter to the *Daily Telegraph* on the 3rd October went further, suggesting that 'the perpetrator is a being whose diseased brain has been inflamed by witnessing the performance of the drama of 'Dr Jekyll and Mr. Hyde' (ibid.). It's also noteworthy that Mansfield's production was brought over to London's Lyceum Theatre by the actor-manager Henry Irving and so would doubtless have been seen by Irving's personal assistant – and struggling author - Bram Stoker. Whether or not Stoker saw a connection between Hyde and the Ripper, the Whitechapel murderer is surely an influence on Dracula, a character who is both a worldy, civilised aristocrat and a bloodthirsty killer of women.

Indeed, it is significant that, as Judith Flanders points out, Dracula kills five women, the same number attributed to the Ripper. On a related note, Dracula's appearance seems to have been modelled on the tall, thin and saturnine Irving. The actor-manager was also one of the celebrity attendees at the ticket-only Old Bailey trial of one Robert Wood. Wood was charged with the gruesome near-beheading of a prostitute, Emily Dimmock in September 1907 in a case which became known as the Camden Town Murder, considered by some at the time to be another Ripper murder and immortalised by the aforementioned Walter Sickert who produced four paintings on the theme. There may also be something of the Ripper in Oscar Wilde's *The Picture of Dorian Gray* (1890), the story of a debauched sensualist turned murderer, the respectable gent who hides a dark secret. Indeed, for many the author himself was such a character, a husband and father and 'posing Sodomite', to use Lord Queensberry's description.

Ripper substitutes are a regular fixture in British horror, from *Gaslight* (1940) to *Dr. Jeykll and Sister Hyde* (1971) and beyond, a long line of killers clad in top hat and cloak, the murdered prostitutes, the serial killer as supernatural force, the mysterious figure penning lurid letters in spidery red ink. And this iconic figure shows no signs of going away. In *Deep Breath*, the first episode of the 8th season of *Doctor Who* from August 2014, the titular Time Lord goes up against a villainous cyborg responsible for a series of mutilation murders in Victorian London who is unsurprisingly kitted out in the traditional Ripper garb of top hat and black overcoat.

DEAR BOSS... FROM HELL

As with the murders themselves, there is some debate about the provenance of the letters and postcards which purport to be from the killer. Given the sensational nature of the case and the publicity surrounding it, it's no surprise that the authorities received hundreds of letters and postcards, some naming suspects, some confessions and others taunts. Particular attention has been paid to three such items, two letters and a postcard. The 'Dear Boss' letter was received by the Central News Agency on 27 September 1888. Written in red ink and littered with mis-spellings, the tone is mocking and defiant:

> I am down on whores and I shant quit ripping them till I do get buckled... The next job I do I shall clip the ladys ears off just for jolly wouldnt you... Good luck. Yours truly, Jack the Ripper.

On the 1st October 1888, the day after the murders of Stride and Eddowes, a postcard was received by the Central News Agency. It appeared to be written by the same person and made reference to a 'double event this time number one squealed a bit couldn't finish straight off'. The last letter was received by the leader of the Whitechapel Vigilance Committee, George Lusk on the 16th October and differed slightly from the others, being much less literate and making no reference to Jack the Ripper:

From Hell… I send you half the Kidne I took from one women prasarved it for you tother piece I fried and ate it was very nise. I may send you the bloody knif that took it out if you only wate a whil longer.
Signed Catch me when you Can.

The letter also contained half a kidney preserved in wine, which was discovered to be human. The provenance of these communications is debatable (like virtually everything else about the case). The references to ear-snipping may be significant (Eddowes certainly had her ears nicked although this may have been an accident) but this detail – and the fact that the murderer struck twice on the 30th September, the 'double event' mentioned - would have been known by some at the time the letters were sent, especially journalists covering the case. As for the kidney, the killer did remove one from Catherine Eddowes but it was never proven that it was the one that was sent to Lusk and both letter and organ have since been lost. Certainly, these communications may well have been written by journalists, keen to build up an already sensational story. One journalist was identified as the writer of at least one of the letters in 1913 while another claimed authorship in the 1930s.

Authenticity isn't the point, however. What is certain is the fact they have proved to be the ur-text for murderers' letters. While it's tempting to say the communications are, in one sense, too good to be true, brim full of horror, mocking and callous, revealing a showy kind of cunning, letters written by later killers often demonstrate the same love of the theatrical, the gloating and the bravado (not to mention the same woeful grammar and lack of punctuation). They also sometimes display some odd poetry and some striking images. Consider: 'I love to hunt. Prowling the streets looking for fair game — tasty meat. The wemon of Queens are prettyist of all. It must be the water they drink' (David Berkowitz aka Son of Sam); or 'The best part of it [killing] is thae when I die I will be reborn in paradice and all thei have killed will become my slaves' (The Zodiac).

Also, the process of 'branding' seen in the Ripper communications has also become familiar, with Zodiac, Son of Sam and Dennis Rader, aka BTK (Bind Torture Kill), coming up with their own nicknames in their communications, the latter two going as far as to provide a number of alternatives: David Berkowitz could have ended up as Mr. Monster (letter to police, 1977) while the indecisive Rader seems to have regarded the authorities as a kind of focus group, suggesting they pick a name from choices which included Witchita Strangler, Poetic Strangler, Bond Age Strangler, The Garote Phatom [sic.] and Asphyxiater [sic.]. Sometimes the brand doesn't catch on, as when the Yorkshire Ripper, Peter Sutcliffe, attempted to rebrand himself as The Streetcleaner in a poem sent to a Sheffield newspaper in 1979, which went unnoticed by investigators (see Caputi 1987: 45). However, Sutcliffe, a lorry driver, did have a habit of putting a cardboard sign in the window of his cab when he slept upon which was written in block capitals 'In this truck is a man whose latent genius if unleashed would rock the nation, whose dynamic energy would overpower those around him. Better let him sleep?' – which offers some insight into the messianic self-regard of the serial killer.

In *The Lodger, A Story of London Fog* (1927), often described, not least by the director himself as 'the first true Hitchcock film' (Martin 2012), the press is given a prominent role. At the start of this tale of a Ripper-ish serial killer known as The Avenger killing blondes in London, we see a reporter calling in from a murder scene. We then follow the story through newsroom (where we get a glimpse of the director), printing press, delivery vans and ending with a very busy paper seller on the streets (who says of the Avenger's modus operandi, 'It always happens Tuesdays. That's my lucky day'). An intertitle makes it clear that this is a 'MURDER wet from the press'. The fact we then cut from the paper seller to a radio news reporter and then to the dressing rooms of a fashion house underlines the fact that this is all showbiz. Indeed, the very first shot suggests that murder itself and not just the reporting of it is just another form of showbiz. A close-up of a screaming blonde victim is followed by a neon theatre sign which reads To-Night Golden Curls.

Whatever their provenance, the letters and postcard of autumn 1888 played a crucial role in the Jack the Ripper story but they also display features which would recur throughout the British horror tradition. Amid the taunting, the mis-spelling and the childish scrawl, the letters display black humour, a kind of vicious glee at wallowing in gory excess, a grim theatricality, both the tone and imagery straight out of the Penny Bloods. The author casts himself as an evil genius, a kind of artist or anti-hero. The communications feed into the enduring image of the serial killer as a little man with a big secret, making his way through the squalor of the East End like Dracula passing through the throng at Piccadilly Circus.

The Ripper may be the best-known example of a killer repackaged as a monster but he isn't the first. After the Ratcliffe Highway murders in East London in 1811, two gruesome and very violent attacks that left 7 people dead, the police arrested a young sailor called John Williams. The unfortunate suspect, who in actual fact was extremely unlikely to have had anything to do with the murders, committed suicide before he could be tried and his corpse was buried with a stake through the heart while his skull ended up behind the bar of a local pub. But the sheer terror generated by the murders – and Williams' subsequent suicide – led to the dead man being convincted in the public imagination. As Colin Wilson put it:

> It was the first time in English history – probably in European history – that a crime had created widespread panic. Why? Because it was generally accepted that they were committed by one man. In fact, it is rather more probable that they were committed by two, or even by a gang... If that had been believed, there would almost certainly have been no panic – gangs of thieves were still a familiar hazard in 1811. It was this notion of a lone monster, a man who stalked the streets on his own, lusting for blood that terrified everybody. (1985: 461)

So Williams, a good-looking, slightly effeminate young man was transformed into a demon. The mischievous Thomas De Quincey described him (with deliberate inaccuracy) as a pale man, dressed all in black and recast, somewhat fancifully as 'a Miltonic ruined god' (Flanders 2011), a 'domestic Attila, or "Scourge of God"' whose 'face wore at all times a bloodless ghastly pallour' (De Quincey 1827). This process, whereby an inconsequential man on the margins is transformed into a figure of dark glamour, a personification of evil is still in evidence in the form of that great modern monster, the serial killer.

Even if one rules out the aforementioned self-dubbed likes of the Son of Sam, one still has to consider the nicknames – the Yorkshire Ripper, the Black Panther, the Night Stalker, the Hillside Strangler – with the sadsack reality to see this process of mythologising is still with us. The child killer Ian Brady, giving evidence to a mental health tribunal in June 2013 spoke of what he described as the public obsession with the 'theatricality' of his crimes and the crimes of others:

> Why are we still talking about Jack the Ripper over a century on? Because of the dramatic background: the fog, the cobbled streets… it fascinates them. With the Moors it's the same: *Wuthering Heights*, *Hound of the Baskervilles*, that sort of thing. (Pidd 2013)

The aforementioned Victorian fascination with violent crime is pinpointed in the sub-title of Judith Flanders' book, The Invention of Murder: How the Victorians Revelled in Death and Detection and Created Modern Crime. *The Daily Mail*, never knowingly understated, put it in much starker terms in a review of the book, writing of The Death Junkies: Victorians who lived for Murder (Lewis 2011). Certainly the rigidly conformist character of the period – and the emphasis placed on emotional restraint – meant that those who violently transgressed these social norms became an object of fascination. This led to a kind of Golden Age of Murder.

In December 1888, a woman was found disembowelled in Gateshead, leading to fears that the Ripper had moved north. The killer was revealed to be the young woman's boyfriend, who after killing her when she refused sex, decided to make it look like a new Ripper murder. In October 1890, Mary Pearcey violently murdered her lover's wife and 18 month-old baby, pushing the corpses in a pram through the streets of Hampstead. Pearcey told investigating officers that the blood splashes in her house were from mice, later chanting 'Killing mice' over and over again like a mantra. For a time, she was even considered a Ripper suspect. In 1896, Amelia Dyer was hanged for the murders of six infants. Dyer was a 'baby farmer', who took in illegitimate children for a fee. Estimates have suggested Dyer's victims may have numbered as many as 600. Perhaps inevitably, she too has been considered a Ripper suspect. In 1899, George Nunn, a teenage farm labourer in Wortham, Suffolk approached mother of six Eliza Dixon and offered her sixpence for sex. She refused and Nunn attacked her, raping her before stabbing her 14 times in the head and neck.

Newspapers and scandal sheets created a number of these 'grotesque celebrities' (Spoto, 1983: 35), but, in truth, the Victorians were simply the most extreme examples of a fascination with murder that goes back much further. It may well be, as Hitchcock (who was born during this Golden Age, in 1899) was wont to suggest that such a fascination is 'a particularly English problem… The British take a peculiar interest in crime' (in Spoto 1983: 33). One could argue that the Victorian fixation on the grim details of murder, visits to the sites of famous crimes and the sale of relics associated with them is positively restrained when compared to public executions and the displaying of the severed heads of traitors on London Bridge, a practice which lasted more than 350 years, the heads dipped in tar and boiled to protect them from the elements before being stuck on iron spikes as a ghastly reminder that the wages of sin are not only death but also dismemberment and public decomposition. Indeed, the excesses of the Penny Bloods and Video Nasties seem positively wholesome when compared to what used to pass for popular entertainment. As Harold Schechter points out:

> Our popular culture may be saturated with synthetic gore but at least we don't spend our leisure time watching real people have their eyes put out, their limbs pulverized, their sex organs amputated and their flesh torn to pieces with red-hot pincers. (qtd. in Peters 2006)

The case of Maria Marten and what would become known as 'the Murder in the Red Barn', is a perfect illustration of the way real tragedy could become transformed into entertainment, from news stories and porcelain figurines to theatrical and film adaptations. At first sight, there was little that was exceptional about the case – in Polstead, Suffolk in 1827, a young squire, William Corder, arranged to meet his lover, Maria Marten, a mole-catcher's daughter and young mother, at a local landmark called the Red Barn, whereupon he killed her (either shooting, stabbing or strangling her) and hid her body in the barn before fleeing for London. Corder wrote letters, claiming that he and Maria had settled in the Isle of Wight but after her step-mother dreamt that the girl was in the barn, her body was discovered and Corder was tracked down, tried and hanged. However, the cocktail of class divide, illicit passion, gruesome murder and the supernatural led to the case becoming a *cause celebre*, inspiring numerous newspaper articles, ballads and associated media.

The fascination was immediate, with ticket-only admittance to Corder's trial and plays being performed before he had even been convicted. Corder was hanged on 11th August 1828 in Bury St. Edmonds and according to some sources there were as many as 20,000 spectators. The exploitation of the case was staggering, offering one of the most dramatic illustrations of the appeal of what is now known as murderabilia: the hanging rope was cut into pieces that sold for a guinea each; Corder's scalp (with one ear still attached!) was displayed in Oxford Street; and one could even buy a recreation of the Red Barn made by Staffordshire potters. An estimated 200,000 'murder tourists' visited Polstead in 1828. Not only was the notorious barn stripped but Maria's gravestone ended up completely chipped away by souvenir hunters. After being dissected and his skull examined for criminal traits, Corder's skeleton was displayed, first in Suffolk and later in London, while his skin was tanned and used to bind an account of his crime. The skeleton was finally cremated in 2004. The story was very quickly transformed into a generic melodrama, turning the messy and ambiguous facts – Colin Wilson pithily describes the protagonists as 'a sluttish countrygirl of loose morals and a weak young man of criminal tendencies' (1985: 465) – into a pre-existing narrative of good and evil. In order to make her into a pure and innocent Victorian heroine, Maria's children by other men were written out (indeed, it may be the case that a child she bore by Corder was killed soon after birth by one or both of them) while Corder was made not only monstrous but, even worse, old.

The first filmed adaptation came as early as 1902, *Maria Martin* [sic.]; or, *The Murder in the Red Barn* (the recurrent mis-spelling of the victim's name indicates the film-makers' familiarity with earlier films rather than the case itself). *The Red Barn Crime; or Maria Martin* followed in 1908 while *Maria Martin; or The Murder in the Red Barn* (1913) was marketed as having been shot on location in the actual Red Barn (which sounds impressive, until one discovers that the barn had burned down in 1842). There was *Maria Marten* in 1928 before the best-known adaptation of the story came along in 1935 with the barnstorming Tod Slaughter as Corder (and we'll hear a lot more from Slaughter in the next chapter).

Madame Tussaud's was also in on the murderabilia game early. They bought the pram which Mary Pearcey used to transport her victim through the streets as well as her kitchen furniture. On the first day of the Pearcey exhibition in 1890, 31,000 people turned up to the museum. Madame Tussaud's would eventually end up acquiring such additional grim mementoes as one of the three baths in which George Joseph Smith drowned one of his three wives and the electric chair which killed Bruno Hauptmann, convicted of the Lindbergh baby kidnapping and murder. Given this deep-seated fascination with murder and the macabre, the gothic and the weird, both in fiction and reality it's worth taking the time to consider just why it took so long for the horror film to establish itself in Britain long after it was a popular genre in Germany and the US.

CHAPTER 1: 'IT'S ALIVE!' THE BIRTH OF HOME-GROWN HORROR

Even if we regard British horror cinema as starting decades before Pirie does – he argues that 'there seems little of real interest' (2007: 14) until the 1950s - the question of why it took so long to become established is still a valid one. There are a number of examples of the macabre, the spooky and the weird in the early British cinema, although nothing to rival the likes of *Nosferatu* (1922) or *The Phantom of the Opera* (1925) – at least not until *The Lodger* in 1927. A significant number of silent films of a horrific or supernatural bent were adaptations of literary properties with which the audience would have been at least vaguely familiar and which have been revisited on and off in the intervening years.

There were the couple of versions of the W.W. Jacobs story *The Monkey's Paw* (1913 and 1923) and six versions of *Faust* made between 1910 and 1927. There were also four versions of H. Rider Haggard's *She* – which would later be filmed by Hammer – made between 1911 and 1925. Julian Petley goes back even further, to the trick films such as *The Big Swallow* (1901) an ostensible comedy where a filmed subject appears to eat both the camera and its operator, which must have induced just as much awe and fear in the viewer as it did laughter. But if a 'heritage of horror' was taking a while to establish itself over here, it was certainly making its presence felt in the US and British talent played an important role in the development of Hollywood horror. *Frankenstein* (1931) was directed by James Whale (born in Dudley) and had two English leads, Colin Clive and Boris Karloff (born William Henry Pratt in Camberwell). Elsewhere, the scarred Russian hunter Count Zaroff in *The Most Dangerous Game* (1932) was Scouser Leslie Banks, Doctor Moreau in *The Island of Lost Souls* (1932) was Yorkshireman Charles Laughton, and the lead in *The Mystery of the Wax Museum* was Lionel Atwill, originally from Croydon. The latter may be the consummate English horror performer of this time, nondescript in appearance, debonair and charming as well as sinister, his appeal boosted by his somewhat outré private life (watching murder trials, screening porno films and hosting orgies – lying about the latter in court led to a conviction for perjury in 1942). Then as now, it seems, Englishness, especially the slightly effete, cultured, eccentric kind, suggests villainy. Those old colonial wounds run deep.

The enormous popularity of these imported American horror films led to a certain amount of unease in the UK, especially at the British Board of Film Censors, who had already demonstrated a dislike for controversial imports (the BBFC had considered a ban on *The Cabinet of Dr. Caligari* [1919] for fear it would upset viewers with relatives in asylums [see Kermode, 2002], and *Battleship Potempkin* [1925] would be refused a certificate until 1954). *Frankenstein* was heavily cut and both *Freaks* (1933) and *Island of Lost Souls* were banned outright. Their solution to the perceived problem of these gruesome offerings was the creation of the H (for Horror) certificate, which was intended to be advisory (although some councils implemented a ban on under-sixteens seeing H films). The H would last in various forms until 1951 when it was replaced by the (even) more restrictive X certificate. Considering the deeply-ingrained fascination with the horrific and macabre noted above, it's a considerable irony that the film widely considered the first British horror film – and in fact the first film to receive the H certificate – was in such obvious thrall to German and American styles.

THE GHOUL (1933)

Karloff as the title character in *The Ghoul*

The Ghoul has a remarkable pedigree. It was produced by Michael Balcon, the man who gave Hitchcock his first directing job and who would go on to head Ealing Studios. The unusually heavyweight cast included Cedric Hardwicke, Ralph Richardson and the cult star Ernest Thesiger. (Balcon, Hardwicke and Richardson would all receive knighthoods, while Thesiger would have to make do with a mere CBE.) The director, T. Hayes Hunter was an American with something of a track record in the macabre, having made his debut with the US serial *The Crimson Stain Mystery* (1916) and making a number of thrillers after his move to Britain. His 1932 film *The Frightened Lady* anticipates *The Ghoul*, being an old dark house murder mystery based on an Edgar Wallace story (one of the screenwriters was Angus McPhail who would go on to write for Hitchcock and contribute to *Dead of Night*). But the main draw was undoubtedly Boris Karloff, returning to these shores to play the title character in a vehicle which drew heavily on his already-iconic persona.

The Ghoul was a very loose adaptation of the novel by Frank King, which had in turn become a popular play. It deals with the eponymous super-criminal and owes much to the work of the aforementioned Wallace, an English writer whose considerable influence on the genre will be considered later in this chapter. But Hunter's film jettisons the bulk of the novel, although the setting – a mansion near the Yorkshire moors – remains. The story is simple enough. Professor Morlant, a collector of ancient Egyptian artifacts and 'a fellow of queer fancy' is near death and demands to be buried with the jewel known as the Eternal Light bandaged into his hand in the belief that this will grant him immortality. But the jewel is stolen and passed from person to person while Morlant rises from the grave to reclaim it. Of course, like a great many would-be supernatural films and plays of this period, the occult events have a more prosaic explanation, as it is discovered, after what appears to be Morlant's second death, that the first was simply an attack of catatonic shock, which led to him being buried alive. Karloff has few lines – he is first seen on his death-bed and later stalks the house and the people in it, worldlessly clawing at the air in a manner which owes less to his creature in *Frankenstein* and more to Conrad Veidt's silent somnabulist in *Caligari*, one of many Germanic touchstones in the film. He does, however, look impressively hideous, with a monobrow and skin like old parchment. In the most remarkable scene, he kneels before a statue of Anubis and uses a knife to carve an ankh into his sunken chest.

Richardson overdoes it as the vicar who may not be what he seems while Hardwicke broods and glowers impressively as a sinister lawyer. The romantic leads are bland (as they tend to be in the genre pieces from this – indeed, any – period) and, equally predictably, Kathleen Harrison's comic relief is fairly irritating. The most noteworthy performer after Karloff is Thesiger, sporting a club foot and thick Scottish accent. Thesiger is best remembered today for his memorably flamboyant turns for James Whale (such as his demented Doctor Pretorius in *Bride of Frankenstein* [1935]) and compared to his usual manic manner, his performance – although very good – is almost restrained. It's an irony that a film such as this – a thin, familiar plot enlivened by some remarkable visual flourishes – needed four screenwriters. There are a few nice exchanges ('We're only ships that pass in the night'. 'Do you want a drink or do you want to pass now?') but the most memorable thing here is the striking imagery, courtesy of imported European talent. Cinematographer Gunther Krampf was an Austrian with a remarkable back catalogue, including such landmark films as *Nosferatu, The Hands of Orlac* (1924), *The Student of Prague* (1926) and *Pandora's Box* (1929). Krampf would go on to work with that great admirer of German Expressionism, Hitchcock on a couple of World War II propaganda films. Meanwhile *The Ghoul*'s sets were built by the German Alfred Junge, who had worked for UFA and would go on to work on a number of British Hitchcock pictures and Powell and Pressburger's *Black Narcissus* (1947).

Some of Junge's sets are staggering, such as the vast expanse of the Morlant house or the burial vault, with the enormous door covered in hieroglyphics and illuminated by a hanging lamp fashioned into a cobra. Even the lawyer's office is startling, shelf after shelf of ledgers and files stretching up to the ceiling. Unlike so many films of the early sound period, with their often static tableaux, here there is always some motion in the crowded frames, with guttering candles and the shadows cast by tree branches moving in the wind while there's also an array of distorting devices used – heavy shadows, ornate mirrors, frosted glass and an eerily fog-bound street.

Unsuprisingly, there is a marked Teutonic look to the handsome set-pieces, including the late night torch-lit funeral procession from the house to the vault and the spooky sequence where Karloff is resurrected, the lid of his sarcophagus slowly being pushed back and an arm protruding, the bandage dangling from the wrist revealing that the jewel has been stolen. If the visual style owes much to the German cinema of the 1920s, the dominating influence elsewhere is that of Universal – in particular a couple of films made the previous year, both of which starred Karloff. Indeed, the atmospheric score by the alliterative duo of Louis Levy and Leighton Lucas bears this out, sounding like a cross between Wagner and the kind of classically-inspired scores of the Universal horrors.

The mansion setting may have been present in King's novel but the gloomy and gothic Morlant abode seems to have been inspired much more by that most British of Hollywood horrors, the emblematically-titled *The Old Dark House* (1932). James Whale's adaptation of J.B. Priestley's 1927 novel *Benighted* may not be his best film but it's certainly the most fun and one that has cast an appropriately long shadow over the British horror film. On a stormy night, a mixed bag of travellers – ex-soldier, courting couple, showgirl and self-made millionaire – end up at the titular dwelling which is inhabited by the deeply weird Femm family. The gallery of grotesques include a deaf, god-bothering sister, a gin-swilling neurotic brother (Ernest Thesiger, as highly-strung here as he is restrained for Hunter) and a mute, scarred butler (Karloff). The screenplay by Benn Levy and R.C. Sheriff ditches most of the novel's political content but it's still hard to avoid the implication that the Femms, isolated, hidebound and oddly out of time represent Olde England, clinging to a way of life as the world outside is changing. This idea – which owes something to Poe and his story *The Fall of the House of Usher* – is returned to time and again in the genre.

Kim Newman has identified the debt that this strand of horror cinema owes to Agatha Christie and her country house murder mysteries (see Newman 2002), where a motley cast of characters is assembled in an isolated locale before one or more of them are bumped off, going on to identify the way that the 'shadowed and decayed Gothic trappings' of these rambling, frequently decrepit manses reflect the warped, weird and/or broken mind of many a screen psycho (2002: 73). This is certainly the case in *The Ghoul*: as one character comments 'curious house, this', the reply is 'curious owner'.

Of course, the decrepit castle/mansion house/abbey has been around at least since the gothic novel – Walpole's novel was named after one such abode and the term 'gothic' itself comes from the style of architecture. The large house is traditionally the dwelling of the villainous and/or dissolute aristocrat so there is also a frisson of class resentment. (In addition, as Hammer would later discover, renting a country house would often work out cheaper than shooting on a number of different locations, so there are economic reasons too for the proliferation of such locations in British horror.) The irony of *The Old Dark House*, an adaptation of a (very) British novel by a British director being made in Hollywood was not lost on Priestley, who expressed dismay that no native producers had shown interest (see Conrich 2009). In this context, Hunter's film could be seen as an attempt to, pace Bob Dylan, 'bring it all back home' to Europe with this British gothic made in a German style. In much the same way as *The Ghoul* borrows from *The Old Dark House*, the motif of Egyptology may have been fashionable at this time – the clearing of Tutankhamun's tomb was only finished in 1932 – but its presence here more than likely reflects the box-office success of *The Mummy*.

This fascination with the exotic recurs throughout the horror films of this period (consider, for example, the Tibetan flower which creates *The Werewolf of London* [1935]) and it could be regarded as Orientalism (a phrase coined by Edward Said in an influential 1977 book) or colonial guilt. Maybe both. This exoticism certainly plays a role in a remarkable amount of British horror films – Hammer alone produced *The Stranglers of Bombay* and *The Terror of the Tongs* (the latter directed by Anthony Bushell, who played the romantic lead in *The Ghoul*) as well as such imported monsters as *The Reptile* (1965) and the undead workers in *The Plague of the Zombies* (1965). This fear of the repressed, colonial Other returning to wreak revenge should be regarded in much the same way as the slaughter of the indigenous population of North America keeps recurring in US genre films, from the Navajo Indian who is transformed into the titular monster in *The Werewolf* (1913), the evil medicine man of *The Manitou* (1978) and the native burial grounds which crop up in *The Amityville Horror* (1979), *The Shining* (1980) and *Poltergeist* (1982). *The Ghoul* does acknowledge this romantic fascination with all things exotic through the strange relationship, played for laughs, between the lovestruck comic relief Kaney (Harrison) and Aga Ben Dragore (Harald Huth) where she shares her breathless fantasies of 'slave girls, lovely as sin, stripped to the waist and lashed'. The first line of the film is also telling, when a man wearing a fez arrives at a house only to be told by the maid 'We don't want to buy no lino or nothing'.

The film performed disappointingly at the box-office and this didn't help the parlous state of the genre. After a brief re-release in 1938, *The Ghoul* was thought to be lost until the late 60s when the author and collector William K. Everson found a subtitled copy in a very poor condition in Czechoslovakia. In the early 1980s, an original negative was discovered in the entirely-fitting location of an abandoned vault at Shepperton Studios. The version available at the time of writing on Region 1 DVD is, despite some occasional softening of the image, beautiful and does justice to Krampf's stunning photography.

QUOTA QUICKIES

The Cinematograph Act of 1927 established an exhibition quota for British films with the aim of boosting home-grown production. The quota offered a lifeline for British film-makers while also having the unintentional effect of widening the gap even further between prestige pictures and what would in the US be called B movies; that is low-budget comedies, thrillers and comedy-thrillers. This meant that the so-called quota quickies often have important value, providing a useful document of the popular culture of the period – music hall performances, variety acts – chosen as subjects because they were cheap and required little if any rehearsing. The Quickies also served as an excellent training ground for talent, giving a boost to a small company called Hammer as well as the likes of David Lean, Vivien Leigh, James Mason, Errol Flynn and Michael Powell, as well as Britain's first horror star. Enter Tod Slaughter!

THE STRONG MEAT OF SLAUGHTER

Watching Slaughter perform is a bizarre experience. He is a burly man with his hair parted in the centre and teased up into wings and a remarkably expressive frog-like face. He is constantly emoting – smugly gloating, glowering menacingly, leering, sniggering, cackling, stroking his glued-on facial hair and contorting his face into a demon mask – and he never knowingly underplayed. He was a big man (it's hard to find a description of him that doesn't use the phrase 'barrel-chested') but his performances were always bigger. In a good example of nominative determinism, Slaughter was his real name, although his first name was Norman and he'd been treading the boards since he was 20.

He started off playing lead roles in the same kind of Victorian melodramas he would become known for but after a short spell as a chicken farmer in the early 1930s, he began to play a series of larger-than-life, hissable villains. Rather than look to the classics for inspiration, Slaughter's material came from the likes of The Newgate Calendar and Police Gazette, as well as some creaky old music hall standards like *Maria Marten* and *Sweeney Todd*. Slaughter was 50 by the time he made his first film, the aforementioned 1935 adaptation of *Maria Marten or The Murder in the Red Barn*, playing the emblematic role of Squire Corder, both respectable gent and rapacious murderer ('I will make you a bride, a bride of death!'), the first of his trademark Jekyll and Hyde roles. The film was produced by George King, who would go on to direct six Slaughter vehicles: *Sweeney Todd The Demon Barber of Fleet Street* (1936), *The Crimes of Stephen Hawke* (1937), *The Ticket of Leave Man* (1938), *Sexton Blake and the Hooded Terror* (1938), *The Face at the Window* (1939) and *The Crimes at the Dark House* (1940).

King was a master of the quota quickie and although he would eventually move on to more respectable work, he is still best known for the Slaughter films. The actor also made a number of gothic melodramas for other directors, including *The Greed of William Hart* (1948), a thinly-disguised version of the Burke and Hare story. The film fell foul of the BBFC's insistence on not naming criminals, so the bodysnatching duo are redubbed (somewhat unconvincingly) as Moore and Hart. It's largely notable for the screenwriting contribution of John Gilling, an important figure in British horror who would not only revisit the Burke and Hare story in 1959 but also make a series of films for Hammer, including the impressive 'Cornish' double bill of *Plague of the Zombies* and *The Reptile*. Gilling represents an important bridge between the twin traditions of Slaughter melodramas and Hammer horrors and he's not alone, with production designer Bernard Robinson also making his debut on a Slaughter film.

Away from his trademark 'strong meat' melodramas, Tod also made a couple of cop thrillers as well as the odd sentimental romance. Without a doubt, the Slaughter films have dated terribly, far more than the Universal pictures from around the same time. But it's a mistake to do what many critics have done and simply write them off as filmed theatre. In fact, this is a moot point as, rather than shying away from the theatrical origins of their best-known projects, the director and star wholeheartedly embrace them as a means to foreground performance. So *Maria Marten* opens with the costumed actors being introduced to us and *Stephen Hawke* has an old-fashioned variety show as wraparound, featuring singers and interviews including one with Slaughter himself. In much the same way, the actor's often laughable, hissable villains are not broadly played by accident but rather by design. As the opening titles of *The Face at the Window* puts it, after a few sentences of exposition detailing a recent crime wave:

> A wave of terror which inspired this melodrama of the old school – dear to the hearts of all who unashamedly enjoy a shudder or a laugh at the heights of villainy.

Slaughter also seems to anticipate the response of many in the audience to his barnstorming schtick, which was pretty dated even in the 1930s. When, for example we return to the framing device in *Stephen Hawke*, we discover the film has sent the interviewer to sleep. Despite a strong emphasis on the performative, King's direction often consists of more than simply pointing a camera and shooting. *Maria Marten*, for all its self-conscious theatricality has camera movement and the murder scene is very cinematic, a mixture of close-ups and long-shots, an expressive use of shadows and sound effects, particularly the boom of thunder.

In *Sweeney Todd*, the cinematic technique is far beyond the merely rudimentary. Aside from a number of hokey devices familiar from low-budget films of the period – poor back projection, stock footage inserts – and some unconvincing jungle scenes (replete with a black manservant called Snowdrop), the camera placement and use of cross-cutting is often suprisingly effective. In an early sequence set on the docks, Todd watches the young woman he covets with the man she loves. Another pair of lovers, principally there for comic relief, are also present. When the subject of money comes up, its importance to the plot is emphasised by a series of quick cuts from Todd/Tod to one couple then the other. Although the film-makers were forbidden by the BBFC from depicting the cannibalism which is integral to the original story, there is a clever scene where characters theorise as to how Todd disposes of his victims' remains. The discussion quickly moves off-screen as the camera stays fixed on one of their number as he eats a (comically large) pie. When asked directly what he thinks happens to the corpses, he answers 'How do I know?' with his mouth full.

The Face at the Window is the film which most obviously tips over from murder melodrama into full-blown gothic horror (the title alone is indicative of that). The King/Slaughter vehicle was the third film version, the first being made in 1920 and the second, which starred Raymond Massey, in 1932. In King's version, Slaughter plays the wealthy investor Chevalier Del Gardo who is also the murdering thief known as the Wolf. The setting is Paris, which not only has associations of glamour and sleaze but was also the home to the *Grand Guignol*, the (in)famous theatre in Pigalle that specialised in graphic depictions of extreme violence. During the war, after George King moved on to a more upmarket collaboration with Leslie Howard, Slaughter returned to the stage, presenting a number of *Guignol* pieces alongside his usual overblown turns as, amongst others, Jack the Ripper and the French murderer Landru. The Gallic setting of *Face* enables Slaughter to cut more of a dash than before, wearing a floppy hat, cloak and (ridiculously phony) beard. The Wolf's murders provide stronger meat than usual, heralded by the hideous titular apparition – a snaggle-toothed, straggly haired, drooling man – and a wolf howl, before an unseen assassin hurls a knife into the victim's back. There is also a sub-plot centred on the Frankensteinian exploits of a Professor ('and they dared call me mad!') who claims he can use electricity to reanimate the dead. In the frenzied finale, Del Gardo is not only exposed as the Wolf but his mis-shapen accomplice is revealed to be his foster-brother, who is kept in a cage between murders. As the gendarmes approach, the caged man grabs Del Gardo by the neck and they both, along with the cage, fall into the river.

Slaughter's speciality was dual roles, upstanding philanthropist and/or pillar of the community and rapist, robber, killer. So in *The Ticket of Leave Man*, his respectable role as the head of the Good Samaritan Aid Society is simply a cover for his nefarious activites as 'The Tiger'(and they are pretty nefarious – he garrotes two coppers in Peckham at the opening of the film) while in *It's Never Too Late to Mend* (1937), Slaughter is Squire Meadows, a Justice of the Peace who we first see dressed in his finery, leaving a country church after a Sunday service and praising the sermon with a heavily-ironic 'I feel a better man already'. But behind this facade, he is a cheat, a conman and a sadist who enjoys the excessive punishments he visits on his unfortunate charges who he describes, more than once, as his 'children' (anticipating the vicious puritans of Pete Walker's *House of Whipcord* [1974]).

We see him inspecting a row of sorry-looking prisoners, asking one if he's 'getting a little more used to the cat?' and telling another 'They'll be glad to see you when you get home – if ever you do' and later sneers at a 15 year-old prisoner, who was convicted for stealing a loaf of bread for his starving mother. It's worth bearing in mind that Meadows, for all his pantomime villainy (he actually, shamelessly, fondles his moustache as he plots his dastardly deeds) is one of the less-excessive Slaughter characters – he isn't a murderer or a rapist, just a corrupt and sadistic bastard and this is reflected in the fact that he isn't killed off in the hysterical climax but locked up in his own prison, bedraggled and babbling. Although this film is stagey even by Slaughter standards, the director David MacDonald manages to make good use of the settings, composing shots that go way beyond the merely functional; the punishment cell with the shadows of the bars projected on the wall and the J.P.s sitting at a table, top-hatted and cigar-smoking with the cat o'nine tails hanging on the wall behind them.

It's hard to know which is more disturbing – the oily fake virtue of Slaughter's characters is sometimes even more unsettling than his violent lechery. Certainly, the cackling, gurning killers are, to say the least, broadly-drawn. But for the working-class audience these films were aimed at, they puncture notions of bourgeois respectability while also feeding into a suspicion which is still with us today – that our social betters, for all their piety and wealth and philanthropic boasts, are greedy, lecherous, murderous hypocrites.

Kim Newman has observed how the protagonists in these films are 'stiff and ridiculous' (2002: 69) and he connects the Slaughter films to the 'anti-establishment' films of Pete Walker, which also feature ineffectual heroes powerless against their corrupt yet charismatic elders. Slaughter's characters, for all their lechery, greed and cruelty are always the most alive and his strange, stylised performances and undoubted presence mean it's easy to have sympathy for his parade of old devils. There's certainly little chance of him being upstaged by the bland nondescript heroes or the parade of cowering, screaming ingenues.

As well as seeing Slaughter's characters as 'direct precursors of the Hammer anti-heroes' (Richards 2001: 59) such as Dracula and Baron Frankenstein, Jeffery Richards also stresses his influence on a British strand of sensational popular film-making:

> If one can with justice describe the Slaughter films as a series of variations on a handful of basic themes, it would also be true to say that those themes were refreshed and revisited both by Gainsborough and by Hammer in a continuing cinema of excess. (ibid.)

It comes as no surprise to discover that the director Ken Russell, another advocate of excess was an admirer of the great barnstormer. As Joseph Lanza puts it, '"Tod Slaughter, yes!" Russell cheers at just the mention of his name' (Lanza 2007:10).

Pirie and Rigby are too quick to dismiss Slaughter. The former considers *The Crimes at the Dark House*, by any measure one of the actor's lesser vehicles (a bastardised, diluted version of the Wilkie Collins novel, *The Woman in White*). He describes Slaughter displaying 'little more than the boorish villainy of the golf club cad' (2007: 15), but this is understating the gleeful cruelty of Slaughter's characters – he is a golf club cad but one who happily slaughters children. As 'The Spinebreaker' in *The Crimes of Stephen Hawke*, he is interrupted by an interfering (and deeply unsympathetic) little boy. 'Come here, my little man' cajoles Slaughter and there follows an off-screen scream and the sound of a spine being snapped. Elsewhere, we are told that his Sweeney Todd has gone through 8 boy apprentices in 8 weeks and it's made clear they've ended up as pie filling. For Rigby:

> Slaughter's acting style would die with him…British horror in its halcyon years would be dominated by Christopher Lee and Peter Cushing, actors whose work is everything that Slaughter's is not – sleek, subtle, sophisticated and frequently sensual. (2000: 29)

This is undoubtedly true. One couldn't argue that there was anything sexy or subtle about the gurning Tod. But I think the Slaughter influence on British horror comes not from his acting style (which was dated even for the 1930s) but from the tone of his films. For Richards, Slaughter's work, this 'Cinema of Excess', stands in opposition to other traditions in the British cinema of the time, be it the epics of Alexander Korda or the comedies of Gracie Fields and George Formby, both traditions sharing a 'downplaying of sex and sexuality and the playing up of duty and self-denial' (2001: 140). The cruelty and savagery of the Slaughter films still carries a charge, which is not diluted by the frequent lurches into comedy. On the contrary, the tonal shifts from murdered children to comedy characters, from garroted coppers to treacly love scenes, create a kind of disorientation in the viewer. The work of Slaughter, with its distinctive blend of black comedy, violence and stylisation offers a vital link between Victorian music hall melodrama and British horror cinema.

The reliance on 'human monsters' in British cinema of the 1930s resulted from a number of factors. In part, it was a response to the oft-expressed social concerns around horror films while also reflecting the fact that many of the classic monsters – many of whom, ironically had been created by British writers – had been copyrighted by the major studios in the US. A focus on psycho killers rather than supernatural beings can also mean saving money on costly special effects. But it also springs from this fascination with murder, making the psycho killer sub-genre an enduring one which is stil in evidence today.

SHOCKERS AND COMEDIES

In the 1930s, the visceral dislike of the genre evidenced by the BBFC led to a situation where film-makers had to smuggle 'horror into comedies and thrillers rather than attempting to make outright horror films' (Conrich 1997: 228). The thriller, in all of its many guises, from Hitchcock's spy and chase narratives (*The Man Who Knew Too Much* [1934], *The 39 Steps* [1935]) to near-horror films [*The Dark Eyes of Midnight* [1939]) was enormously popular in the British cinema of this period. James Chapman, who refers to these films as 'shockers'[2] has estimated that:

> Some 350 thrillers were produced in Britain between 1930 and 1939, a figure which approximates to about one-fifth of all feature films made in the country...in sheer numbers it was surpassed only by the comedy. (Chapman 2001: 75)

For Chapman, the thriller, 'which makes no pretence of realism and which routinely foregrounded the sensational and the extraordinary' (2001: 93) deserves to be located squarely in Petley's Lost Continent. One of the best examples of the horrific thriller is another quota quickie, shot in Teddington Studios in Middlesex. *They Drive By Night* (1938) was directed by Arthur B. Woods (and shouldn't be confused with the Bogart film of the same name made two years later). What begins as a Hitchcockian 'wrong man' story set in a convincingly tawdry downmarket milieu – dance halls, smokey cafes, back-room poker games – becomes a study in psychosis.

Shorty (Emlyn Williams), fresh out of Pentonville prison, goes on the run after finding his dancer ex-girlfriend strangled. He masquerades as a trucker, finding some sort of refuge in the transport cafes and dark, forbidding provincial backroads before returning to the city to try and find the real killer, who the press have dubbed The Silk Stocking Strangler. The murderer turns out to be the amateur student of 'abnormal criminal psychology' Walter Hoover, played by our old friend, Ernest Thesiger. Hoover is a good example of the stereotypical British screen psycho, being sexually ambiguous and effete (with his silk smoking jacket and immaculately slicked-down hair), intellectual and cultured (speaking French and owning books such as The Thrill of Evil and Sex in Relation to Society). Thesiger, with his precise diction, fastidious manner and that astonishing nose seems at first to have come from a different film entirely: indeed, the film is nearly over by the time he makes his first appearance (57 minutes into the 79 minute running time), gluing newspaper clippings about the murder into a scrapbook. But his malign presence is anticipated from the outset. The world of the film is a very grim one, with anonymous locations and a persistent howling wind, dead leaves which are blown past the crowd waiting outside a prison where a man is to be hanged, the rain bucketing down.

It's a world steeped in murder, discussed in cafes and the subject of lurid billboards and headlines. In one telling moment, Shorty hides out in a newsreel cinema only to have to leave when a show called Famous Murderers begins. There is a persistent sense of impending doom which anticipates classic noir, emphasised by some striking directorial flourishes (such as the lamp fringes that obscure Shorty's eyes as he denies being the murderer) and the climactic plunge into horror mode comes as no surprise. In a startling moment, Shorty and the woman he loves are hiding out in one of those old abandoned mansions which keep cropping up in the gothic tradition when Thesiger's face, wide-eyed and cadaverous suddenly appears at one of the windows.

Robert Murphy may be exaggerating a bit when he talks of:

the atmosphere of unrelenting wind, rain and gloom which makes the average American film noir look bright and breezy in comparison (1997: 183)

but not much – this is a tough, bleak film. In contrast to Thesiger (whose character, we are told, 'always gives things a queer twist'), Emlyn Williams plays a strangely passive, largely reactive protagonist with a shifty, haunted look about him. He was no stranger to psychosis off-screen, being the author of the celebrated play Night Must Fall, about a charming killer with a severed head in a hat-box, filmed twice (in 1937 and 1964). He would also write an account of the Moors Murders, with the emblematic title Beyond Belief (1967). Arthur Woods joined the RAF when war broke out and was killed in a head-on plane crash over Hampshire in 1944.

In much the same way as horror was smuggled into thrillers, the addition of humour, while by no means unique to British genre items, was particularly pronounced at this time. Spooky goings on are revealed to be the work of smugglers or brigands or, after war breaks out, Nazi spies. The *Ghost Train* (1941), based on a play by Arnold Ridley (who went on to play Godfrey in the sit-com *Dad's Army*) is a typical example. This, the fourth adaptation, stars Arthur Askey who discovers that the titular train is not supernatural but merely a cover for fascist sympathisers. The popular comedian Will Hay had starred in a rip-off of Ridley's play, *Oh, Mr. Porter!* (1937) but his film for Ealing, *My Learned Friend* (1943) is much darker stuff.

Hay's comedy often revolved around a foolish character inserted into a stock setting and creating chaos, but *My Learned Friend* points toward the later (and far more celebrated) Ealing 'comedies of murder' such as *The Ladykillers* (1955) and *Kind Hearts and Coronets* (1949). Hay plays an ex-barrister who turns up on the 'kill list' of a disgruntled (and insane) former client, played with considerable intensity by Ealing regular Mervyn Johns. Anticipating Vincent Price vehicles such as *The Abominable Dr. Phibes* (1970) and *Theatre of Blood* (1973), Johns dons a variety of disguises in order to carry out his 'six little dramas of retribution, all beautifully staged'. The film, directed by Hay and Basil Dearden, features a brief appearance by Thesiger as a mischievous lunatic and a well-staged climactic struggle on top of Big Ben, with Hay and his doltish sidekick (Claude Holbert) chased across the clock-face by the demented yet always softly-spoken Johns. The ghoulish nature of *My Learned Friend* shouldn't come as a surprise given that a number of people who worked on the film – Dearden, producer Robert Hamer, screenwriter MacPhail, actor Johns – would reunite for the landmark *Dead of Night*.

It may be the case that the deep-seated English prejudice against horror and fantasy has encouraged film-makers to adopt a blackly comic tone: after all, if a genre isn't worth taking seriously, then it can only be regarded as comedy. It's undeniable, though, that horror and humour are close cousins and the British have traditionally excelled at both. Despite his stated dislike of the form, Pirie (2007) does acknowledge the black humour in Hammer, perhaps best-exemplifed by the cut in the *Curse of Frankenstein* from a murder to the Baron at breakfast requesting that his fiancée 'Pass the marmalade'. (Indeed, a popular website devoted to British horror films takes its name from this phrase.) Indeed, gallows humour is an enduring element of British horror and it's hard to imagine the sole reason directors from Whale to Hitchcock, Polanski to Pete Walker have indulged in it is down to the lowly status of horror in the popular imagining. For Hitchcock, it seems to be a device to help the horror go down - 'I hope to offset any tendency toward the macabre with humor [sic], a typically English form of humor' (in Spoto 1983: 270) – and I'm not convinced the oft-expressed notion that humour has a neutering effect on horror holds water. To use two of the more celebrated examples of this form, both *Psycho* (1960) and *Frenzy* are very funny and yet also shock and horrify. The humour adds a disturbing quality to the horror, making it hard for an audience to know how to react and this can be troubling in the best way.

If it didn't feel slightly incongruous invoking the Russian philosopher Mikhail Bakhtin in defence of the likes of Slaughter, Antony Balch and Pete Walker, it's not too much of a stretch to see their black comic excesses as a carnivalesque attack on the status quo through a combination of mocking humour, bad taste and chaos (see Bakhtin 1965). It's also surely significant that British horror has been celebrated to an almost fetishistic degree not in dramas but in two recent comedy shows. *The League of Gentlemen* (1999 -2002) is a kind of extended riff on horror movie conventions (village full of lunatics that persecute outsiders, nasty deeds that take place against a peaceful rural backdrop). Their Christmas Special was an Amicus-style anthology and the spin-off film *The League of Gentlemen's Apocalypse* (2005) pays extensive homage to *Blood On Satan's Claw*. Less successful, but even more obsessively detailed was *Dr. Terrible's House of Horrible* (2001) created by Graham Duff and Steve Coogan. The show featured a number of genre pastiches including another anthology, lesbian vampires and *Scream Satan Scream*, a witchfinder tale. There are also some well-chosen cameos from the likes of Angela Pleasence and Sheila Keith, the latter doing her *Frightmare* tarot card schtick.

BLIMEY!

The first British film to be slapped with the new, more restrictive version of the H certificate, *The Dark Eyes of London* (1939) aka *The Human Monster* stands out as the most sadistic home-grown shocker of the 1930s. This is the story of Dr. Orloff, a Tod Slaughter-style philanthropist/monster who runs a home for the 'destitute blind' as a cover for his nefarious deeds, getting a mis-shapen hulk called Jake to drown hapless victims and then dumping their bodies in the Thames in order to claim on their life insurance. It's another Edgar Wallace adaptation, this time from a 1926 novel and the author's contribution to the cinema is a notable one. For Chapman, the author 'provides a bridge between the literary and cinematic versions of the [thriller] genre' (2001: 82). In addition to writing more than 200 novels, a number of plays and reams of journalism, Wallace also produced and directed a number of adaptations of his work in the 1920s and wrote the original draft of *King Kong* (1933) before his death in 1932.

His novels also formed the basis of the influential series of German horror/thrillers known as *krimis* made from the late 1950s through to the early 1970s. This strange sub-genre anticipates both the Italian *giallo* films and American slasher movies, with a focus on bizarre crimes committed by fiendish masked killers in an expressionistic London of spooky mansions, fog-wreathed graveyards and shifty butlers recreated on a soundstage. Indeed, one such *krimi* was a remake of *Dark Eyes of London*, *Die toten Augen von London* (*The Dead Eyes of London* [1960]). Like *The Ghoul*, *The Dark Eyes of London* borrows heavily from the visual style of the Universal films, an influence emphasised by the presence of Hollywood horror star Bela Lugosi. Lugosi plays the dual role of Orloff and the supposedly-blind Dearborn, disguised pretty effectively with a walrus moustache, long wig and dark glasses and with his extremely distinctive voice redubbed by the English actor O.B. Clarence. It's a typical Lugosi performance, weird, stylised and not really very good and yet that intense gaze, strange intonation and those incredibly expressive hands give him an undeniable presence. While the film is a bit static in places, with lengthy scenes of exposition and the unnecessary presence of a irritating 'wise-cracking' Chicago cop, director Walter Summers manages to create some unsettling images.

The opening scene, with a shot of Tower Bridge followed by a body floating in the river would be echoed more than three decades later in Hitchcock's Frenzy. While the British cinema of the 1930s has nothing to rival the sadism and grue of American pictures such as The Most Dangerous Game and Murders in the Zoo (1933), the shots of twisted corpses lying in the mud provide a ghoulish charge. The scenes in the blind home are very creepy, as Dearborn reads from a braille bible – 'Give us a sign that we may see' – as an organ plays and the blind men sit around a table, almost completely immobile, the only movement the steam rising from their bowls of soup. Elsewhere, they are more like the undead in the earlier Lugosi picture, the deeply strange White Zombie (1932), shuffling around. In one startling scene, the 'brilliant but unbalanced' Orloff uses an electric charge to deafen one of his charges, after telling him 'You are blind and you can't speak. But you can hear and that will never do.' It's a pity that one of the murders – when Jake drowns a man in his bath – is rendered comical by the victim's cry of 'Blimey!' as he is pushed under the water. The Dark Eyes of London, more than any other British film of this period, illustrates the kinship between the 'shocker' and the horror picture, repeatedly sliding from one to the other. The critical reaction was one of predictable indignation. 'The Cinema' wrote:

> This adaptation of one of Edgar Wallace's best-known thrillers has an 'H' certificate and deserves it. The macabre nature of the story… is emphasised by its grisly concomitants. (Chapman 2001: 89)

Another Wallace adaptation released a year later was The Case of the Frightened Lady. This was directed by George King, based on a play which had been filmed in 1932 by The Ghoul's T. Hayes Hunter (which had starred Emlyn Williams), with sets designed by Bernard Robinson and a screenplay by Edward Dryhurst, who had just written Crimes at the Dark House for Slaughter and King (the British genre scene of the 1930s was a pretty incestuous one). The cast also includes Felix Aylmer (who would end up being victimised by The Mummy [1959]) and Patrick Barr (who would appear in three Pete Walker films). Frightened Lady has most of the elements familiar from the 1930s shockers – a country house complete with locked room and secret passage, some shifty servants, family secrets, murders and some scares.

The 'exotic horror' theme of The Ghoul is developed further here in the portrait of an established aristocratic family infected by a colonial evil. There is also a touch of the iconoclasm of The Old Dark House as the killer is revealed to be Lord Lebanon (Marius Goring), the sympathetic heir to the Lebanon family name, driven insane through years of in-breeding and introduced to Thuggee-style strangling – 'It's wonderful when people die quickly!' – while stationed in Delhi. It all ends on an apocalyptic note very apt for a country at war, with Lebanon shooting himself and his mother intoning mournfully 'a thousand years of history gone out like a candle in the wind'.

The German and British authorities shared a similar view of horror in war-time. Indeed, the Nazis didn't even wait for war to clamp down on a genre they regarded as morbid and decadent. The German horror film had effectively been killed off with the election of Hitler in 1933 and foreign films including Reuben Mamoulian's *Dr. Jeykll and Mr. Hyde* (1932) and James Whale's *The Invisible Man* (1933) were banned outright. Indeed, stills from *The Cabinet of Dr. Caligari* were included in the infamous exhibition of 'degenerate art' in 1937.

There's a common misconception that the BBFC operated an official ban on horror films in the second half of the 1930s; David Skal, for example, in his *The Monster Show: A Cultural History of Horror* (1994) specifically refers to such a ban (Skal 1994: 201). But this seems not to have been the case, although the BBFC, along with the American Production Code Administration, certainly had their misgivings about the genre. Alex Naylor suggests such rumours were part of a deliberate strategy by the PCA.

> The PCA, who interpreted the complex, decentralised and often confusing British censorship process for Hollywood studios, talked up and simplified British censorship organisations' dealings with horror films, to the point of suggesting to studios that the BBFC had instituted a 'ban' upon horror films. The PCA were at this time openly discouraging studios from making horror films as part of their attempt to guide studios towards 'inoffensive' types of filmmaking. (Naylor 2014)

Despite the efforts of the PCA, the genre continued to be successful in the US but there were no out-and-out horror films made in the UK between 1939–44 , although there were a couple of shockers, such as *The Door with Seven Locks* (1940; yet another Wallace adaptation) and *The Night Has Eyes* (1942). There were also a couple of ghost films in 1945, the Noel Coward adaptation *Blithe Spirit* and Gainsborough's *A Place of One's Own* which should come as no surprise, given that there had been a lot more dying than usual going on. The best example of an English ghost story from this period isn't actually English at all but a Paramount film shot in the US. *The Uninvited* (1944), directed by Lewis Allen deals with a brother and sister (Ray Milland and Ruth Hussey) who move into a haunted cliff-top cottage in – a very Californian – Cornwall. It's an elegant, restrained film, if a bit too talky which owes a lot to Hitchcock's *Rebecca* (1940) with some high-profile admirers (Martin Scorsese selected it as one of his '11 Scariest Horror Films of all time' [2009], alongside *Night of the Demon* [1957] and *Psycho*). Allen's film is noteworthy in that it takes the supernatural seriously, unlike so many previous spook shows which offered up all manner of unconvincing explanations (the smugglers and spies in *The Ghost Train*) or played it for laughs (*The Ghost Goes West* [1936]). Allen – who would go on to make the exciting Frank Sinatra thriller *Suddenly* (1954) – offers up some chills, such as the moment where Milland and Hussey prattle on, failing to notice how the flowers between them wither and die in seconds and when we finally get to see the apparition, a vengeful ectoplasmic female, it's extremely effective (too effective for the BBFC who removed the special effects sequences). *The Unvited*'s very civilised, understated horror anticipates *The Haunting* (1961), even down to the inclusion of a heavily-coded lesbian character (Cornelia Otis Skinner's stylish and charismatic Miss Holloway provoked the Legion of Decency to complain to Paramount). Shockers and spooks had replaced the visceral terror of *The Ghoul* and *The Dark Eyes of London* and the Americans were colonising the rural English chiller. But the British horror film was about to return with a vengeance.

DEAD OF NIGHT (1945)

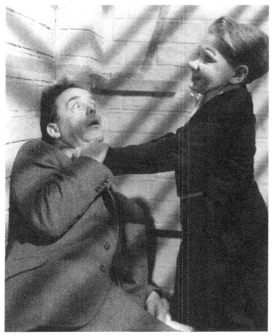

It's tempting to see this celebrated Ealing portmanteau film as a false start before Hammer kicked off the gothic cycle in earnest a decade later. But rather than anticipating the future, *Dead of Night* feels much more like the last gasp of an earlier kind of horror. Indeed, in so many important ways – the anthology structure, the focus on obsession, morbid psychology and dreams, the elaborate visual style – it reflects the way European horror was still in thrall to German Expressionism.

It is a truth commonly observed that so much horror is concerned with external threat – Dracula heading west from the east or the exotic origins of so much 1930s

The unfortunate Craig meets Hugo: *Dead of Night*

horror. Even when the locale is a familiar one, as in *The Ghoul* or the soundstage Wales of *The Wolfman* (1941), the menace has a distinctly foreign flavour – an Egyptian jewel or a gypsy curse. In the Universal horror films, the monsters, sadists and killers were almost always from overseas; the Hungarians Lugosi and Lorre, the British Karloff, Atwill, Clive, Rains. But *Dead of Night* seeks to locate its horror in a very recognisable England of country cottages, suburban bus routes and brightly-lit Chelsea apartments. It stands out amongst the eerie thrillers and ghost stories of the 1940s for its disturbing depiction of the way the irrational and the chaotic can erupt into a comfortable bourgeois England. The idea of the film as an aberration among the cosey output of Ealing still persists, although there have been a number of recent attempts to challenge this view, as in the 2012 'Ealing Light and Dark' film season at London's BFI Southbank. As well as the black comedies for which the studio is justly celebrated and the less celebrated noirish thrillers

(*It Always Rain on Sunday* [1947]) a film such as *Went The Day Well?* (1944), divorced from its war-time context is a chilling view of rural England, the remarkable scene where an old woman chucks pepper in a Nazi soldier's face before axing him to death looking forward to *Frightmare*'s psychotic rural granny.

The portmanteau film had been around for a long time, with Griffith's *Intolerance* (1916) being an early example. There have been numerous non-horror portmanteaus but the abiding association of the form with the horror genre started early in Germany with *Unheimliche Geschichten* (1919), Fritz Lang's supernatural fantasy *Der Müde Tod /Destiny* (1921) and *Das Wachsfigurenkabinett /Waxworks* (1925), which featured an early screen outing for Jack the Ripper (played by Caligari himself, Werner Krauss) who had become an important figure in German art: he appeared in Frank Wedekind's play *Die Büchse der Pandora /Pandora's Box* (1906), later filmed to great acclaim by GW Pabst and the Ripper was also referenced by the painters Otto Dix and George Grosz. This Teutonic influence, both structurally and thematically can be identified in *Dead of Night*.

The stories in the Ealing film are woven into the wraparound narrative with considerable skill. Architect Walter Craig (Mervyn Johns, here twitchily anxious rather than menacing) is invited to a cottage in the country where there is a gathering of people. Craig, visibly agitated, explains to the guests that he has had a recurring dream about the cottage and everyone who is there. This encourages some of the other guests to share their stories of supernatural events – a premonitory dream, a meeting with a child ghost, a haunted mirror, a golfing spook – as a German psychiatrist attempts to provide a scientific explanation for the increasingly bizarre events, before providing a story of his own about a mad ventriloquist.

Unlike the later Amicus anthologies, the film is a collaboration between a number of directors, all of whom would go on to bigger, if not better, things. The Hearse Driver and the framing story were directed by Basil Dearden, the co-director of *My Learned Friend* who would make *The Blue Lamp* (1950) for Ealing. Dearden would team up with writer/producer Michael Relph (art director on *Dead of Night*) for a series of well-crafted thrillers which deal with social issues (*Victim* [1961]) about the laws against homosexuality and *Sapphire* [1959] about race). The Hearse Driver is a slim, mildly creepy affair, best-known for the 'Just room for one more inside' line given to the undertaker/bus driver played by Miles Malleson. The next story, Christmas Party, was one of two directed by Alberto Cavalcanti and is another pretty thin, if atmospheric ghost story. The crime in the the story, the murder of a young boy, Francis Kent, by his older sister Constance in 1865 may have been familiar to British audiences of the time. It had been referenced in novels by Wilkie Collins (*The Moonstone* [1868]) and Dickens (*The Mystery of Edwin Drood* [1870]) and inspired the recent non-fiction book *The Suspicions of Mr. Whicher* (2008) by Kate Summerscale. Cavalcanti was a Brazilian surrealist and documentarian who had directed *Went the Day Well?* and would go on to make the tough British noir *They Made Me a Fugitive* (1947).

The third story, Haunted Mirror, is arguably the best. The title succinctly sums up the story, which begins when Joan (Googie Withers) buys a mirror for her fiancé, Peter (Ralph Michael) which appears to be possessed by the man who used to own it, an embittered aristocratic wife murderer. The segment is directed by Robert Hamer, a gifted director undone by a pronounced self-destructive urge. It's a story about two distinct worlds, the normal world of the brightly-lit airy apartment and the dark, threatening yet seductive world of the gloomy, ornately-furnished mirror room, Hamer conjuring up a very real sense of the irrational and the horrific which threaten the security of what we think of as reality. The complacent, arid, passionless existence of Peter and Joan is emphasised from the outset, the episode beginning with her explaining the difficulty in buying presents for men ('they all seem to have everything they want'). When she brings her present home, Joan tells Peter 'I thought you'd like to look at yourself', the exchange emphasising their claustrophobic, hermetic cosiness. It appears Peter has everything he wants – except a pathway into a libidinal world of passion and murder. As the couple stand and gaze at their reflection, Joan remarking 'Hmm, a handsome couple' Peter's expression suddenly changes and he glances over his shoulder. 'I thought I saw something', he tells his fiancée but he doesn't know what it was.

Watching this scene today, there is a horrible irony in Joan's subsequent suggestion that Peter may be hallucinating due to lunchtime drinking. Hamer's crippling alcoholism would eventually lead to terrifying bouts of delirium tremens and on one occasion he was chased back to his Chelsea flat by a mutilated lobster which he saw emerge from the lake in Battersea Park, hearing its legs crunch as he trapped them in the lift door (see Jackson 2004). There are continued reminders of the affluent complacency of Peter and Joan, the way normality is asserted after Peter's scare with the suggestion that they 'dress up and spend a lot of money' and her description of wedding preparations and the move into a palatial Chelsea apartment as 'usual chaos'. The room beyond the mirror, with its gloomy romance, flickering fire and four-poster bed, wood panelling and ornate décor, takes an increasing hold on Peter and as with Jekyll and Hyde and any number of werewolf stories, there is a strong sense of wish fulfilment in his obsession. While all Joan sees reflected in the mirror is an 'ordinary room with you and me in it', for Peter the dark bed chamber 'almost becomes the real room and my own bedroom imaginary'. When Joan returns to the shop where she purchased the mirror, she is told the tale of Francis Eddington, a 'handsome man' of 'dominant character (and) a violent temper'. There is even a coy reference to his 'enormous energy', Eddington with his passion and cruelty being everything her fiancé is not. When she smashes the mirror as Paul attemps to strangle her, order appears to be restored. But as Charles Barr puts it:

> The effect is to restore the status quo, this time definitively: he no longer remembers the nightmare, and they are free to go back to being a charming young couple, which is what they presumably will do. It is like a lobotomy. (Barr 1999: 57)

It's also tempting to read the story as dramatising the tensions in British cinema, with both Jonathan Rigby and Mark Duguid seeing the world beyond the mirror as representing the same dark and passionate forces at play in films by Gainsborough and, later, Hammer (see Rigby 2000; Duguid et al 2102). Certainly it is not hard to imagine Eddington being played by James Mason or Christopher Lee. Charles Barr finds something similar, the 'dark world' representing the kind of desires that 'form a current running underground, surfacing only intermittently, for instance in the line of lusty Gainsborough productions of the 'forties… and in the films of Michael Powell' (ibid.). Barr considers that the tyranny of 'good taste' in the early '50s led to sex and violence having to 'force their way up again like the *Dead of Night* visions – most spectacularly in the explosion of British horror films, a cycle to which Powell contributes with the most execrated film of his career, *Peeping Tom*' (1999: 58).

Certainly Hamer, like his protagonist, was drawn to the dark side. He memorably stated his desire to 'make films about people in dark rooms doing beastly things to each other' (in Bygraves 2012) and would go on to make what is arguably the best of the Ealing comedies, *Kind Hearts and Coronets*. He also made a handful of evocative gloomy thrillers. *Pink String and Sealing Wax* (1945) and *It Always Rains on Sundays*, both of which rework the theme of Haunted Mirror, the eruption of the dark past into the normal world, while his *The Long Memory* (1953) is a tough British noir shot on location in Gravesend and Shad Thames. His tantalising unmade projects include an underworld story set in Soho and a film about a young man who sets out to commit a murder to be famous. Hamer's last film, *School For Scoundrels* (1960) had to be finished by others, as his drinking finally got the better of him and he collapsed on set more than once. He died in 1963, aged 52. It's hard to argue with David Thomson, for whom Hamer's career is 'the most serious miscarriage of talent in the postwar British cinema' (2002: 367).

The fourth tale, Golfing Story, is by far the weakest, less due to its being so tonally different but more because it really isn't funny. The director Charles Crichton would go on to the likes of *The Lavender Hill Mob* (1951) and *A Fish Called Wanda* (1988) but his contribution here relies on clumsy innuendo and stupid sight gags. Cavalcanti's second entry is the last, and best-known story, Ventriloquist's Dummy. Michael Redgrave is both sad and very creepy as Maxwell Frere, bullied and browbeaten by his dummy, Hugo who appears to have a mind of his own. There's some irony, given the film's title, that many of the other stories have scenes that take place in broad daylight (the bus crash in the Hearse Driver or the first sight of the Haunted Mirror), but in the climactic story the whole thing has an increasingly claustrophobic, shut-in quality. This is necessary for budgetary reasons in the opening scene, which purports to take place in Paris but the spaces gradually shrink, from nightclub to bar to hotel room to finally, a padded cell. Jonathan Rigby (2000) has identified the way the final scenes – when Frere has 'become' Hugo – anticipate the end of *Psycho* but the theme of losing one's will, of becoming an automaton is repeated throughout the film. Maxwell becomes Hugo just as Paul loses (gives up?) his sense of self in the haunted mirror and at the end of the framing device the now-murderous Craig will explain to his would-be victim, 'If only I'd left here when I wanted to, when I still had a will of my own'.

This notion of falling under a malign spell was a recurring theme in Expressionism, the most celebrated example being that of the somnambulist Cesare in *Caligari*, and the film's debt to the Germans is nowhere clearer than in the closing section, where the framing device comes full circle (one can't correctly refer to it as 'the end'). Early on, Craig predicts that the real horror will begin when the psychiatrist breaks his glasses and when this happens (the moment given a chilling emphasis), the room empties, leaving the architect alone with the doctor. The cosy living room of earlier is now a place of gothic gloom, the light dim, the open fire casting flickering shadows. Craig is now 'in the grip of a force that's driving me towards something of unspeakable evil… a nightmare of horror'.

The montage sequence that follows Craig's murder of the psychiatrist is quite unlike anything else in British horror up to that time, an extraordinarily explosive depiction of the way dark forces can consume the unwary. Craig is propelled through the stories in a remarkable waking nightmare wherein he appears among the kids playing games at the Christmas party before fleeing up a shadowy flight of winding stairs (shot at an Expressionistic canted angle). As the image ripples and distorts, he begs to be allowed to hide in the room beyond the mirror only to see his own corpse splayed out on the bed. He is attacked by a crowd of hideous, garishly-made up revellers, dragged to the floor and carried to a cell where the jailer (Malleson again) informs him that there is 'just room for one more inside'. Locked in, the now-animate Hugo advances upon him, while, in a very disquieting image, the faces of the transfixed guests are pressed up against the cell door. As Hugo strangles Craig, the hysterical score fades out to the sound of a telephone. Craig wakes in bed and answers the phone. It's Foley, inviting him to his country cottage for the weekend. It's clear when Craig tosses a coin to decide whether to go or not what the answer will be. Malign fate has marked the unfortunate architect and the final shots of the film – Craig driving up to the cottage, meeting Foley – are the same as the first, the whole story one endless loop.

The framing device is arguably the strongest of the stories, in marked contrast to the later Amicus anthologies, where the writers seemed to be in an increasing hurry to gather a bunch of characters together so the tales could be told. The oft-employed 'It was all a dream' device is rightly regarded as a cop-out, letting both characters and audience off the hook – 'this is what could have happened, be thankful that it doesn't'. Fritz Lang's otherwise excellent noir *The Woman in the Window* (1944) exemplifies this approach. But in *Dead of Night* the dream is employed as an integral part of the horror, a character trapped in an endless nightmare which won't ever stop. This idea of an unending terror, a dream from which one cannot ever wake also comes from Weimar cinema: consider the importance given in Expressionism to the spiral, which goes on and on. The German title for *Dead of Night, Traum ohne Ende/Dream Without End* is extremely apt. (The cosmologist Fred Hoyle reportedly came up with his Steady State theory – which posits that the universe has no beginning or end – after watching the Ealing film.)

For decades, *Dead of Night* would seem to have had little influence on the British horror film. The thriller *Three Cases of Murder* (1955) employed a similar structure, as well as being a three director collaboration. There are watchable enough segments from David Eady and George More O'Ferrall (the latter story possibly featuring some uncredited input from its star, Orson Welles) but In the Picture, directed by Wendy Toye is an extremely effective and unusually unpleasant story about an unfortunate who ends up trapped in a painting in an art gallery (the story was reworked for the *Night Gallery* pilot [1969]). But the anthology form was revived with a vengeance in the 1960s by Amicus, a small production company formed by two American ex-pats, producer Max J. Rosenberg and screenwriter/producer Milton Subotsky and based at Shepperton Studios.

AMICUS

Rosenberg and Subotsky had worked together in the US making low-budget musicals such as *Rock, Rock, Rock* (1956), for which the latter wrote nine songs. In 1955 they approached Hammer with the idea of making a Frankenstein film in colour. James Carreras may not have liked their pitch (or Subotsky's script) but he liked the idea enough and the end result was *The Curse of Frankenstein* (1956), a huge hit for the company. Although Subotsky's script was never used (and the contribution of both men never acknowledged publically by the company) the concept alone was enough to net Rosenberg and Subotsky a pay-off of 15% of the net profits (for more on the Rosenberg/Subotsky Frankenstein, see Pirie 2007; and for an analysis of Subotsky's script, see Nutman 2008).

Both men came to England in the late 1950s and worked on *City of the Dead* aka *Horror Hotel* (1960), although Rosenberg was uncredited. This is a striking monochrome gothic which feels very American, owing a considerable debt to the writing of H.P. Lovecraft and the extremely atmospheric B-movies produced by Val Lewton at RKO. Despite being shot in Walton-on-Thames by a British director (John Moxey) and a largely British cast (Christopher Lee, the very creepy Patricia Jessel) it was set in the US and the finished film has a curious, mid-Atlantic feel.

Peter Hutchings has suggested that for many critics, 'there was always something suspiciously "foreign"' about Amicus' (2008: 132) and this was only reinforced by the way that, unlike Hammer, they largely eschewed home-grown gothic subjects in favour of US sources. Some of their scripts were written by the noted genre author Robert Bloch (who famously quipped that 'Amicus is Latin for low-budget' [qtd. in Nutman 2008: 53]), who would mail them over from his home in California while the anthologies *Tales From The Crypt* (1972) and *Vault of Horror* (1973) were adaptations of stories from the EC comics of the same name.

Ironically given the name of their company, Rosenberg and Subotsky had a difficult relationship that would ultimately end badly. Subotsky was a gentle, geeky film and theatre buff while Rosenberg, a lawyer who was often regarded as 'the outside man' was more hardnosed and spent a lot of his time back in New York.

Both men also seemed to have a curious distaste for horror films. Rosenberg said the genre was 'never a favourite of mine' (qtd. in Nutman 2008: 34) while Subotksy was more outspoken, saying 'I don't want to put on the screen anything which dehumanises, brutalises or degrades people'. When asked why he made horror films, Subotsky joked that 'it was the only kind of cinema where you could avoid sex and violence' (Pirie 2007: 133). Was Subotsky joking – or explaining? This equivocation about the horror genre may be why they worked so frequently with Freddie Francis. Francis was an excellent cameraman, particularly when working with black and white (*The Innocents* [1961], *The Elephant Man* [1980]) but he was a lacklustre director at best and had little if any interest in horror. Although he worked at Hammer, directing such shoddy fare as *The Evil of Frankenstein* (1964) and *Dracula Has Risen from the Grave* (1968), he claimed to have never seen a Terence Fisher film. (He also turned down the chance to photograph David Lynch's *Blue Velvet* [1986], after reading the script and describing it as 'terrible'! [in Perks 1995: 43]).

As was the case with Hammer, the Amicus output was more varied than they are often given credit for. As well as the celebrated anthologies, there were musicals (*It's Trad, Dad* [1962] the directorial debut of Richard Lester); a couple of *Dr. Who* spin-offs; would-be prestige literary adaptations *The Birthday Party* (1968), directed by William Friedkin and *A Touch of Love* (1969) as well as a series of horror and sci-fi pictures. Most of these single-story genre films were poor – *The Deadly Bees* (1966), *The Terrornauts* (1967), the Hammer-ish period film *And Now the Screaming Starts* (1973) – but there were some interesting misfires.

These include the Jekyll and Hyde-inspired *I Monster* (1970), directed by the 21-year-old would-be wunderkind Stephen Weeks and intended to showcase a new kind of 3D, which in the end failed to work while *The Beast Must Die* (1974) was a weird mixture of Agatha Christie and Blaxploitation notable mainly for the William Castle-style 'Werewolf Break' which appears towards the end. (While the US title, *Black Werewolf*, is much better, the British title is an example of Subotsky's curious habit of buying the rights to the titles of existing, unrelated books and re-using them. *The Beast Must Die* was originally the title of a crime thriller by the poet Cecil Day-Lewis (writing as Nicholas Blake) which had itself been filmed twice, and Subotsky unsuccessfully attempted to purchase the title *I Have No Mouth But I Must Scream* from Harlan Ellison, leaving him to settle for the more prosaic *And Now the Screaming Starts*. *Dr. Terror's House of Horrors* [1964] was borrowed from a little-seen compilation film from 1942.)

The often slapdash approach that the company took to their material can be seen in two of their more interesting films, the Robert Bloch adaptations *The Psychopath* (1965) and *The Skull* (1965). The former film, a serial killer story which anticipates some of Dario Argento's inconherent narratives of the 1970s without his delirious set-pieces, although creepy in places was fatally flawed when Subotksy changed the identity of the murderer during post-production! This was the kind of interference that led Freddie Francis to quip that 'Milton apart from wanting to be a writer, wanted to be an editor' (in Nutman 2008: 40). In the case of *The Skull*, Subotsky's shooting script was only 40 pages long, although this is what ended up giving the finished film such a strange, extremely atmospheric quality. Director Francis had to pad out the running time with the help of some eerie lighting, a prowling camera and some impressive cinematography, particularly the repeated trick of filming events through the eyeholes of the skull.

Jonathan Rigby describes the end result as 'style over substance' (2000: 146) and the film is certainly unlike anything else Amicus attempted, with its nightmare logic, sparse dialogue and long scenes where little happens but the atmosphere of foreboding increases. There is a genuinely scary scene when Cushing is taken from his home by two men claiming to be cops and endures an eerie drive to a house where he is forced to play Russsian roulette in front of a silent judge. The camera stays close in on Cushing during this sequence – sweaty, his hair awry, huge expressive blue eyes registering fear then relief as the trigger clicks on an empty chamber.

The Skull also represents a couple of the other strengths of Amicus. Firstly, the strident score by the celebrated composer Elisabeth Luytens, one of a number she wrote for the company. It also has a very good cast – Peter Cushing, Patrick Wymark, Christopher Lee, Jill Bennett, Nigel Green with small roles for Michael Gough and Patrick Magee (even if they are given very little to do). In fact, such unusually starry casts can be regarded as an Amicus trademark, particularly in the anthology films where an actor could get paid for a couple of days work. Ralph Richardson, David Warner, Diana Dors, Herbert Lom, Jack Palance, Terry-Thomas, Joan Collins and Donald Sutherland were a few of those who appeared alongside established genre stars like Cushing, Lee, Gough and Donald Pleasence.

Amicus's main claim to distinction lies in the seven anthology or portmanteau films they produced between 1965 and 1974: *Dr. Terror's House of Horrors, Torture Garden* (1967), *The House That Dripped Blood* (1970), *Asylum* (1972), *Tales From the Crypt, Vault of Horror* and *From Beyond the Grave* (1974). The lesser-known anthology film *Tales That Witness Madness* (1973) was not made by Amicus but by an outfit called World Film Services although one could be forgiven for thinking it was, what with Freddie Francis directing and a good cast (Donald Pleasence, Jack Hawkins, Kim Novak). But the stories are much sillier, particularly the one where an artist betrays his wife, played by a wooden Joan Collins with his non-human lover, an even more wooden tree.

The anthology films all share their same basic premise with *Dead of Night*: a group of characters meet up in an unfamiliar environment (fairground, crypt, backstreet antique shop) where a mysterious stranger relates a series of stories that illustrate what has happened/will happen/could happen. Each story is 15–20 minutes long and has a twist ending. When all the stories are told, the mysterious stranger is revealed to be undead/ Death/Satan and the characters discover they are dead/in Hell. Even when the framing device is different, the end result is essentially the same with a handful of stories and a 'shock' ending. So, in *Asylum*, a newly-arrived doctor is greeted by a creepy warder who tells him he must interview four patients in an attempt to discover the identity of his predecessor, Dr. Starr. After the stories are told, the warder confesses that he is Starr then kills the doctor.

The films are more playful than those of Hammer, hokey and self-conciously reflexive and yet they are also, at times, more vicious. This playful quality is embodied in the central character in most of the films, the 'master of ceremonies' to use Peter Hutchings' phrase. In a number of the films, this character – whether it's the fairground performer Dr. Diabolo in *Torture Garden* (Burgess Meredith), the Cryptkeeper in a monk's habit in *Tales From the Crypt* (Richardson) or a Yorkshire-accented antique shop owner (Cushing again) in *From Beyond the Grave* – ends the film by breaking the fourth wall and directly adressing the audience. So Diabolo talks about those lucky few who escape his domain before looking straight into the camera (wearing a ridiculous would-be devilish eyebrows-and-beard combo) and asking 'But will you?' while the Cryptkeeper ends with 'Who's next? Perhaps you?' *Vault of Horror*, however does away entirely with the narrator and while Cushing's tarot-reading German Dr. Schreck clearly performs as a 'master of ceremonies', he does it without addressing the audience directly.

This playful quality is also evident in the number of self-reflexive moments: a character in *Vault of Horror* reading the novelisation of *Tales From the Crypt*; a copy of Lotte Eisner's *The Haunted Screen* appearing during the credits of *The House That Dripped Blood*; the silly bit in *Vault of Horror* where Robin Nedwell and Geoffrey Davies, two of the stars of the *Doctor* series of sit-coms (1969–77) appear as graverobbing medical students, and the striking moment in *Dr. Terror* where Roy Castle's character spots a poster for the film he's appearing in, with the actors' names replaced by those of the characters. The anthologies have, like most of the single-story Amicus films and in sharp contrast to Hammer, contemporary settings.

This means that they have either dated hideously or acquired a kind of retro-chic, depending on how you look at it. There is a real charge in the horrendous acts being carried out in groovy bachelor pads (David Warner's place in *From Beyond...* 'just off the Edgware Road'), home counties splendour and grotty suburban living rooms. Just how important a sense of place is to the anthologies is indicated by the credit sequences, which all, with the exception of *Dr. Terror...*, feature a prowling, sometimes subjective, camera tracking around an old house (*The House That Dripped Blood*), a fairground (*Torture Garden*), a cemetery (*Tales From the Crypt*), the Thames and riverside apartment block (*Vault of Horror*) and Highgate Cemetery (*From Beyond the Grave*) while in *Asylum* we follow a character as he arrives at the mist-shrouded institution set in a huge gothic mansion (actually New Lodge in Winkfield, Berkshire, which was also home to the titular caveman in *Trog* [1970]).

These lengthy scenes go way beyond traditional establishing shots and offer a perfect illustration of the Amicus tone, both semi-parodic (the creaky doors and rolling mist) and genuinely creepy (the murky, daylit cemetery in *From Beyond...* complete with a burst of off-screen gibbering). There is a sense of the chaos that lurks in the corners of the everyday – a wrong turn taken on a guided tour or getting into the wrong train carriage. A striking example of this is the opening of *Vault of Horror*, when a scene of anonymous characters in sober suits (and a boho Tom Baker looking very like his Rasputin in *Nicholas and Alexandra* [1971]) entering a lift one by one is accompanied by hysterically portentuous music.

Subotsky's contribution (as producer, if not screenwriter) is often undervalued and despite his dislike for the genre, he deserves to be regarded as an important figure in British horror cinema. He was instrumental in Amicus being Hammer's main rival throughout the 1960s and early 70s and even if one considers just the anthology films, they have a distinctive quality and charm all their own. However, his *laissez faire* approach to a lot of the films and his general lack of insight doesn't help his cause. As well as his underwritten scripts and slash-and-burn approach to post-production, he was dismissive of the remarkable *Scream and Scream Again* (1969), a co-production between Amicus and AIP. Although he must have been wounded when the film-makers ditched his script, for him to suggest the film's success was down to the title rather than its many virtues is baffling. (The film, directed by Gordon Hessler, feels much more AIP than Amicus and so it is discussed in Chapter 3.)

Kim Newman describes the Amicus anthologies as 'about fifty mini-movies in which something supernaturally horrid happens to an embarrassed guest star' (1988: 18) but this is a criticism of the format just as much as it is of the films. As Hutchings suggests, 'it is in the nature of the portmanteau film...to be uneven and inconsistent' (2002: 144), going on to point out that most of the attention paid to *Dead of Night* focuses on the haunted mirror and ventriloquist's dummy tales. Subotsky, who unsurprisingly – even unnecessarily - described *Dead of Night* as 'one of my favourite films' (in Nutman 2008: 34) seems to have been particularly taken with the Haunted Mirror episode, remaking it twice in *From Beyond...* with both a haunted door and mirror!

It is undoubtedly true, though, that some of these 'mini-movies' are very good and the best of them showcase that very EC nastiness – vicious, blackly comic tales of Old Testament-style retribution. In Poetic Justice (*Tales from the Crypt*), warm-hearted binman Grimsdyke (nicely played by Cushing) is driven to suicide by his snobby neighbour who, as the culmination of a campaign of cruelty, sends him Valentine's cards with malicious rhymes in them. One year later, Grimsydyke returns as a zombie to tear out his tormentor's heart, leaving it wrapped in a love letter. In the even grimmer Blind Alleys (also *Tales from the Crypt*), an ex-military sadist (Nigel Patrick) with a pet Alsatian becomes the head of a school for the blind. After his tyrannical regime ends in the death of one of their number, the blind men take revenge and imprison both dog and owner in separate cells. When the Major is freed, he has to navigate his way through a makeshift maze lined with hundreds of razor blades only to emerge in front of the room which contains his very hungry, very angry dog. The door opens, the dog charges out and the light goes out. Perhaps the best of the Amicus stories is the genuinely eerie An Act of Kindness. The put-upon (and aptly-named) Lowe (Ian Bannen), unhappily married to Mabel (Diana Dors) and with one unhappy son, has what appears to be a chance encounter with a blind ex-serviceman, Jim (a creepy Donald Pleasence), who introduces him to his daughter, Emily (Pleasence's real-life daughter, the even creepier Angela). They start an affair and Emily stabs an effigy of Mabel, which results in her death. On the day of Lowe and Emily's wedding, when the time comes to cut the cake, she instead cuts into the figure of the groom on the cake and Lowe is killed. Jim and Emily tell Lowe's son that 'We always answer children's prayers...one way or another'. With its seedy suburban setting, this segment offers a nightmarish kind of kitchen-sink horror, full of supernatural menace in a humdrum setting – Dors having a lock of her hair cut off while travelling on a bus or the weird song Emily sings to an uncomfortable Lowe. David Pirie accurately described the episode as 'Pinterish' (see Pirie 2007) and indeed, it can be regarded as the missing link between the Amicus horrors and their adaptation of The Birthday Party. As with Poetic Justice (middle-class creep plots to shift binman out of a pleasant neighbourhood) and Blind Alleys (ex-officer treats his lower-class charges as inferiors), there is a strong, most un-American emphasis on social class in these stories – Lowe is not just a bad husband and father but he's also a liar who pretends to be something he's not, falsely claiming to be the recipient of a Distinguished Service Medal.

Indeed, for all their in-jokes and self-referentiality, the world of the anthology films is a chaotic place of greed and cruelty, a place where, as Peter Hutchings puts it:

> wives kill husbands (Tales From the Crypt, Vault of Horror), husbands kill wives (Dr. Terror's House of Horrors, Vault of Horror), brothers kill sisters (Vault of Horror), sisters kill brothers (Asylum), nephews kill uncles (Torture Garden) and children kill parents (The House that Dripped Blood) or arrange to have their parents killed (From Beyond the Grave). (2002: 140)

The brevity of the stories, and the resulting lack of characterisation, only adds to this atmosphere of brutal misanthropy, where characters gleefully bump each off as a result of domestic strife, marital disharmony, greed or just plain spite. For all Subotsky's oft-stated dislike of graphic excess, the Amicus anthologies, with their grim humour and numerous stories of twisted families doing terrible things in shabby suburban surroundings, come closer to the seedy nastiness of Pete Walker than the period fantasies of Hammer.

Rosenberg and Subotsky had an acrimonious split in the mid-seventies. As gothic horror faltered, the last Amicus productions were a series of rubber monster movies adapted from Edgar Rice Burroughs (The Land That Time Forgot [1975], At The Earth's Core [1976]).

Rosenberg continued his career in the US, and his post-Amicus work includes *The Incredible Melting Man* (1977) and Paul Schrader's *Cat People* (1982), a reworking of the 1942 Jacques Tourneur film, which Subotksy had planned to remake back in the 1960s. His last feature was Alex De La Iglesia's *Perdita Durango* (1997) an overheated, violent thriller which Subotsky would, no doubt, have hated.

Subotksy, meanwhile, made a couple of disappointing anthologies, *The Uncanny* (1977) and *The Monster Club*. The former, shot in Canada offered a collection of silly stories about evil cats. He had long wanted to make a portmanteau horror for children – *The House That Dripped Blood* was originally intended as an A certificate until the distributor Rank balked – but *The Monster Club* is awful, neither scary nor involving and notable only for the inclusion of some terrible pop acts (BA Robertson) and the sad spectacle of Vincent Price and John Carradine disco-dancing.

CHAPTER 2: HAMMER — STUDIO AS AUTEUR

The story of Hammer horror has become familiar through repetiton. After more than twenty years of making low-budget comedies and thrillers, a small production company based in a series of country houses in the home counties exploited the new-found freedoms that came in the wake of the X certificate to make a series of costume gothic horror films in colour. They became the most important and influential makers of genre cinema since Universal — in part by reviving most of the Golden Age monsters and reworking them for a thrill-hungry public, injecting a heretofore unprecedented amount of graphic gore and sex. The leap from country house production company to global success seems like something out of an Ealing film, the Little Horror Studio That Could. Then came the inevitable fall as their stylish reworkings of oft-told stories suffered due to cost-cutting in the face of rising production costs in the 1960s, followed by market saturation, self-parody, soft-porn and Kung Fu in the 1970s.

Looking at Hammer's output today, it can be hard to see what all the fuss was about. The remarkable qualities of their early films — the vivid use of colour, the overtly sexualised horror, the dynamic physicality — can easily be overlooked after an endless series of imitations, reworkings and parodies. The enormous affection fans have for Hammer may also be part of the problem. They've become a cosy national treasure and thus neutered. Their rise to fame was accompanied by howls of outrage and consequently they were always wary of being accepted. As the executive/producer/director and eventual owner, Michael Carreras remarked:

> When the National Film Theatre gave us a two-week season, I was terrified. I thought if they made us respectable, it would ruin our whole image. (Hutchings 1993: 187)

They had already managed to avoid such respectability after receiving the Queen's Award for Industry in 1968 but it's hard to avoid the thought that, what with Royal Mail releasing a series of Hammer stamps and *Dracula* recently recertificated in the UK as a 12A (!) that Carreras's fears have finally been realised. But then this is surely the nature of things, with genres and traditions shifting over time from consolidation to exhaustion and then renewed elsewhere — what John G. Cawelti refers to as 'the life cycle characteristic of genres' (2003: 260) — with yesterday's ghastly shocker becoming today's cosy institution. Hammer, perhaps more than any other production company, steered a perilous course between outraged scorn and admiring acceptance.

The importance of Hammer can scarcely be overstated. Consider that the first British vampire film came as late as 1952 with *Old Mother Riley Meets the Vampire* and a very tired Bela Lugosi playing second fiddle to Arthur Lucan's music hall drag act. (The film was directed by the aforementioned John Gilling, one-time Tod Slaughter screenwriter on his way to a notable directorial career at Hammer). Only 6 years after this woeful parody of what had become a very tired sub-genre, *Dracula* (1958) would make stars of Christopher Lee and Peter Cushing and revive the fortunes, not only of the vampire film but the horror genre, injecting graphic gore, a lot of sex and action set-pieces, along with gaudy Eastmancolor and the novel addition of fangs. (The Count has fangs in Stoker's novel and Orlock in *Nosferatu* [1922] has rat-like teeth but Lugosi's Dracula is fang-less.)

Given this newly-discovered respectability, it can be both instructive and shocking to re-visit the critical revulsion heaped upon Hammer in the late 1950s. There are plenty of examples to choose from. Take C.A. Lejeune in *The Observer*, May 1957:

> Without any hesitation I should rank *The Curse of Frankenstein* among the half-dozen most repulsive films I have encountered in the course of 10,000 miles of film reviewing. (Hutchings 1993: 6)

Or the oft-quoted remarks from *The Daily Telegraph*'s Campbell Dixon from the same month:

> But when the screen gives us severed heads and hands, eyeballs dropped in a wine glass and magnified, and brains dished up on a plate like spaghetti, I can only suggest a new certificate – SO perhaps; for Sadists Only. (ibid.)

Or how about the best-known attack on Hammer and their imitators, 'The Face of Horror' by Derek Hill, published in *Sight and Sound*? Hill starts as he means to go on:

> Only a sick society could bear the hoardings, let alone the films. Yet the displays, the posters and the slogans have become an accepted part of the West End scene. So, too, have the queues. The horror boom, despite occasional trade rumours, is still prospering. Why? (1958/9: 6)

For Hill, who is principally concerned with Hammer, although he also finds time to castigate science fiction films like *The Trollenberg Terror* (1958) and *The Fly* (1957) it's not just a question of the graphic gore. It's that the films are worthless in themselves:

> Hammer Films' revival of the Frankenstein legend was marked by a total disregard for the qualities of the original James Whale films of the 'thirties. Instead of attempting mood, tension or shock, the new Frankenstein productions rely almost entirely on a percentage of shots of repugnant clinical detail. There is little to frighten in *The Curse of Frankenstein* and *The Revenge of Frankenstein* but plenty to disgust. (1958/9: 9)

Hill doesn't think it's worth acknowledging that Whale's *Frankenstein* was heavily cut both in Britain and the US – only being shown uncut in 1999! – but he goes on to employ the favourite argument of all enemies of the genre, the idea of 'the corruption of taste' (1958/9: 10). He quotes Dr. Frederic Wertham, an American psychiatrist whose 1954 publication, *The Seduction of the Innocent* (an extremely apposite title) inspired the anti-horror comics crusades of the 1950s. Although Wertham's work has been largely discredited – not only for his questionable research methods but also due to claims such as Wonder Woman's strength and intelligence are 'proof' she is a lesbian – it is still useful for the insights it offers into the mind-set of those who seek to protect us from 'harmful material'. Hill quotes approvingly an anecdote from Wertham's book:

> A ten-year-old girl from a cultivated and literate home asked me why I thought it was harmful to read *Wonder Woman* (a horror comic)…'Supposing' I told her, 'you get used to eating sandwhiches made with very strong seasonings, with onions and peppers and highly spiced mustard. You will lose your taste for simple bread and butter and for finer food. The same is true of reading strong comic books. If later on you want to read a good novel it may describe how a young boy and girl sit together and watch the rain falling. They talk about themselves and the pages of the book describe what their innermost little thoughts are. This is what is called literature. But you will never be able to appreciate that if in comic-book fashion you expect that at any minute someone will come along and pitch both of them out of the window'. In this case the girl understood and the advice worked. (Hill 1958/9: 10)

The arguments of Wertham and Hill are essentially the same as those employed against such 'highly spiced mustard' as Penny Bloods and Video Nasties, the idea that such material is actively deleterious, blunting sensibilities, coarsening, even, to quote the legal definition of obscenity, possessing the ability to deprave and corrupt. For Hill, Hammer is not just a 'sandwich made with strong seasonings', it's also rotten, representing, as he concludes, 'the worst that the industry has ever offered' (1958/9: 11).

Even genre afficionados found lots to dislike about Hammer. For Carlos Clarens, author of *Horror Movies* (1971):

> The common denominator of their product is not really horror but sadism. The more jaded the public's palate becomes, the ranker the banquet of effects…mutilations, beheadings, gougings, burning flesh and decaying corpses – all of these are arbitrarily spliced into the scenarios at the expense of characterisation and plot. (1971: 209)

Derek Hill was writing only a couple of years after *The Curse of Frankenstein* but even as late as 1973, Dennis Gifford could suggest that:

> In quantity Hammer films are fast approaching Universal, but in quality they have yet to reach Monogram [a minor independent studio of the 1930s and 40s]. Meanwhile, they can admire their Queen's Award for Industry and scream all the way to the bank. (1973: 208)

These critical attacks were matched in ferocity by the response of the BBFC, under the auspices of John Trevelyan. Trevelyan was a complicated, often contradictory figure whose tenure as Chief Film Censor at the Board ran from 1958 to 1971, a period of enormous change in both film culture and the wider society. In his immensely readable autobiography, *What the Censor Saw* (1973) Trevelyan goes out of his way to paint himself as the very epitome of liberal enlightenment:

There are, and will continue to be some films that might be harmful to some people but I believe that this risk is not great enough to justify the continuance of restricting the freedom of adults. (1973: 229)

However, his belief did not stop some of his excesses such as cutting the shower murder in *Psycho* 'to lessen the sadism'(1973: 160) and deciding to cut death camp footage from the Holocaust documentary *Nuit et Brouillard* (1955) in an attempt to excise 'the worst of the horrors' (1973: 173). But while Trevelyan is keen to boast of his convivial meetings with the likes of Losey and Bergman, he harboured a particular distaste for horror films. On the subject of Mario Bava's visionary *La maschera del demonio* aka *Mask of Satan* aka *Black Sunday*, he explains how

It was refused a certificate in 1961 on grounds of disgust but was eventually passed by the Board in 1968 because by that time it looked rather ridiculous… One help to us was that nobody took these films seriously; this included the people who made them as well as the audiences. (1973: 166)

Or it's more likely that, as Mark Kermode suggests,'no one was allowed to take them seriously for only when they had passed into the realm of ridicule were they finally considered acceptable for public viewing' (2002: 14). In a similar vein, Trevelyan explains how, 'violence in a film, even if explicit and horrifying, was justified if it was there for a valid purpose, particularly to show that violence was inhuman and totally destructive'(1973: 162). His examples of such films are *Soldier Blue* (1970) and *The Devils* (1971) – although the BBFC had demanded changes to the latter – but when it came to *Witchfinder General*, which by any measure portrays violence as 'totally destructive', Trevelyan wasn't convinced and the film was heavily cut.

On the subject of Hammer, Trevelyan describes meetings with 'Jimmy' Carreras where it was decided that the company would 'avoid scenes which people could regard as disgusting or revolting' (1973: 165). But in practice, this 'gentlemen's agreement' didn't work with the BBFC not only demanding cuts to a number of their films but also vetoing some entirely at script stage (one such casualty being what would have been the first film version of Richard Matheson's seminal novel *I am Legend* [1954]). All of this vitriol flung at a company which in David Thomson's words 'was the work of decent men who tended the garden on weekends' (2002: 292), a world away from the politically radical, drop-out visionaries of '60s and 70s American horror such as Romero, Hooper and Craven. Indeed, when producer/screenwriter Anthony Hinds, son of one of the studio's founders, died in 2013, his obituary in the *New York Times* noted how 'he had told his next-door neighbour for twenty years that he was a hairdresser'(Fox 2013). But surely no-one sums up this odd mixture of tweedy English gentility and visceral, sexed-up horror better than Terence Fisher.

FISHER KING

The sheer scope of Hammer's output is daunting, from their celebrated gothic horrors to 'mini-Hitchcocks' (*Paranoiac* [1963]), sci-fi (*The Quatermass Experiment* [1956]) to prehistoric dramas (*Creatures the World Forgot* [1971]), costume romps about pirates (*Pirates of Blood River*) and Vikings (*Viking Queen*), sit-com adaptations (*On the Buses* [1971]), fantasy adventure romps (*She*) and a number of 'historical horrors' such as *Rasputin the Mad Monk* which offer up foreign grotesques and exotic period gore. Indeed, some of the most interesting Hammer films were far from the period horror they tend to be closely associated with: *Never Take Sweets from a Stranger* (1960), *The Damned* (1963), *The Anniversary* (1968), *Quatermass and The Pit* (1968), *Taste of Fear* (1960) and *Hell is a City* (1960).

Hammer were very much a family business; founder Will Hinds and his partner Enrique Carreras were joined early on by their respective sons and Enrique's grandson would eventually take charge. So it's appropriate that they assembled a trusted team of regular collaborators with which they could develop a strong house style. Indeed, one of the problems the company faced in the 1970s was the fact that a number of key personnel were dying, retiring or moving onto pastures new. The Hammer family included set designer Bernard Robinson, composer James Bernard, the cinematographers Jack Asher and Arthur Grant and the screenwriters John Elder (a pseudonym for producer Anthony Hinds) and the prolific Jimmy Sangster. As well as Terence Fisher, the most acclaimed of their directors, they also worked regularly with a number of other talented film-makers including Roy Ward Baker, Val Guest, Seth Holt, Don Sharp and the aforementioned Gilling.

The case of Terence Fisher and his leisurely journey to auteur status is illuminating. Born in 1904, he had been in the Merchant Navy before entering the industry in 1933. He trained as an editor and worked for a number of different companies including Gainsborough (he edited *The Wicked Lady*). When he started directing, he took whatever he was given, from light comedy through to romances until he ended up at Hammer and after a number of films landed *The Curse of Frankenstein*. In the 1950s Fisher's slow rise through the industry wasn't unusual but seen from the perspective of today, after the auteur theory and the French New Wave, Cassavetes and Tarantino, his career path seems torturous. His unassuming persona, too seems to come from another era and reads almost like a parody of Englishness, diffident, gentle and fond of a drink. Certainly Fisher saw a connection between his nationality and his work:

> Continental film critics acknowledge the English as the world experts in horror. It's because we're timid. Shyness breeds shadows and shadows breed vampires. (Fisher 2000 [1964]: 67)

It's also striking how he came to display such a talent for horror having come to the genre so late and certainly not by any overarching design – the success of the gruesome horror-tinged sci-fi film *The Quatermass Experiment* paved the way for the gothics that the director would excel at. This instance of a director finding his metier almost by accident is not unprecedented – Jack Arnold graduated from shorts and documentary subjects to some of the best science fiction films of the 1950s – but Fisher's case may be the most striking. Some of his numerous pre-*Curse* films touch on the supernatural and the fantastic - the mystery of *So Long at the Fair* (1950, co-directed with Anthony Darnborough) and the sci-fi *Four-Sided Triangle* (1953). But the physicality and energy of his period gothics is still evident, even when they have been imitated by so many over such a long period of time.

Fisher famously claimed his films were not horror but 'fairy tales for adults' (in Leggett 2002: 2) and his portrayal of the struggle between good and evil is often commented upon ('Manichean' is to discusssions of Fisher what 'barrel-chested' is to Slaughter). Fisher's films are essentially Christian; as he told Paul Jensen 'you've got to say something about Good and Evil in every film you make…Ultimately and inevitably, Good must be triumphant' (in Jensen 2008: 62). Thus his dislike of *Witchfinder General* makes sense ('I found it, in a strange way, not satisfying but upsetting' [ibid.]). Indeed, Fisher's stylised romanticism could seem stilted or just silly were it not allied to his incredible dynamism. It's also not always as black and white as it seems: Fisher's Baron Frankenstein may well be evil – he's a narcissist, graverobber, murderer and rapist – but he possesses a vitality and spirit lacking in any of the would-be heroes. The director's Victorian sensibility was noted by Török who in 1961 pointed out how:

> All of Fisher's films are set in the late nineteenth century in this striking Victorian era, the era of nonsense and the ghost story and the English golden age of the occult and the irrational. (2002 [1961]: 70).

Fisher would go on to make a number of contemporary films, including the underrated Planet double-bill *Island of Terror* (1966) and *Night of the Big Heat* (1967) but these tend to be neglected in favour of his lush period stylings.

THE MUMMY (1959)

It's not hard to see why so much attention has been paid to *The Curse of Frankenstein* and *Dracula*. Not only are they exciting and important films in their own right but they also serve as dramatic introductions to Hammer's two most enduring anti-heroes. They also managed to succesfuly reinvent characters that had become tired and repeatedly spoofed as the Universal series had shifted from innovation to exhaustion. But this reinvention was a choice borne of necessity: the Universal versions of the Count and Baron were under copyright and so screenwriter Jimmy Sangster had to go back to the source novels. Thus, Lee's Dracula could not refer to howling wolves as 'children of the night', yet he was also prevented from travelling by boat to England – the whole film taking place in a vaguely-delineated Romanian setting – as the budget wouldn't stretch to a sea voyage. In the case of *The Curse of Frankenstein*, the reinvention of what Hammer called The Creature was even more radical, with make-up man Phil Leakey using Shelley rather than Karloff as inspiration. Her description of Frankenstein's creation as having

> yellow skin scarcely covering the work of muscles and arteries within… hair of lustrous black… watery eyes that seemed almost of the same colour as the sockets in which they were set, his shrivelled complexion and straight black lips (1998 [1818]: 37)

is uncannily close to Lee's hideous car-crash visage. When Universal saw just how profitable the Hammer gothics were, they decided to license a number of their other monsters. The resulting reworkings are a distinctly mixed bag and Pirie has noted that none of the monsters that Hammer inherited from Universal proved as successful or as durable as their adaptations of Shelley and Stoker (see Pirie 2007).

While the glossy *The Phantom of the Opera* (1962) – intended at one time as a vehicle for Cary Grant –was handsome but oddly flat and *The Two Faces of Dr. Jekyll* (1960) an interesting failure, *The Curse of the Werewolf* (1961) is a fascinating reworking of Universal monster lore. Hammer's only lycanthrope film, *Curse* is richly-detailed and exciting with the young Oliver Reed giving great wolf, aided by some excellent make-up by Roy Ashton which replaces Universal's yak-haired Yeti look with something much more lupine. The source novel was Guy Endore's *The Werewolf of Paris* but the cost-conscious company had already built some sets for a proposed film about the Inquisition (scuppered by the BBFC at script stage), so the action was relocated to eighteenth-century Spain. Some of the more sensational elements (blasphemy, rape) were snipped by the censor and Warren Mitchell as the cockney-accented Spanish shepherd Pepe is a mistake but the film is as good as any of the better-known Hammers.

Lobby card for *The Mummy*

The Mummy was another of the revivified Universal monsters and unlike Hammer's werewolf, this did spawn three sequels. Two of them, *Curse of the Mummy's Tomb* (1964) and *The Mummy's Shroud* (1967) were pretty awful (although *Shroud* did have one of the best taglines in British horror history with 'Beware the beat of the cloth-wrapped feet') but *Blood from the Mummy's Tomb* (1971) is a powerful, if muddled film – undoubtedly due in part to its troubled production history with director Seth Holt dying half-way through the shoot and being replaced by Michael Carreras. But this enjoyably overheated story of reincarnation and curses adapted by Chris Wicking from Bram Stoker's novel *The Jewel of the Seven Stars*, is a mummy film in name only.

Although they share a title, Fisher's The Mummy is not a remake of the Universal film. Screenwriter Sangster watched Freund's film and there are some obvious lifts (reincarnation, the mind-snapping effect the mummy's resurrection has on an unfortunate observer) but he seems to have been influenced much more by the sequels, unashamed monster movies that replace eerie atmospherics with a shambling killing machine. The plot of The Mummy's Hand (1940), with the monster bumping off a group of archaeologists one by one seems to have been a particular influence as well as the origin of the names Kharis and Karnak. The idea of killing off the monster in a swamp, meanwhile comes from The Mummy's Curse (1944).

The plot of Fisher's film is much simpler than the fragmented narrative with a bunch of Victorian explorers followed to England (or Ireland; see below) by a mysterious Egyptian and a reanimated mummy who will wreak revenge on them, killing them off one by one until the creature is distracted by the reincarnation of his lost love. Sangster's script includes some lengthy flashbacks, which portray the death of the Princess Ananka, the attempts by High Priest Kharis (Lee in heavy eyemake-up, a skull cap and leopard skin robe) to resurrect her with the Scroll of Life and his subsequent punishment, having his tongue amputated before being mummified and entombed alive.

The Mummy reveals Fisher's strengths as a director, showcasing as it does an intoxicating mix of stylised, dream-like imagery and dynamic, visceral action. It is surely significant that the director declined to watch Freund's film for fear it would influence his approach. It may actually be the case that the unusually convoluted Sangster script means even more emphasis is placed on the dazzling set-pieces and directorial flourishes.

Fisher, more than anyone else, is responsible for turning horror into an action genre. There were, of course, bursts of dynamism in the Universal films, especially where Karloff's creature was concerned and there was The Wolf Man, that most athletic of monsters. But Hammer moved far further from the gloomy atmospherics of German Expressionism than Universal ever did, rendering the clash between good and evil with a remarkable physicality. Whereas the Count is staked off-screen in Tod Browning's (uncharacteristically listless) Dracula, the climax of the Hammer version is still thrilling, Van Helsing's charge across the table, leaping to tear down the curtains and let in the light, Lee's pained recoil, all of this powered by James Bernard's hysterical relentless score. Fisher's direction was a large part of this dynamism; consider that remarkable tracking shot into the face of the unmasked Creature in The Curse of Frankenstein.

The action sequences in The Mummy are off-set by a strange, heightened sense of artificiality – the green light which washes the interior of Ananka's tomb, the strange reddish tinge which plays over the swamp. In one startlingly surreal moment, we see Kharis stomping down a quiet idyllic country lane in the half-light. This is not only an emblematic image for the film, an ancient colonial evil in this most incongruous of settings but it also serves to perhaps illustrate the appeal of so much of Hammer's output, setting an exotic monster story in an idealised bucolic setting.

Yvonne Furneaux would go on to dismiss much of her horror work as 'real rubbish' (in Del Valle 2010: 50), which is a bit rich given how wooden she is here. She is also oddly bloodless for a Hammer heroine, although she is given little to do except scream, faint and look like Ananka. (She would acquit herself much better in *Repulsion*, which is discussed in Chapter 5 — although this may be down to director Roman Polanski, a far harsher taskmaster than the genial Fisher.)

Lee is very good at portraying Kharis as a kind of proto-Terminator rather than the tottering shambler of popular imagination. Tall, lean, long-limbed and caked in glistening black mud, he creates what is undoubtedly the screen's most frightening mummy, clambering through the asylum window set high in the wall and smashing through doors. He manages to express a great deal of emotion under the circumstances, his soulful gaze reminding one of the words of Zita Johann, the female lead of the Universal film who described Karloff's reanimated corpse as possessing 'eyes like shattered mirrors' (Del Valle in the DVD documentary, *Mummy Dearest*). The startling image of burning eyes staring out from behind bandages is repeated in *Blood from the Mummy's Tomb* and to unpleasant effect in two Continental horror films, Franju's *Les yeux sans visage* (1960) and Polanski's *The Tenant* (1976).

There is a nice contrast set up between unstoppable monster and all-too-human protagonist when Kharis smashes through the locked front doors of the Banning house to attack Whemple (Raymond Huntley) while Cushing's character is in the next room fumbling to find the right key to unlock the glass gun-cabinet. With the possible exception of the aptly-named John Hurt, has any actor taken a beating as well as Cushing? He is shoved and strangled and knocked around, loose-limbed, hair flopping over his face. In the most memorable scene, Kharis bursts in through the French windows and charges at Banning, who shoots him twice with a shotgun, tearing holes in his chest. Banning dives across a desk, grabbing a harpoon off the wall and thrusting it through Kharis before the mummy grabs him round the neck and forces him backwards. Again, as with *Dracula* — where the actor suggested making a cross from two candlesticks in order to force the Count into the sunlight — Cushing deserves credit for his input into the action scenes. After reportedly seeing a promo poster which showed a torch beam shining through a hole in the monster's chest (Hammer habitually designing the posters before the film was finished), the actor explains that he inquired how it got there.

> 'Oh' said the publicity man 'that's just to help to sell the picture'. Oh, I thought — that's just not on…So I asked Terry if I could grab a harpoon hanging on the wall of Banning's study and during the struggle for survival, drive it clear my opponent's body. And that's what I did, thus giving some sort of logic to the illuminated gap on the posters. (Cowie 2007: 94)

The dynamism of the scene, Cushing's frenzied attacks on the relentless, seemingly indestructible monster has a real nightmarish charge. The action scenes make up for the lack of Hammer's trademark gore, with little spurting blood and few dismembered body parts with the exception of Kharis's tongue amputation – which was snipped by the censor. There is also the shocking moment where Mehemet Bey is killed by the mummy, forced backwards over the monster's until his spine snaps.

Unlike the climax of *The Mummy's Curse* where Kharis and the rapidly aging Ananka sink beneath the swamp water, Fisher adds a posse of armed cops who blast away at the half-submerged mummy, blowing big bits off him, one shot even tearing his head open before he sinks out of sight. One problem with the film, identified by Jonathan Rigby (2000) – although on reflection hard to miss – is the setting, which appears to shift from England to Ireland seemingly at random. Although we are told it is England in the year 1898, the film is full of Irish characters, including familiar company mascot Michael Ripper, who are, true to stereotypical form drunken, feckless, superstitious and lazy. This uncharacteristic carelessness would become a regrettable feature of the cash-strapped Hammer of the early 70s. In contrast, the flashback scenes are extravagant and well-mounted, the hordes of wailing extras and the long funeral cortege looking forward to the lavish spectacle of *She* while the removal of Kharis's tongue anticipates the exotic nastiness of Fisher's *The Stranglers of Bombay*.

Rather than the Carter expedition, the film reflects a very contemporary anxiety about Britain's foreign escapades, particularly the recent Suez Crisis of 1956 where military action was taken against Egypt under President Nasser. The strange scene which comes towards the end of the film, where Banning and the fez-wearing Bey (played by the all-purpose ethnic villain character actor, George Pastell, a Cypriot) debate belief (where the former arrogantly describes Karnak as 'a third-rate god') serves to lay bare the 'clash of civilisations' narrative which informs so many of these exotic colonial horrors.

THE HAMMER EFFECT

The enormous success of *The Curse of Frankenstein* encouraged a number of imitators to come up with lurid romps of their own. Many of these films are interesting in that, despite the clear debt they owe to Hammer, they take their inspiration not from the Universal reworkings of European monster tales but rather from the gory excesses of British history. A good example is the Boris Karloff vehicle *Grip of the Strangler* aka *Haunted Strangler* (1958), directed by Robert Day. The film shares a Victorian setting with *Curse...* but feels more like a retread of the stylish black and white period films the actor made 10 years earlier for RKO, such as *Bedlam* (1946) and *The Body Snatcher*. But the pronounced Englishness of the film's gothic horrors is striking. The film opens in 1860 with a public execution at Newgate Prison, a practice that actually began in 1783 – the gallows set up in the street across the road from the prison, which stood where the Old Bailey now stands – and continued until 1868 after which the hangings took place within the walls until the institution closed in 1902.

This tale of Rankin, a novelist and social reformer (Karloff at his gentlest) investigating a decades-old series of murders committed by the Haymarket Strangler only to find he himself was the killer is a (very) thinly-disguised riff on Stevenson's Jekyll and Hyde. Rankin is actually physically transformed when he handles the killing blade into a grotesque, tousle-haired fiend (who looks a bit too much like the actor Bill Owen). The contrast between respectable middle-class life (family, a big house and servants) and the temptation of lower-class depravity (The Judas Hole, a dive/brothel where upper-class men quaff champagne with can-can dancing floozies) also owes much to Stevenson's novella.

There is also the aforementioned connection between Mr. Hyde and the Ripper. Like the Ripper of myth, Rankin is upper-class and possesses medical knowledge, while we are told the Haymarket Strangler, like the Ripper (and Stoker's Dracula) had five female victims. There is one strange error related to the Whitechapel murders; when we see Rankin researching criminal cases 20 years after the opening scene, the first file is marked Jack the Ripper – even though, as it's 1880, the murders won't happen for another 8 years.

By far the film's most memorable scene is that opening, showing an expectant crowd gathered outside the prison. The crowd is a veritable gallery of grotesques – a drunken old woman swigging from a bottle, a whore leaning out of a window eating an apple, a horny butcher canoodling among the sausages and a broadside seller who moves through the crowd, touting an issue detailing the crimes of the strangler. There is an emphasis on the pleasure derived from the spectacle of death – lips licked, the hush of anticipation followed by cheering and cackling. When the whore and a middle-aged spectator exchange glances, the connection between death and sex is made clear. Day seems to want to have his cake and eat it, a common ploy used when tackling sensational material, criticising the self-same love of excess and horror on which the film-makers hope to capitalise.

The film also displays a post-Hammer level of explicitness, with scenes of a corpse in quick lime, a rat crawling over a skull, the bloody back of a flogged convict and a generous cleavage splashed with champagne. The sensationalism is also generously applied – with scenes in asylums, prisons, graveyards, brothels – as are the gothic touches – even a minor character who arrives to deliver Rankin to the madhouse is a hunchback with a limp. Day would go to direct the thematically similar *Corridors of Blood* (1958), a gruesome nineteenth-century melodrama with Karloff as a drug-addicted surgeon who falls foul of a band of brigands, including a bodysnatcher called Resurrection Joe (Christopher Lee).

BAKER AND BERMAN

Like Hammer, the team of Robert S. Baker and Monty Berman had been knocking around for a while, making quota quickie comedies and thrillers since the early 1940s. In 1958 they came out with the Quatermass-ish sci-fi film *The Trollenberg Terror*, also based on a TV show and written by Hammer mainstay Jimmy Sangster. They followed this with *Blood of the Vampire* (1958) a full-colour rip-off of the Hammer style which made it to the screen scarcely a month after *Dracula* opened. In a very 1950s twist, Dr. Callistratus is less a supernatural vampire than a scientific one, revived from the dead by means of a transplanted heart and siphoning blood from confined lunatics to keep going.

The gaudy colours and ugly, patently phony backdrops make *Blood*… seem much more tacky and disreputable than its Hammer counterparts. In a pre-credit sequence, we see the doctor having an iron rod hammered into his chest and the credits play out over a close-up of his bloody shroud. The film also contains a deformed hunchback (a shockingly bad make-up job), floggings, mad dogs and a noteworthy cast including John Le Mesurier, Bernard Bresslaw and an unbilled Pat Phoenix. The main point of interest is the presence of the noted Shakespearian stage performer Donald Wolfit as Callistratus. If, as a number of critics have suggested, Tod Slaughter would not have cut it at Hammer, he'd certainly have felt at home in a Baker and Berman production. Indeed, watching Wolfit, it feels as if he's consciously channelling Slaughter. Well-fed and deathly white, wearing a ridiculous false nose and some bizarre bushy eyebrows, he shambles around, over-enunciating his silly dialogue while dressed in a gore-spattered leather apron. This costume is significant: before the Whitechapel murderer became known as Jack the Ripper, he was referred to in newspapers and flyers as Leather Apron (a name actually given to a Polish Jewish shoemaker John Pizer, considered a suspect at one stage, although later exonerated). Henry Cass, the director of this lurid mess was also a devoted member of the grandly-named Campaign for Moral Rearmament, a faith-based pressure group whose aim to 're-arm the nation morally' sits slightly at odds with the gory activities of the blood-boltered, beetle-browed Callistratus.

Baker and Berman followed this with a couple of monochrome horror films based on notorious real-life crimes. *Jack the Ripper* (1959) starts as it means to go on, with fog-wreathed streets, hansom cabs, drunken prostitutes in big, feathered hats and a killer in a top hat and frock coat carrying a doctor's bag. The script, another from the ubiquitous Sangster, is both police procedural – with the irritating American TV star Lee Patterson playing a visitor from the NYPD (!) – and whodunnit, although both elements take second place to the usual Ripper movie staples: volatile proletarian mobs, brawling pocket-picking men, drunken cackling women, can can dancers and a string of red herrings, including a grinning, scalpel-wielding hunchback in yet another leather apron.

The film is flatly-directed and pedestrian and save for the oddd canted angle, looks very like the kind of television show Berman and Baker would go on to make at the end of the decade. It is, however, notable for a couple of things. It was the subject of what David Pirie calls '*the* most protracted production versus censorship battle of the 1950s' (2007: 123; emphasis in original) with BBFC objections over, amongst other things the mentions of prostitutes, an 'orgiastic' can can dance, surgical procedures, knives – indeed, the whole concept of a film about such a notorious series of murders. The lengthy bargaining process between Trevelyan's BBFC and an impressively tenacious Monty Berman is explored in detail in Pirie 2007. On a related note, as was the case with a number of other British genre films (even the semi-prestigious likes of *Witchfinder General*), extra footage was shot for *Jack the Ripper* to spice up what were known as 'Continental versions'. This includes some backstage scenes featuring an array of topless chorus girls and repeated shots of champagne sprayed over cleavages, that familiar visual shorthand for the theme of decadent well-to-dos slumming it for sex with floozies.

The end of the film – despite the best efforts of the BBFC – is a grim delight, with the killer, surgeon David Rogers (who looks and sounds disconcertingly like the late British Foreign Secretary Robin Cook) trapped in a lift shaft as the elevator descends. The sequence is drawn-out and extremely tense, ending with the crushed man's blood squirting through the lift floor. In an inspired exploitation touch, colour was used for this scene in US prints (although none of these survive). It's also interesting that the killer has a conventional motive – he is searching for the prostitute he holds responsible for his son's suicide. It seems fairly certain that if the Whitechapel murders were the work of one man, he was a sexual psychopath killing for personal gratification but the apparently-motiveless murder is rarely explored outside of slasher movies, perhaps because it appears to be unknowable. Indeed, the psychological backstory of the typical slasher movie villain is not too far removed from that of many a real serial killer, with an unresolved trauma leading someone to repeatedly slaughter strangers (even if that trauma is something far more baroque – tricking someone into bed with a corpse, for example in *Terror Train* [1980] - than run-of-the-mill physical and sexual abuse). A number of films do attempt to depict motiveless murder, while at the same time trying to downplay some of the mythology - Fritz Lang's *M* (1929) and the Losey remake as well as *Henry Portrait of a Serial Killer* (1986) all manage this. (The German title for *Jack the Ripper* was virtually the same as the alternative title for Lang's film, *Eine Stadt sucht einen Mörder*). But it's interesting to note the inability of writers and film-makers to explore the crimes of the prototype serial killer without resorting to conspiracies or other mundane motives.

THE FLESH AND THE FIENDS AKA MANIA (1959)

In 1959, Gilling returned to the Burke and Hare story with this richly-detailed brutal film laced with a very modern kind of black comedy. The familiar story of the Irish graverobbers (George Rose and Donald Pleasence) in Edinburgh who turn to murder in order to supply fresh corpses to Dr. Knox (Cushing) for dissection is told surprisingly straight. There is a seemingly superfluous romantic sub-plot between one of Knox's students and a tart with a heart but that is given a startling twist when she is murdered by Hare only to end up on the slab at the medical school. Rose and Pleasence are an effectively ghastly double act and Gilling conjures up some nightmarish images, notably the very protracted murder scenes, including one where Hare leaps up and down dancing a kind of horrible jig as Burke suffocates a woman. So skewed is the dark world on show here, even the pictures on the wall of the Burke house hang at an angle. Jean-Paul Török, a great admirer of the British horror of this period seems distinctly ambivalent about Gilling's film. It 'exerts an attraction that is not far removed from necrophilia' and he goes on to compare the 'shameful' pleasures of the film to the joys experienced by people who like to watch executions' (2002 [1961]: 70).

This idea of horror films as appealing to the prurient and the ghoulish conjures the spectre of George Selwyn, an eighteenth-century English nobleman who enjoyed watching executions and who led Pirie (2007) to coin the term Selwynism for a national variant on sadism. Török concludes:

> In the history of the horror film, Mania is important because it reveals the mechanics of pleasure we derive from it. (2002 [1961]: 70)

Török's comment is reminiscent of Nigel Floyd's perceptive review of the gruelling Australian film *Wolf Creek* (2005):

> The violence is flat, ugly and remorseless, our sense of powerlessness overwhelming… By making us feel the pain, Greg McLean's ferocious, taboo-breaking film tells us so much more about how and why we watch horror movies. (2005)

This is an important aspect of graphically violent/sadistic horror, the way it induces a kind of masochistic self-examination. Of course, Gilling's film pales somewhat when placed alongside *Wolf Creek* – and yet as we're often reminded, one generation's shocking gorefest is another's quaint nostalgia.

SADIAN

But the most striking work produced in the wake of Hammer's breakthough came courtesy of Anglo-Amalgamated, who came up with three remarkable Eastmancolor shockers in rapid succession. The sensationalism which had become a staple of the British genre film in the wake of Hammer's success is foregrounded here with true crime, surgery, pornography and the circus used as motifs. *Horrors of the Black Museum* (1958) was directed by Arthur Crabtree, who was no stranger to the lurid and the overheated, having directed films for Gainsborough Studios and the exciting, slightly daft flying brain movie *Fiend Without a Face* (1958). But the film bears the authorial stamp of its producer and co-screenwriter Herman Cohen, an American who made a number of brilliantly-titled, teen-orientated exploitation flicks in the US (*I Was a Teenage Werewolf* [1957], *I Was A Teenage Frankenstein* [1958]). Cohen was a showman and unapologetic about his lurid genre offerings:

Children of all ages should be allowed to see horror films. I am sure that Frankenstein and Dracula would not have any serious effect on children's minds. After all, I saw them myself when I was a kid and they didn't affect me. (in Gifford 1973: 185)

Inspired by Scotland Yard's infamous Black Museum (which also spawned a 1951 radio show starring Orson Welles), it's the story of Edmond Bancroft (a very over-the-top Michael Gough), a crime writer and murderer. The plot – Bancroft keeps drugging the young man who helps him run his private crime museum so he'll commit a series of murders that Bancroft can then write about - is merely a way to string together a series of extremely effective and very graphic set-pieces (a woman stabbed in the eyes with spiked binoculars, another beheaded by a guillotine attached to her bed). Indeed, the film really comes to life in the murder sequences, anticipating the slasher movies of the late 1970s and early 80s. There is a telling line of dialogue, when a police officer describes the guillotine murder room as 'the most gruesome sight I've ever seen'. Cohen and Crabtree certainly hope so.

'The most gruesome sight I've ever seen': *Horrors of the Black Museum*

Black Museum feels prescient in other ways, too. Cohen was open about his reasons for casting youngsters ('I always try to put in the young teen, so the teenagers can identify with somebody in the film' [in Rigby 2000: 74]) and while the acting of Graham Curnow and Shirley-Anne Field leaves a lot to be desired (to put it mildly), this theme of the younger generation manipulated by corrupt elders which had been around since at least *Caligari* would go on to become one of the dominant themes in British horror. Gough's Bancroft seems to have the hots for his young assistant Rick, at one point describing him as 'sound of body, fleet of limb' and exploding into a jealous rage when he discovers Field's character in his museum, telling him that 'no woman can hold her tongue. They're a vicious, unreliable breed,' even at one point warning against Field's ability to 'set off a toboggan that will crush us' (the script is full of such over-ripe, semi-meaningless dialogue). Indeed, Cohen was still repeating this homo-erotic formula of scenery-chewing older star grooming a callow youth as late as 1974 with *Craze* (1974) which features Jack Palance in a lot of hokum about a magical African doll.

Crabtree's film also tackles head-on the aforementioned British obsession with murder and violent death. Cohen would claim that all of the killings portrayed were based on real British murders but this claim seems fanciful. Bancroft is working on a book called The

Poetry of Murder and at one point, he reassures someone concerned that the killing spree is over with 'we can always rely on London to provide another murder'. A scene on the banks of the Thames where a newspaper vendor plies his trade while a random collection of Londoners (bowler-hatted city gents, a nurse and so on) gossip about the murders looks forward to *Frenzy*, where a similar scene takes place about 5 minutes walk away. Some of the film really doesn't work – it feels a bit stagey in parts, with long takes and a lot of talk and there's a very odd sequence where June Cunningham as Gough's mistress stomps her way through a deeply unsexy dance in what has to be London's least fun pub, wearing a tight red dress and matching heels. The US release was accompanied by a turgid 10 minute introduction (although it feels much longer) as a hypnotist called Emile Francel, warns us agains trying to 'hypnotise an idiot, imbecile or fool'. But Crabtree's film has verve, energy and cruelty, although it would pale alongside the next Anglo film.

Circus of Horrors (1960) was directed by Sidney Hayers from a script by George Baxt, the screenwriter of the eerie proto-Amicus pic *City of the Dead*. This is another bizarre and hysterical story with an even-icier-than-usual Anton Diffring as Dr. Rossiter, a renegade plastic surgeon who masquerades as the owner of a circus, repairing the faces of a series of scarred women then killing them off in very public ways when they threaten to expose him. The film mixes a series of exploitation elements – plastic surgery gone wrong and circus-themed murders, prostitution and lots of bare flesh – in a fast-paced pulp fashion which makes the Hammer gothics look almost tasteful (one can only wonder what Derek Hill would have made of it all). George Baxt was frank about what was asked of him – 'They wanted lots of beautiful girls with big tits wherever possible' (Rigby 2000: 89), and the film certainly delivers on that score with a lot of censor-baiting revealing costumes and a distinctly unwholesome air of kinky sadism The doctor seems to be sexually stimulated by the scarred faces of the women he operates on, while the women themselves (including Erika Remberg, Hayers' wife) make very cute victims, usually semi-naked when they're mauled by lions, fall from high wires and in the most graphic scene, stabbed through the neck when a knife thrower misses his target. There's a telling moment when an investigating cop, masquerading as a crime reporter coins the phrase 'circus of horrors' only to have this dismissed as 'sensational'.

Hayers' film looks lovely for a low-budget film, photographed in rich, gaudy colours and benefitting from the use of a real circus. The scenes in France, the pavement cafes, beaded curtains and berets, are clearly not shot there (rather at the end of the Metropolitan Line in Amersham old town) and some of the effects are poor – both Bosco the killer bear and the gorilla that attacks Rossiter are terrible costumes, moth-eaten and shapeless. But the lion attack sequence is very well done, mixing stock footage with a fake lion head with some skill and the whole thing has a deliriously frenzied quality. David Pirie regards the three Anglo films – *Black Museum*, *Circus of Horrors* and *Peeping Tom* – as a 'Sadian trilogy'. But as Ian Conrich has pointed out *Circus…* can be just as easily be seen as belonging to a 'larger group of British horror films that featured operations, surgery and biological experimentation' (2009: 101). He dubs this group of films 'surgical horrors' in contrast to Derek Hill's more salacious term, 'clinical cult' (ibid.). Conrich has also pointed out how Pirie's grouping ignores other similar films such as *Berserk* (1967), another Cohen production with a big-top setting. Circus settings are entirely appropriate for horror films, gaudy, sensational, appealing to the senses. This is a tradition that goes back to German Expressionist horror films including *Caligari*. As Seigfried Kracauer has pointed out, the fair stands as 'an enclave of anarchy in the sphere of entertainment' (1947: 73-4) and Hitchcock, who worked at UFA Studios in Weimar Germany often used a circus or fairground setting (*Saboteur* [1942], *Strangers on a Train* [1951]).

Peeping Tom is by far the best-known of the Anglo films and perhaps the most critically lauded film to appear in this book. It's certainly unique in the way responses to it have so dramatically changed, from revulsion and outrage to its recently-acquired (and much deserved) status as modern classic. *Witchfinder General* has followed a similar path, from spluttering indignation to glowing acceptance and yet the reponse to Powell's film was so vitriolic it is in a class of its own. *The Daily Express* described it as, 'sadism, sex and the exploitation of human degradation' (in Powell 2007 [1992]: 10), *The Spectator* considered it. 'the sickest and filthiest film I remember seeing' (ibid.) and for *The Daily Worker* it was 'wholly evil' (in Powell 2007 [1992]: 11). Our old friend Derek Hill didn't mince his words either:

> The only really satisfactory way to dispose of *Peeping Tom* would be shovel it up and flush it swiftly down the nearest sewer. Even then, the stench would remain. (Powell 2007 [1992]: 10)

The story of Mark Lewis (Carl Boehm), a sad, baby-faced killer cameraman who films his murders, Powell's film certainly has a number of thematic and stylistic similarities with the other Anglo horrors: the gleeful breaking of taboos, a fascination with voyeurism and a focus on the sensational and the taboo – murder, deformity, pornography, surgery. What's striking is the way that Powell's film – being so bold and multi-layered, so personal and ultimately so vilified – had few imitators, whereas *Black Museum* and *Circus*... seem incredibly prescient, despite being lesser films (perhaps precisely because they are lesser films). A better comparison – and one made often - would be with *Psycho* and it is remarkable that two of the greatest British film-makers should choose the same year to release these innovative, deeply shocking and yet intensely personal films, stories of murder with sympathetic protagonists that foreground voyeurism and implicate the viewer in their exposé of that weird process of sitting in the dark watching strangers. Powell didn't manage – or rather didn't even bother trying – to obscure just how personal his dark fantasies were, certainly not to the degree Hitchcock managed to, passing off *Psycho* as a gothic black comic romp. But then how could he? He appears in the film as the sadistic father to the unhappy young Mark, with his own son Columba the boy in scenes shot in the director's own garden.

There was always something very un-English about Powell and Pressburger, the visual excess, the emotional intensity, the way their work is so keen to slough off the dead hand of naturalism. But the reaction to Powell's move into the horror genre – especially horror so tinged with deviant sex – was ridiculous, suggesting that unlike Hammer and even Hitchcock, the master showman, he should have known better.

Peeping Tom, written by the former codebreaker Leo Marks (a name too similar to that of the protagonist for comfort) is an odd film which altenates between an almost parodically English restraint – washed out colours and the courtship between Mark and Helen (wan Anna Massey) – and an alarming high-pitched hysteria – bruised prostitutes and snuff films along with bursts of appropriately hellish red. It's an endlessly reflexive film, the story of a man who, just like us, can't stop looking, fascinated by what the camera can do, how it gives life and takes it away, unable to take his eyes off all of that beauty and horror. As well as the milieu of the film, which exposes the connections between the legitimate industry and its sleazy relations – Soho vice, porn, 'glamour' photos sold under the counter in newsagents – Powell uses a score which conjures up that most visual of forms, the silent film.

While Boehm wasn't the director's first choice (that was the more remote Laurence Harvey who wasn't available) he is excellent, his German accent lending him the same kind of alien-ness as the American Vincent Price in *Witchfinder General* (surely it's no coincidence that Germany was the first country to turn horror into a recognisable film genre). Unlike Robert Hartford-Davis, Pete Walker, Norman J. Warren, Stanley Long *et al*, who moved from the twilight world of softcore sleaze into the (only slightly more respectable) world of horror, Powell was heading the other way, fearlessly stepping into the dark and murky side of the industry. One of the models Mark photographs is Pamela Green, a popular glamour model and the future star of *Naked as Nature Intended* (1961). There are also references to other lurid Anglo horrors. The casting of Shirley Ann Field in the film-within-a-film is surely a reference to her performance in *Black Museum* while the deeply perverse scene where Mark is aroused by the scarred face of a model seems intended to evoke a similar scene in *Circus of Horrors*. Martin Scorsese, a great champion of Powell's film described it significantly in the Region 2 DVD documentary as 'like a tabloid – but in colour'. While Ian Christie goes on to identify the influence of *Peeping Tom* on the likes of De Palma and Polanski, one below-the-line comment on a review in *The Telegraph* suggests another, more sinister connection:

> I have often wondered if Ian Brady had seen this film because a few years later he too would enjoy photographing and recording his victims' death agonies. (Gritten 2010)

It's surely one of the only times that a film-maker has consciously gone over to the other side, at least through choice. (Roland Joffe may have gone from glossy big-budget extravaganzas like *The Mission* [1996] to the sleazy and derivative *Captive* [2007] – where a kidnapped woman is forced to drinking a smoothie made from body parts – but that move doesn't appear to have been through choice). It almost definitely ended Powell's career. But he knew what he was doing; as one character tells Mark by way of warning, 'all this filming, it's not healthy…'.

FOG AND RAIN AND LONG WINTER NIGHTS

Sidney Hayers and George Baxt were reunited for the extremely effective witchcraft story *Night of the Eagle* (1964), the latter teaming up with the classy duo of Richard Matheson and Charles Beaumont to adapt Fritz Lieber's novel *Conjure Wife*. Eschewing the gaudy colours and sexed-up nastiness of *Circus of Horrors*, it's a taut and brooding tale shot in a gorgeous monochrome. Norman (Peter Wyngarde) is a sort of proto-Richard Dawkins, a professor newly-arrived at a rural school. When he discovers his wife Tansy (Janet Blair) is surreptitiously using witchcraft to protect him, he forces her to stop, leaving them both at the mercy of the malign magic of Flora (Margaret Johnston), the outwardly-respectable school secretary. Wyngarde, a talented actor best-known for playing the crime-fighting fop Jason King before a couple of arrests for cottaging derailed his career, is excellent here as the academic who goes from icy arrogance to wild-eyed terror. This transformation from disbelief to awareness is a staple of occult horror: consider the plaintive cry of the title character in *Rosemary's Baby* (1968), 'This is no dream! This is really happening!' Indeed, the creepy and underrated *Skeleton Key* (2005) is a well-crafted play on this idea. In Hayers' film it's dramatically expressed, the film opening with Norman writing I DO NOT BELIEVE on a blackboard, only to end up obscuring the NOT as he reels away from the claws of a demonic eagle. Hayers' style here is restrained but not without some dramatic expressionistic flourishes such as the catatonic Tansy's distorted point-of-view shots of a spooky Cornish graveyard as she is carried upside-down or the moment when she and Norman struggle for possession of a knife and their shadow falls across a framed photo of the pair in happier times. But if Norman is the target of all this bad magic, the central conflict in the film is between two women, Tansy and Flora. Occult powers and femaleness are connected throughout, with references to hysteria and women being variously described as eccentric and mad. In a lecture, Norman declares: 'If we were to investigate all the strange rituals performed by women based on their so-called intuition, half the female population would be in asylums.'

The credit sequence is composed of a black screen with one illuminated, elegantly made-up eye (presumably belonging to Tansy). This opening would find an echo in *Repulsion*, another film concerned with what Barbara Creed has dubbed 'the monstrous feminine' (see Creed 1993). The setting, the rarified tweedy world of academia, complete with Friday night bridge parties is well-realised, the bitchy bourgeois wives and their dull husbands a striking contrast to Tansy and Norman (as Leon Hunt writes 'witchcraft is synonomous with bitchcraft' [2002: 91]). Flora's motive is ostensibly professional rivalry stemming from Norman's being promoted ahead of her ineffectual husband but there is a suggestion that the younger man's vitality and good looks are also a factor (Wyngarde appears semi-naked in a couple of scenes, his physique conspicuously eroticised). The contrast between this superficially staid world of petty rivalries and the realm of dark occult forces is mirrored in the shift from the school setting to an eerily desolate Cornwall photographed in startlingly realised day for night photography.

Night of the Eagle is one of a series of elegant black and white films from the 50s and 60s which reject the full colour excesses of Hammer and its imitators. These films – *Eagle, Night of the Demon, The Innocents* and *The Haunting* – found the kind of critical favour that long eluded many of their British genre contemporaries – Carlos Clarens, for example describes *Night of the Demon* as 'the diametrical opposite of the Hammer way of doing things' (1971: 210). This is, in part, due to their perceived good taste, shot in an icy, restrained monochrome and showcasing talent untarnished by the horror tag. *The Innocents*, for example, is based on a Henry James novella, *The Turn of the Screw*, stars Deborah Kerr, had script input from, amongst others Truman Capote and John Mortimer and was directed by Jack Clayton. But they are also concerned with the supernatural, which lends them some degree of respectability, matters metaphysical being considered more worthy of contemplation than the visceral and violent. Jeremy Dyson has written about these moody and atmospheric horrors, arguing that they're something:

> that we in this country seemed to do well…Maybe it's something to do with our climate – fog and rain and long winter nights are effective stimulants to the fantastic imagination. (2004: 10)

Ironically given the very obvious Englishness of these films, they can be seen as harking back to the suggestive supernatural scares of Val Lewton's output at RKO, an output which accrued a certain amount of positive critical attention. The Lewton influence was also there in a direct form, with both Jacques Tourneur (*Night of the Demon*) and Robert Wise (*The Haunting*) being his protégés. Despite the creative input of a number of Americans (director Tourneur, producer and co-screenwriter Hal E. Chester and star Dana Andrews), *Night of the Demon* is steeped in a very English kind of horror. This is in no small part due to the source material, the short story *Casting the Runes* by M. R. James. James is renowned for his ghost stories, elegantly-crafted tales which typically feature slightly tweedy intellectual men (not unlike the author) who unwittingly unleash a malevolent supernatural force. The titles alone are often creepy – *O Whistle and I'll Come to You, My Lad, A Warning to the Curious* – and James, a scholar and provost of Eton College who wrote stories as a hobby, locates his horrors in a series of familiar settings.

Although Chester has a screenwriting credit, it increasingly appears he did little of the writing with the original script by Charles Bennett (who wrote a number of Hitchcock films including *The 39 Steps* and *Sabotage* [1936]) rewritten by Cy Endfield, an American refugee from HUAC who would go on to a distinguished career as a director with the likes of *Hell Drivers* (1957) and *Zulu* (1965). (See Earnshaw 2004 and Meikle 2008 for more on Endfield's contribution.) Tourneur's film keeps the contemporary backdrop but substitutes a hard-nosed American scientist for James' typically bibliophile academic protagonist. Dana Andrews plays the lead, Dr. John Holden, yet another of the debunking Dawkins-esque scientists so beloved of occult horror but this time with an edge of film noir grit (the actor had starred in Otto Preminger films such as *Laura* [1944] and *Where the Sidewalk Ends* [1950]) although by all accounts he was unhappy making a horror film.

Andrews would become one of a number of alcoholic fading American stars who ended up in British horror, along with Brian Donlevy, Lon Chaney Jr. and Joan Crawford.

'NIGHT OF THE DEMON' X
DANA ANDREWS · PEGGY CUMMINS and NIALL MacGINNIS

The most un-Lewton reveal of the monster: *Night of the Demon*

Night of the Demon opens with a shot of Stonehenge and Tourneur, the talented director of *Cat People* (1942) and *I Walked with a Zombie* (1943), eschews gothic hokum in order to create a very recognisable, deceptively naturalistic setting. In his carefully-drawn vision of a slightly-rarified England of the British Museum reading room and the Savoy, home counties railway stations and board games in a country house drawing room, the director conjures up the likes of *The Seventh Victim* (1945) a satanic cult chiller set in Greenwich Village and looks forward to *Rosemary's Baby*, another occult film with one foot in the real. (In contrast, Hammer's *The Devil Rides Out*, despite its swashbuckling energy and charm, fails on this score, the 1920s Boy's Own-style setting acting to distance us from the diabolic goings-on.) As one character says to Holden 'Take it easy on our ghosts, we English are rather fond of them'. The villain of the piece is Nial McGinnis's Julian Karswell, a charming and urbane intellectual who is himself terrified of the forces he conjures up (at one point telling his dotty mother 'You don't get nothing for nothing'). Karswell is – like most British fictional devil-botherers – clearly modelled on Aleister Crowley, even down to the not-so-subtle hints of sexual deviancy; he has never married because he is 'so fussy'. Much has been written about the post-production meddling that went on, with both Bennett and Tourneur claiming that a meddlesome Chester and MGM added footage showing the demon against their wishes. But Tony Earnshaw has debunked this, revealing that the demon's appearance is mentioned in the screenplay.

Showing the monster may be a most un-Lewton thing to do but truth be told, it's actually pretty scary, all fangs, boils and claws, wreathed in smoke – it's certainly a much better special effect than the one employed when Holden is attacked by Karswell's cat in the form of a leopard (!) *Night of the Demon* is one of the great achievements in British horror, pitched as it is somewhere between parochial cosiness and supernatural terror. Both aspects are combined in the creepy sub-plot about the catatonic farmer and

Karswell cultist, Rand Hobart who is played by Brian Wilde, an actor who would go on play put-upon wimps in long-running sit-coms such as *Last of the Summer Wine* (1976– 2010) and *Porridge* (1973–7).[3] There is also the surreal pleasure of what Leon Hunt describes as 'fire demons materialising on the 8:45 to Southampton' (2002: 83).

Clayton's film, *The Innocents*, is a ghost story-cum-Freudian psychodrama. It bears a striking resemblance to Stanley Kubrick's *The Shining* (1980), another chilly literary adaptation which seems to have been intended as more than just a genre film. Both Clayton and Kubrick appear to tip their hand early on, making their respective protagonists – Deborah Kerr's repressed governess and Jack Nicholson's struggling writer – obviously unhinged. But just as with the eerily empty Overlook Hotel, Bly House does seem to be genuinely haunted, with some startling daylight appearances by restless spirits. Both films also look ravishingly beautiful. *The Innocents* is shot in Cinemascope by Freddie Francis, who always was a better cinematographer than he was a director.

The sexual undercurrents of James' story are underscored by Clayton – the children enacting the very adult things they witnessed taking place between the saturnine Quint and their former governess – and the film feels a bit like a forerunner of Polanski's *Repulsion*, a tightly-controlled case-study of a hysterical woman both fascinated and repelled by sex slowly coming undone. If there's a problem with Clayton's film, it's the faint air of what Andrew Sarris called 'strained seriousness' (see Sarris 1968), the sense that the writers and director feel that they're engaged in something deeper and richer than a mere genre film. This is ironic given that the most effective moments in the film are the most generic – Quint's face appearing at a window, the glimpses of supernatural figures in the gardens and on battlements.

The Haunting has become a bench-mark for post-Lewton subtle horror. It certainly looks all the better since the disastrous remake directed by Jan De Bont in 1999. An adaptation of Shirley Jackson's *The Haunting of Hill House*, Wise's film tells the story of a disparate group of strangers led by the paranormal researcher Professor Markway (Richard Johnson) who move into the supposedly-haunted Hill House in New England. They include Theo the psychic lesbian (slinky Claire Bloom), the irritating youngster Luke (irritating Russ Tamblyn) and Eleanor (Julie Harris), the kind of lonely, borderline hysterical female familiar to anyone who's seen *The Innocents*. Hill's novel has become a classic of the genre and there's a very literary feel to the script by Nelson Gidding. It's as if he's scared to stray too far from the novel, so there is an inordinate amount of voice-over in the early stages of the film but any problems with the screenplay are swept away by the sheer style of the thing. Wise was a disciple of Orson Welles who worked as an editor on *Citizen Kane* (1941) before going to direct a bewildering variety of projects, from a couple of Val Lewton films (*Curse of the Cat People* [1944] and *The Body Snatcher*) to the big-budget musicals *West Side Story* (1963) and *The Sound of Music* (1965). His work on *The Haunting* suggests an effective blend of Wellesian style – the deep focus photography, the intricate *mise-en-scène* – with a chilly ambiguity straight out of Lewton.

Many of the restrained scares here, the pounding walls, the creaking doors, ghostly hands grabbing in the dark, may try the patience of some viewers, with the film determined to avoid the lurch into *Grand Guignol* which characterises many later haunted house stories, from the similar *The Legend of Hell House* (1973) to *Poltergeist*. There's also some irony in the fact that the scariest bit in a film so lauded for its subtlety and creeping sense of unease is a good old-fashioned jump moment when, after a long, very tense climb up a rickety staircase, Markway's bedraggled wife makes a startling appearance. But there are some unnerving details early on, jarring children's music playing while Eleanor argues with her sister and the disturbing dissolve which turns a child into a crone, a whole wasted life passing by in seconds. The location for the film, Ettington Hall in Warwickshire is now a luxury hotel, a fate that has befallen a number of locations for British horror films including Grim's Dyke in Harrow, which appears in *The Curse of the Crimson Altar* and *Cry of the Banshee*, the Edgewarebury Hotel in Elstree featured in *The Devil Rides Out* and Hammer's old haunt, Oakley Court.

Witchcraft (1964) is a B-movie counterpart to this monochrome supernatural cycle. Instead of the respected likes of Kerr and Andrews, the star here is Lon Chaney Jr., an actor who was no great shakes during his 1940s heyday but was a washed-up alcoholic by the 60s. The plot is hokey enough: Vanessa Whitlock, a witch buried alive in the eighteenth century is revived when a graveyard is bulldozed and she seeks revenge on the descendants of her tormentors. But Sharp handles the whole thing with considerable style, the refined gentility of the English village setting providing an effective backdrop to the gloomy gothic goings-on. Sharp is aided immeasurably by the Welsh actress Yvette Rees as Vanessa. She is a remarkable looking woman, strikingly beautiful yet cadaverous and cruel and the film relies heavily on her presence. She doesn't have a line of dialogue but all of the best moments in the film are hers, whether appearing in the back seat of a car, stalking an old woman down the stairs or distorting her features into a gargoylian mask. The most memorable scene is her resurrection, the sound of heavy rain as the camera moves slowly from the smashed gravestone to her standing there, gaunt and feral. She pulls her shawl over her head in an all-too human gesture before skulking away into the night. *Witchcraft* owes something to the earlier *City of the Dead* and an even bigger debt to Bava's *Mask of Satan* but it's an eerie little chiller which deserves to be better known. Chaney Jr. would be unexpectedly affecting in a bizarre cult item from that same year, *Spider Baby* aka *The Maddest Story Ever Told* – where he even provides the title song! – before descending into ill health and a series of dire films such as *Hillbillys in a Haunted House* (1967). He died in 1973 and to avoid the cost of a funeral, left his body to science.

Meanwhile and in marked contrast to all that tasteful supernatural monochrome, Robert Hartford-Davis joined the 'clinical cult' with *Corruption* (1967), a key work in the radical shift in British horror from the period gothic of Hammer to the suburban gothic and excess of the 1970s. Hartford-Davis is an extremely important, if largely-forgotten, figure in British exploitation cinema whose wildly diverse filmography includes the sci-fi rock musical *Gonks Go Beat* (1967), the sappy comedy *The Sandwich Man* (1966), the sexploitationer *The Yellow Teddybears* ([1963], inspired by a *News of the World* story!) and the amazing variant on the women-in-prison film *School For Unclaimed Girls* aka *The Smashing Bird I Used To Know* (1967). Two of his films (debut feature *Crosstrap* [1962] and *Nobody Ordered Love* [1971]) are considered lost and appear on the list of 75 films being sought by the British Film Institue (also on the list are *The Public Life of Henry the Ninth* [1935], the first Hammer film and *Symptoms* [1973] from Jose Larraz, which is discussed in Chapter 5). After a move to the US in the early 70s, he even turned out a couple of blaxploitation efforts, *Black Gunn* (1972) and *The Take* (1974) before a fatal heart attack in an elevator in 1977. Sadly, his 1969 adaptation of Shakespeare's bloodiest play, *Titus Andronicus*, which would have starred Christopher Lee and Lesley Anne-Down, was aborted but it's hard to imagine a better illustration of British horror's commingling of high and low cultures than that. Hartford-Davis's horror films include the atmospheric *The Black Torment* (1964), which borrowed heavily from Italian genre films and *Incense for the Damned* (1967), an interesting take on the vampire mythos with a troubled production history which was taken away from the director (who consequently refused a credit). Hartford-Davis has a kind of crazed energy – rapid cuts, quick zooms, distorting lenses – which easily tips over into hysteria, as well as a fondness for nudity and graphic violence. *Corruption* is probably his best-known work, a characteristically lurid and breathless rip-off of Franju's poetic and gruesome *Les yeux sans visage* aka *Eyes without a Face*. Hartford-Davis's film is still at the time of writing unavailable uncut on DVD and Jonathan Rigby is undoubtedly correct when he dubs it 'the film many Peter Cushing fans would prefer to ignore' (2000: 170) while for Ian Conrich it offered 'an indication of the future form of exploitation… unpalatable to most critics, yet it represents an important strand' (2009: 101).

Cushing plays Sir John Rowan, a surgeon attempting to repair the scarred face of his fiancée (Sue Lloyd) using lasers and pituitary glands. After discovering that glands removed from corpses only work for a short time, he has to become a killer, egged on by the increasingly Lady Macbeth-ish Lloyd. Cushing's performance is excellent and multi-layered, with Rowan unsympathetic from the outset, priggish and possessive, his experiments motivated more by guilt than love (he caused the disfiguring accident) and it's only after a couple of murders that we see him express some real humanity. The film has an appealing, if unconvincing, Swinging London backdrop, opening with a groovy party where Anthony Booth (now better known as Tony Blair's father-in-law) plays a David Bailey-esque photographer who says things like 'what a crazy scene' and 'what a trip you're on, baby, wild' as he joins in with some bodypainting (an activity which is used in any number of movies from this period as visual shorthand for orgiastic depravity). But like *The Sorcerers*, this is no loved-up Aquarian fable. Indeed, the gang of hippies who turn up at the end turn out to be misfit criminals who end up slaughtered, along with all of the other lead characters, by a runaway laser. It's a grim, cold, remarkably intense film which is well-served by the director's hysterical approach. Like a lot of British exploitation film-makers, Hartford-Davis shot stronger material for the European release and these scenes are very graphic indeed. Rowan's murder of a prostitute, for example, is prolonged and stylishly done, from the disquieting shot of cuddly toys and dolls in her bedsit through to the long drawn-out fight scene which ends with hand-held, crazily distorted shots of a sweaty Cushing, his hair flopping over his face, wrestling the topless woman to the floor, stabbing her, smearing the blood over her breasts before cutting off her head. The scene is bracketed by some (obvious but effective) shots of a decapitated doll. A later murder on a train is less explicit but Cushing is even more creepy, staring at a nervous woman in a train compartment before taking out his scalpel and attacking her. After removing her head, he struggles to shove her body under the seats. This kind of graphic sexualised gore would become a fixture of 1970s horror but it's hard to imagine just how gruelling it must have been to contemporary audiences. Given the unusual ad campaign for the film, it may well be the case that said audiences were composed entirely of men and (heterosexual) couples – the tagline was 'Corruption Is Not A Woman's Picture! Therefore: No Woman Will Be Admitted Alone To See This Super-Shock Film'.

Hartford-Davis was by no means alone in making the move from sexploitation to horror. It's always been easy to switch from exploiting sex to violence and vice versa as the careers of Wes Craven, Bob Kelljan, Abel Ferrara, Ed Wood Jr. and a host of others testify. *Corruption* screenwriter Derek Ford would go on to direct *The Wife Swappers* (1969) and Stanley Long, the director of the likes of *Nudist Memories* (1959) would photograph *The Sorcerers* and do uncredited work on *Repulsion*. Even Lindsay Honey, better-known as porn icon Ben Dover had a go at horror, co-directing the shot-on-video black magic opus *Death Shock* (1981). The increasingly graphic gore appearing in the films of these one-time purveyors of smut from the end of the 1960s and into the 1970s makes Ian Conrich's term 'Flesh Films' an apposite one.

DECADENT AND UNRULY

Meanwhile, back in Bray, Hammer's reliance on full-colour gothic horrors had served them well. Their attempts to diversify were mixed – the Raquel Welch-in-fur-bikini Prehistoric romp *One Million Years BC* (1966) was a huge hit – and there were a well-crafted series of psycho thrillers written by Sangster. Although often described as 'mini-Hitchcocks', a better term would be 'mini-Clouzots' given the obvious debt these twisting and turning narratives owe to the latter's *Les Diaboliques* (1955). A couple of them (*Taste of Fear* [1960] and *The Maniac* [1963]) are even set in France. While these thrillers have received comparatively little critical attention – and for some critics don't even qualify as horror films – they represent an important strand of Hammer gothic which complements their monster series. Although they have contemporary settings and are devoid of supernatural elements, in their hysterical stories of persecuted women in country houses and plentiful shock moments – corpses that appear and disappear, characters going insane, nightmares, hallucinations, stabbings and blow-torch murders – they look back to the gothic novel. Sangster seems to have preferred these thrillers to the gothic horrors – indeed, he was still churning them out for US TV in the 1970s – and Freddie Francis certainly does a better job with *Paranoiac* (1963) and *Nightmare* (1964) than he does with any of his monster flicks. A couple of the later thrillers showcase faded Hollywood royalty as sinister crones, a move clearly inspired by the success of *Whatever Happened to Baby Jane?*): Tallulah Bankhead in *Fanatic* aka *Die Die My Darling* and Bette Davis in *The Nanny* and *The Anniversary*, a very weird, stagey black comedy.

There were also some notable flops. The woeful comedy remake of the James Whale film *The Old Dark House* (1963) was a waste of time while *The Gorgon* (1964), a gloomy, atmospheric attempt at a new (at least on film) monster performed badly at the box-office. The 'space western' *Moon Zero Two* (1968) released in the wake of *2001*, completely bombed. The gothic horrors were still Hammer's most popular films but the company were no longer the sole providers of lurid period grue and as production costs rose, they decided to start shooting films back-to-back to cut costs. The effect of this can be seen in a couple of films from 1966, *Dracula Prince of Darkness* and *Rasputin the Mad Monk* where the Count plunges into what is clearly the same frozen lake that claimed the charismatic Russian.

Hammer were slow to catch onto the social upheavals of the 1960s and the revivifying effect this gave to the horror film, proving either unwilling or unable to tackle the kind of contemporary concerns explored in a variety of genre films from the period. In addition to *Corruption*, a series of British horror films - *Repulsion, Scream and Scream Again, Blood on Satan's Claw* and the work of Michael Reeves – went where Hammer were – initially at least – reluctant to go. Whereas AIP were keen to exploit the abilities of a number of talented young upstarts and film school graduates (including such future luminaries as Martin Scorsese, Francis Ford Coppola and Peter Bogdanovich), Hammer were content to rely on their established writers and directors. As we shall see in Chapter 5, Tony Tenser, the enterprising head of Compton then Tigon had no scruples about employing young, sometimes untried directors and actively sought out fresh talent, such as Reeves and Polanski (Hammer turned Polanski down when he came to them with the script for what would become the highly-regarded *Cul-de-Sac* [1966]). The problems they had with the maverick Americans Robert Aldrich (on the war film *Ten Seconds to Hell* [1959]) and Joseph Losey can't have helped matters. (Amicus would have similar problems with William Friedkin, another talented American director with a singular vision and an accompanying distaste for compromise.)

The story of Hammer and Losey is interesting, in part because the film that resulted, *The Damned* aka *These are the Damned* is one of the best the company released. It illustrates Hammer's willingness to take on a left-field project and also their reluctance to follow through with it. Losey was the gifted American director of a handful of tough genre pictures – such as *The Prowler* (1951) and an underrated remake of Fritz Lang's *M* – who fled to England in 1953 to escape the anti-communist witch-hunts. He started work in the UK under a pseudonym and after filming a short for Hammer, was signed up for the sci-fi film *X-The Unknown* (1956) but was fired after complaints from the star, the rabidly anti-communist Dean Jagger. The director appears to have blamed Jagger, as he was back at Hammer in 1961 to work on an adaptation of H.L. Lawrence's novel *Children of Light*. The fact that it deals with eerie blonde-haired kids – as well as the title change forced on Losey – indicates the company wanted to cash in on the success of the similarly-themed *Village of the Damned* (1960). But Losey's film is darker and stranger, starting out as a youthsploitation film about a gang of leather-clad roughs led by an oddly-accented Oliver Reed in the seaside town of Weymouth and turning into a deeply pessimistic Cold War nightmare. The BBFC were disturbed by the strong hints of incestuous desire as well as the gang violence and Losey's film was held back until 1963. Hammer seemed uncertain what to do with such a bleak, problematic, genre-busting film so cut it (by 10 minutes for the UK release and an unforgivable 20 for the US) and stuck it on a double-bill with the psycho-thriller *Maniac*.

While Polanski would test the patience of Tenser and his partner Michael Klinger with his endless reshoots and Tigon insisted Michael Reeves lose a band of gypsies from *Witchfinger General* as they were reluctant to hire the extras, they didn't treat either of them as shabbily as Hammer treated Losey. Admittedly, the American was more difficult than they were used to, insisting on last-minute script rewrites with a writer of his choosing but *The Damned* more than makes up for it, even down to its oddly memorable quirks (the weird bird sculptures which litter the film, the maddeningly catchy theme song, Black Leather Rock).

The Devil Rides Out may have been released in 1968, a turbulent year of riots, protest and social change but it takes place in a rarified, idealised past, a kind of derring-do John Buchan-esque late 20s. Fisher's adaptation of Dennis Wheatley's novel about the clash between the forces of good (Christopher Lee's imposing Duc De Richlieu) and evil (Charles Gray's camp Mocata) is a curious film, much beloved by fans, exciting and often frightening – albeit hamstrung by some terrible special effects (which were controversially tweaked for the 2012 Blu-ray release). It's fast-paced and creepy but compared to the same year's *Rosemary's Baby*, also based on a vaguely hokey diabolical novel, it seems like a film from another era, the aristocratic characters, the cravats, the parade of ethnic villains and the conspicuous consumption (best demonstrated when a character asks to borrow the Duc's car and is told to 'take any of them'). Of course, the upside to this stubborn refusal to get hip was the fact that Hammer should have avoided embarrassing themselves with would-be youth horror films like *The Curse of the Crimson Altar* (with a very fetching Barbara Steele painted green and wearing a ram horn hat) and *The Haunted House of Horror* (1969) but this was not the case. *Dracula AD 1972*, a film we'll return to later, is not only every bit as bad as any in the 'hipster horror' category but also by the time it was released woefully dated.

Conventional wisdom has it that Hammer lost its way and proved unable to move beyond the same old hoary gothic tropes, producing a series of misjudged reworkings of old ideas (off-beat psycho-thrillers, sexy mummies, swashbuckling heroes and a lot of lesbian vampires). Certainly, late Hammer had its fair share of terrible films (although such is the abiding love for the company, even turkeys like *Lust for a Vampire* [1970] have a considerable cult following). But the company's increasingly desperate 70s incarnation, keen to attract American distributors who were rapidly losing interest in British horror offers up some peculiar pleasures. This includes off-beat stand-alone gothics such as *Countess Dracula*, *Hands of the Ripper* (1971) and *Demons of the Mind* (1972) to the series of decadent, yes, perhaps even desperate experiments which were often compromised by cost-cutting and a fatal reliance on over-production. *Dr. Jekyll and Sister Hyde*, *Blood From the Mummy's Tomb*, *Vampire Circus* (1972), *Frankenstein and The Monster from Hell* (1974) and *The Satanic Rites of Dracula* have a demented, over-ripe, slightly incoherent quality to them. Ian Conrich has dubbed these late films 'unruly' while for Kim Newman they are 'decadent' (1988: 18) and 'display a kind of despairing, end of the road nihilism' (ibid.) but this can be just as satisyfying in its own way as the wild libidinal energy of 1950s Hammer, the grim and gloomy gothic of these last years very fitting for a company coming to an end and taking a whole tradition down with them. There is a sad, elegaic quality to a film like *Frankenstein and the Monster from Hell*, the same kind of autumnal gloom that could also be found in American Westerns of this period like *Pat Garrett and Billy the Kid* (1973) or *The Shootist* (1976), another classical genre on its last legs.

Many of these films were the work of new, younger talents Hammer drafted in at the start of the new decade. These included the critic and screenwriter, Chris Wicking, writer/director Brian Clemens and directors such as Peter Sykes and Peter Sasdy. These newcomers were not only more interested in the possibilities of the genre than their predecessors but they were also more interested in exploring contemporary concerns. Wicking, who had written the way-out *Scream and Scream Again* became the last of the company's resident script editors and his *Demons of the Mind*, directed by Sykes would, like a host of other horror films from this period, tackle the clash of generations, the older and corrupt feeding off the young and vital, conjuring up a convincing air of disillusion and cynicism that was far removed from the moral certainty of much of the studio's former output.

The films Clemens worked on were even more strikingly unusual. A writer on the influential cult TV show *The Avengers*, Clemens had written a number of screenplays including the Hitchcockian 'stalked schoolgirls' thriller, *And Soon the Darkness* (1970). Indeed *Thriller*, the TV show he created which ran from 1973 to 1976 produced a bewildering number of variations on that theme (often with splendidly lurid titles like *I'm the Girl He Wants to Kill* and *A Coffin For the Bride*). But *Dr. Jekyll and Sister Hyde*, scripted by Clemens and directed by the veteran Roy Ward Baker and *Captain Kronos*

Vampire Hunter (1973) which he wrote and directed, are stylish and refreshingly off-beat. The former project — which could easily be pitched on that title alone — is a richly atmospheric twist on Stevenson's story with the idealistic doctor (Ralph Bates) turning into a demonically sexy woman (a ferocious Martine Beswick). Clemens also manages to rope in Burke and Hare (who supply Jekyll with the female organs he needs to continue his experiments) and the Ripper (who is Jekyll/Hyde, when he/she decides to cut out the middle-men). David Whitaker's lush score is memorably melancholy and the film has a rich texture, the gimmicky premise working in no small part due to the startling resemblance between Bates and Beswick. Sadly, *Captain Kronos, Vampire Hunter*, despite another high-concept idea — action meets horror when a swashbuckling hero and hunchback assistant fight the undead — is a bit of a mess. The (dubbed) German actor Horst Jansen isn't bad in the title role and there is a good supporting cast (John Carson, Shane Bryant, Caroline Munro, Wanda Ventham) but the whole thing is a wasted opportunity.

It may be the case that viewers of a certain age find *Kronos*, along with *The Legend of the Seven Golden Vampires*, a let down because they first encountered both films in the pages of *House of Hammer* magazine (1976–78). It may seem strange in these days of Netflix, YouTube and Blu-ray but in those pre-VCR years, *House of Hammer*'s main selling point was comic strip adaptations of films aimed at a readership too young to see them at the cinema and so exciting were a number of these stories that the films themselves couldn't help but pale in comparison.

Hammer even went so far as to hire the vaguely hip genre director Peter Collinson for *Straight on Till Morning* (1972), an uncharacteristically flashy psycho-thriller. A pregnant young woman (Rita Tushingham — another clue that this is a very different kind of Hammer thriller) arrives in London from Liverpool and falls in with a enigmatic and handsome young man obsessed with Peter Pan who also happens to be the killer of a string of women. It's very different to anything else the company would try, a fact evident from the start, which contrasts a fairy tale voice-over ('a wondrous magic garden, where the rain never fell') with rows of grim terraced houses. There is a lot of faux-verite footage of Earls Court and scenes in fashion boutiques and happening parties as well as a restrained, muted quality to the horror — the murders take place off-screen but are tape-recorded, a detail inspired by the excesses of the Moors Murders. Collinson's modish direction, a lot of zooms, crowded frames and an over-reliance on glass, mirrors and jagged, jarring editing is very of its time. Indeed, *Straight on Till Morning* makes more sense when compared to other films by the same director such as the claustrophobic Pinter-inflected home invasion shocker *The Penthouse* (1967) and the proto-slasher *Fright* (1971), with a mini-skirted Susan George being attacked by escaped lunatic Ian Bannen while babysitting. Collinson, who died of cancer aged only 44, is a fairly neglected figure these days, best-known for *The Italian Job* (1968), although he made a number of glossy, semi-exploitation films in a variety of genres (westerns, thrillers, war films) and shot in a range of countries. His work often combines an attention-grabbing, self-conscious style with violent action, as in *Open Season* (1974), a grimly compelling reworking of *The Most Dangerous Game* set in the US but filmed in the UK and Spain. *Straight On…* also fits neatly into a series of British 'shockers' of the early 1970s much more than it does into any comparable Hammer tradition (there are no Jimmy Sangster-style plot twists and double-crosses here). It's an illustration of the chances Hammer were taking, even if as Kim Newman suggests this was possibly driven solely by desperation (see Newman 1988). But the fate of Collinson's film, put out on a sensationally promoted 'Women in Peril' double bill with Jimmy Sangster's *Fear in the Night* (1972) is also typical. The company's more outré or experimental work (including *Demons of the Mind*) ended up as the second feature on a double bill but then this was nothing new, as Joe Losey would tell you.

The best-known late Hammer monster is surely the lesbian vampire, although if truth be told time has not been kind to the so-called Karnstein Trilogy – *The Vampire Lovers* (1970), *Lust for a Vampire* and *Twins of Evil* (1972). The first was a surprisingly straight (pardon the pun) adaptation of *Carmilla* (1872), Joseph Sheridan Le Fanu's story of a predatory female bloodsucker. The role of Carmilla/Mircalla/ Marcilla was taken by the feline, heavily-accented Ingrid Pitt, whose iconic status rests on a relatively slim filmography (as well as her Hammer debut, she made *Countess Dracula* and *The Wicker Man* as well as *Where Eagles Dare* (1968) and a Bond film). There are some nice touches – the vampirised women are tormented by dreams of a monster cat, Carmilla's panicky reaction to a funeral – but these all come straight out of Le Fanu. *Lust for a Vampire* is poorly-written and fatally crippled by the casting of Yutte Stensgard, as wooden as she is beautiful. Ingrid Pitt was too old for the role of Carmilla but she had a kind of feral intensity which is entirely lacking here. The addition of a terrible song, Strange Love is the final nail in the film's coffin. The best of the trilogy, *Twins of Evil* brings elements of the witchfinder sub-genre in the form of the Brotherhood, a kind of nineteenth-century mittel European Taliban who dress like puritans and like to immolate young women. The cold, unusually bleak pre-credit sequence where we see the Brotherhood in action, led by Cushing's icy fundamentalist Gustav Weill is the best scene in the film. Director John Hough does a pretty good job, imbuing the whole thing with a strange tone mid-way between fairytale – the dark woods, the too-blue skies (even at night!) – and Western – the Brotherhood riding around like an evil posse accompanied by Harry Robertson's driving score. The titular siblings, Madeleine and Mary Collinson, the first twins to pose naked for Playboy magazine are fetching enough but not really actors, especially when they're so atrociously dubbed.

A large part of the problem with the Karnstein trilogy is writer Tudor Gates, who is not a bad screenwriter as such but certainly lacked Sangster's ability to find new twists in an old formula. There are also so many moments of camp creeping into the films. Hammer always approached their subjects seriously, even when there were traces of black humour and even when, as in *The Lost Continent*, the plot was really very weird. But the

Early 70s Hammer glamour: *The Vampire Lovers*

over-the-top performance of Damien Thomas as Count Karnstein here, an almost Tod Slaughterish rendering of the old aristocrat stereotype is misjudged, as is the painful bit where mid-coitus, Carmilla half-heartedly masturbates a candle. The films are not even particularly effective as sexploitation, fairly tame when compared to the heady, woozy eroticism of *Dr. Jekyll and Sister Hyde* or the unearthly Valerie Leon in dual roles in *Blood from the Mummy's Tomb*.

There is clearly some serious psychosexual stuff to explore in the lesbian vampire scenario, a sexy female monster feeding off various young women until she is hunted down by a group of men who restore what seems like order by penetrating her with a stake or lopping off her head. But Gates does little with this, unlike the similarly themed European films *Le Rouge aux lèvres* /*Daughters of Darkness* (1971) and *La Novia Ensangrentada*/ *The Blood-Spattered Bride* (1972). The coming of *Vampyres* by Jose Larraz in 1974, discussed at length in Chapter 5 would make the Karnstein films look positively anaemic.

To really get a sense of just how wild and off-beat these late Hammers could be – even a fairly staid example like *The Vampire Lovers* – one could compare them to the handful of 'heritage gothics' produced by Tyburn Film Productions during the same period. Tyburn was the brainchild of Kevin Francis, the son of Freddie and a big fan of old-time gothic horror. They specialised in a kind of retro horror which relied on the input of various old Hammer hands (and some old Hammer stories). Matthew Coniam interviewed Francis in 1995 and asked him why he formed Tyburn, only to get the blunt answer 'I needed to earn a living' (2009).

Coniam points out that, given the prolonged decline Hammer were suffering in the 1970s, Francis's claim that he went into the field in 1974 planning "'to make a living" seems disengenous in the extreme. This was more like suicidal aesthetic defiance'(Coniam 2009). Their first film, *Persecution* (1973) was directed by Don Chaffey, who had made *One Million Years BC* for Hammer. It's a psycho melodrama with a slumming-it Lana Turner tormenting her weak son (Ralph Bates) and ending up smothering his baby son. It's little more than an homage to the *Baby Jane*/mini-Hitchcock cycle. The next film, *The Ghoul* aka *The Thing in the Attic* (1975) based on a script by Anthony Hinds using his John Elder pseudonym, scored by Hammer composer Harry Robertson and directed by Kevin's dad

Freddie, was an improvement of sorts. It had a good cast (a typically pain-wracked Peter Cushing, a young, very intense John Hurt), some eerie business on the foggy marshes and very handsome sets (left over from Jack Clayton's *The Great Gatsby* [1974]). But when the monster is revealed, it's a huge disappointment (a scabby, green Don Henderson in a loincloth) and the film is really just a moderately stylish rip-off of *The Reptile*.

Undaunted, Tyburn went further back into Hammer's back catalogue for inspiration and came up with *Legend of the Werewolf* (1975), which owes a considerable debt to *Curse of the Werewolf*. The make-up for the titular beast is good and for horror fans who first encountered the film through stills in glossily-illustrated 70s horror books, *Legend...* promised great things. But in the end, and typically for Tyburn, it falls flat, despite the vaguely exotic setting (nineteenth-century Paris) and the presence of Cushing. David Rintoul's lycanthrope can't compare with *Curse*'s Oliver Reed, who is convincingly feral even before he is transformed, and Freddie Francis seems even more bored by the material than usual. Francis's 'suicidal aesthetic defiance' failed to pay off and Tyburn hobbled away into TV movies.

Hammer weren't at the Tyburn stage but they were struggling to find their way back to a winning formula in an increasingly competitive horror market. Production costs in the UK were climbing, leading to a lot of American companies upping sticks. Hammer had long relied on major studio US distribution but it wasn't just audiences who were turned off by the recent films. Warner Brothers passed on releasing *Scars of Dracula* and *Horror of Frankenstein* (with good reason, it should be said) and Hammer had to look elsewhere.[4] Their relationship with Rank was already strained and it seems that *Demons of the Mind* was the last straw. Rank broke it off. EMI Films, who had had a good relationship with Hammer were starting to lose patience. Poor old Michael Carreras took over from his father in 1971 in the midst of all this chaos and resorted to screening all of the recent films in an attempt to identify what was going wrong. A lot was resting on…

VAMPIRE CIRCUS (1972)

Developed under the more prosiac title *Village of the Vampires*, *Vampire Circus* was the feature debut of Robert Young, who had a background in short films. Cushing and Lee are absent, as are any of the new generation of stars the company were in the process of grooming: Ralph Bates, Shane Briant and Christopher Neame. A number of the cast were Hammer veterans, however – Thorley Walters had played bumbling oafs in a number of 60s films including *The Evil of Frankenstein*, Anthony Higgins (credited here as Anthony Corlan) had appeared in *Taste the Blood of Dracula* and the musclebound Dave Prowse had played the monster in *Horror of Frankenstein* (1970) (and would go on the play the simian title creature in *Frankenstein and the Monster From Hell* before achieving fame in the dual roles of Darth Vader and the Green Cross Code Man).

The rest of the cast is of considerable cult appeal: Adrienne Corri had appeared in *Clockwork Orange* and John Moulder-Brown was fresh from the dazzling Jerzy Skolimovski picture *Deep End* (1970). Lalla Ward would go on to play the companion to *Dr. Who* from 1979–1981 before marrying the scientist Richard Dawkins while Lynne Frederick would make *Schizo* (1977) for Pete Walker before becoming Peter Sellers' last wife in

The end of Emil in *Vampire Circus*

1977. When he died in 1980 (soon after he and Frederick were divorced), she inherited most of his money and died age 39 in vaguely mysterious circumstances. Count Mitterhouse, the closest thing the film has to a Dracula figure, is played by Robert Tayman, an imposing actor, if not a very good one, who would go on to play Mark E. Desaart (!) in *House of Whipcord*. Here, he comes over as ridiculous, his voice clearly dubbed, wearing a frilly, chest-revealing shirt, a gold choker and way too much mascara. It may be an attempt to keep up with the Bowie/Bolan androgyny of the period but the Hammer vampires seemed to keep getting camper, reaching a high of sorts with John Forbes-Robertson's ridiculous Dracula in *The Legend of the Seven Golden Vampires*.

Corlan is more convincing in the almost dialogue-free role as the werepanther/ vampire Emil. (With his long, frizzy hair and saturnine appearance, he always vaguely reminded me of David Essex, so it's no surprise to find Jonathan Rigby [2000] observing that Essex was a contender for the part.) The screenplay is credited to Judson Kinberg, who was a newcomer at Hammer (and wouldn't work with them again) but the co-writer of the story was George Baxt who, of course, had form where circus settings were concerned, having written the aforementioned *Circus of Horrors*.

In the familiar Hammer setting of a village in mittel Europa, a vampire, Count Mitterhouse is preying on the locals. Anna Müller, the wife of a schoolteacher, is in thrall to the Count and procures victims for him. The villagers attack the castle, kill the vampire and drive Anna out of town after a brutal beating. Fifteen years later, the village now plague-ravaged and under quarantine, the Circus of Nights appears led by a gypsy who is in fact Anna Müller. The performers are vampires and they have returned to wreak revenge on the villagers by killing their children. *Vampire Circus* offers up many of the by now very well-established pleasures associated with Hammer, from the dazzling sets – the eerily empty plague village, the creepy castle crypt – to the weird setting, this Serbian village with a German name (Schtettel) where everyone speaks English, a convention Hammer borrowed from the Universal Frankenstein films (where British and American actors play what the script calls burghers in a fantasy rendering of a German village built on a soundstage).

There are also some concessions to the liberalised climate of the 1970s, with a very high body count and some graphic violence. A bullet leaves a big exit hole in the strongman's back, a family is savaged by a panther (very bright red blood being splashed over the ferns) and in the film's most surprising sequence, Anna watches as the child she has brought to Mitterhouse is tenderly 'groomed' in a scene with a distinctly kinky paedophiliac edge to it. This impression is reinforced by the obvious sexual pleasure the woman gets as she watches the action, which ends with her swooning in ecstasy as the Count bites the child in the neck. This unwholesome subtext was noted by Hammer script editor – and one-time Bond girl – Nadja Regin who felt the scene was 'strongly reminiscent of the Moors Murders' (2013: 41).

As was par for the course in late Hammer, there is some (female) nudity and a couple of fairly graphic sex romps but thematically, too, it reflects some of the contemporary concerns that were cropping up their films from this period. The 'sins of the father' plot echoes the generation gap narratives of the likes of *Hands of the Ripper* while the sexualised thrashing of Anna Müller is reminiscent of the thinly-disguised gang rape portrayed in *Dracula Prince of Darkness*, where the newly-vampirised Barabara Shelley is pinned down by a gang of monks and penetrated. Hammer's view of female sexuality can be regarded as a conservative one, alebit not unproblematically, and this is particularly true of the vampire films, which for all their bouncing breasts and lesbian writhing, seem to regard sexed-up women as a problem to be dealt with, albeit a titillating problem (no pun intended).

Hammer was always looking to cut costs where they could but the situation was getting dire. In a shocking act of disregard for Young and his film, they stopped the shoot after six weeks. This led to a certain amount of creative editing, the result of which is a kind of choppy quality and a very noticeable increase in pace in the second half: indeed, there are times where it feels like a rough edit, with scenes abbreviated and little room to breathe. Jonathan Rigby has identified the 'Euro-style narrative incoherence' (2000: 219) and it's true, this barrage of disjointed images has a vaguely surreal quality *a'la* Jean Rollin but it's also frustrating, given the strange, hallucinatory atmosphere created in the first half.

While some of these scenes, such as the first circus performance are a bit hokey with the flash editing between a panther and Emil lounging in a cage, there is a strangely powerful dance sequence featuring a man with a whip 'taming' a nude, bald woman covered in tiger stripes. It's hard to know how seriously we're supposed to take it, especially the weird moment where the woman starts shaking suggestively and we cut to a caged tiger mimicking her movements but it's a memorable scene nonetheless. There are also some striking images, such as the bat crawling from the eye socket of a skull and the dwarf ringmaster who peels off his facepaint mask to reveal another beneath. Young also uses some odd optical effects, some of which don't work at all (the blinking bood spot that fall onto Mitterhouse's chest) but at least one which is very effective, as the Count appears in the room like something out of a Melies trick film. The killing of Mitterhouse is also notable. Given the sheer number of Hammer vampire outings, the screenwriters couldn't always rely on the usual stakes and crosses to dispatch the undead and so were forced to look further afield, plus Sangster and Fisher set the bar very high with *Dracula* and its swashbuckling climax.

Hammer vampires have been beheaded and impaled on burning beams, killed by showers and sprinklers, caught in hawthorn bushes, killled by flocks of bats, impaled on wagon wheels, even, in the slightly-baffling ending of *Taste the Blood of Dracula*, killed by angry God. Mitterhouse is killed in a less metaphysical but arguably more dramatic fashion, when a villager hooks a crossbow over his head and then fires it, decapitating the Count with the string. His head, still-snarling, slowly falls from his body and tumbles into his coffin. There are enough imaginative touches in the direction to make one wish Young, like Sasdy and Sykes, had stuck with Hammer. His later career has been a disappointment, with turkeys like *Splitting Heirs* (1993), where the very well-preserved 45 year-old Barbara Hershey plays the mother of the nowhere-near-as-well-preserved 50 year-old Eric Idle and the ignominious experience of being removed from *Fierce Creatures* (1997).

THE BARON AND THE COUNT

It's never just about the numbers but they are revealing. *The Curse of Frankenstein* spawned six sequels while there were also the same amount of *Dracula* sequels (and that's just including those starring Lee). As well as a handful of unrelated vampire films, there was also *Brides of Dracula* (1960) – which featured David Peel's blond Baron Meister and the aforementioned *Legend of the Seven Golden Vampires*, which features a very unconvincing, extremely fey Dracula. The Hammer sequels are unusual in that unlike other long-running sagas – the Universal monsters or the *Friday the 13th* films – there was no slow decline. The Universal multiple monster mash-up *House of Dracula* (1945) is fun but not even close to the earlier *Frankenstein meets The Wolfman* (1945) in terms of quality, never mind *Frankenstein* while Sean S. Cunningham's *Friday the 13th* (1980), a derivative and rough-edged yet compelling rural slasher looks all the better when compared to the risible likes of *Jason Takes Manhattan* (1989) and *Jason X* (2001) which sends the hockey-masked killer into space.

However, the law of diminishing returns doesn't apply to the Hammer Frankenstein and Dracula pictures, with some of the sequels being among the studio's best: *Frankenstein Created Woman* (1967), *Frankenstein and the Monster from Hell*, *Brides of Dracula* and *Taste the Blood of Dracula* (1970) – while also, lest we forget, some of the worst: *Dracula Has Risen From the Grave* and *Horror of Frankenstein*. Yet they also offer two very different approaches. The Dracula films were often wild and wayward with a number of different directors and approaches. Kim Newman has written how vampirism was grafted on to an ultra-violent 'meat' movie (*Scars of Dracula*), the pseudo-hip youth scene (*Dracula AD 1972*) [and] a James Bondish superscience thriller (*The Satanic Rites of Dracula*). (1988: 18)

Sometimes the vampirism seems to be tacked on as almost as an afterthought or perhaps as a useful way to brand an otherwise difficult picture. *Taste the Blood of Dracula*, to take the best example, would work just as well, maybe even better, without the Count but like that other dark 'problem picture' *Demons of the Mind*, it may have proved a tough sell.

The Frankenstein series is considerably less wayward, anchored by the presence of Fisher (and the very shoddy *The Evil of Frankenstein* shows just how much the series needed him). Even as the experiments got wackier – soul transplants, head transplants, building an aperman in a madhouse – Fisher manages to maintain a remarkable stylistic consistency. The fact that both cycles drew to their respective close in the same way – a horrible misfire followed by a bold twist – offers not only a pleasing, curious symmetry but also a striking illustration of how the decadent desperation of late Hammer could go either way.

HORROR OF FRANKENSTEIN (1970) / FRANKENSTEIN AND THE MONSTER FROM HELL (1974)

Jimmy Sangster was lured back to gothic horror by the offer to direct an update of Hammer's first Frankenstein film but he really shouldn't have bothered. Some people may regard *Horror of Frankenstein* as a kind of charmless 'Carry on Baron' but it's actually worse than that. It's a serio-comic remake of *The Curse of Frankenstein* starring Ralph Bates but it reeks of the contempt Sangster seems to have for the monster he has created (in more ways than one). When a severed hand is galvanised into life and sticks two fingers up, it feels like the writer/director is giving a v-sign to the gothic tradition for which he felt such ambivalence. Or maybe it was aimed at the audience. Similarly, the climactic scene is completely wasted, the monster given an accidental (and off-screen) acid bath.

Sangster's other gothic directorial outing *Lust for a Vampire* was also poor, although his final film for Hammer, *Fear in the Night* was a vast improvement. Significantly, it was also a return to the mini-Hitchcock/Clouzot tradition with a spooky setting – a rural school

– and a good cast (Cushing, Bates, Joan Collins and Judy Geeson). Sangster increasingly worked in US TV, writing one of the best episodes of the cult show *Kolchak the Night Stalker* (1974-5) and mini-Hitchcock TV movies such as *Scream Pretty Peggy* (1973). He died in 2011.

Sangster's contribution to Hammer is hard to overstate. He was a screenwriter who was as inventive as he was prolific, both of which came in handy when breathing life into old formulae for a cash-strapped company. Although there may be screenwriters of his calibre working today in the UK, it's hard to see how they would get the kind of chances Sangster got to hone their craft.

Frankenstein and the Monster from Hell, the last of the Baron's outings is also Fisher's last and it's an appropriately gloomy, claustrophobic film. All of Frankenstein's various dubious experiments which we have followed for nearly two decades comes down to this, his incarceration in a weirdly phony lunatic asylum. His last creature is fittingly demented, a hideous ape/yeti (played again by Dave Prowse), a bizarre creation for bizarre times. There are some nice touches – the ridiculous wig the Baron sports – along with some very voguish gore – a brain is trodden on and the monster bottles someone. It's not hard to identify something incredibly moving about the end of the film, after the lunatics have torn the monster to shreds, leaving both the Baron and Fisher seemingly stranded, men who've been left behind as time has moved on but who are still possessed of a creative urge, be it film-making or conjuring new life out of corpses stitched together. Fisher never made another film before his death in 1980.

DRACULA AD 1972 (1972)

AD 1972

The reinvention of Dracula was far more radical. In the early 70s, there was a short-lived cycle of US vampire films which radically reinvented the gothic through the use of contemporary settings and a hip, semi-parodic tone. This loose collection, which I have described elsewhere as 'counter-culture vampire films' (see Cooper 2013) include *Blacula* (1972) and the sequel *Scream Blacula Scream* (1973), *The Velvet Vampire* (1971) and *The Deathmaster* ([1972] which reimagined Charles Manson as one of the undead). The pick of this bunch was *Count Yorga Vampire* (1970) and the superior sequel, *The Return of Count Yorga* (1972), which abandoned period trappings and went back to Stoker to locate the title character, an undead Bulgarian count played by a smooth Robert Quarry, in a recognisable setting (in this case, contemporary California). The approach taken by director Bob Kelljan is both playful (such as the scene where a fancy dress vampire asks Yorga 'Where are your fangs?', with the Count snapping back 'Where are your manners?') and genuinely scary (Yorga's slow-motion attacks are animalistic and bloody and his vampire brides are part *Night of the Living Dead*-style ghouls and part Manson Family). In a very telling scene in *The Return of Count Yorga*, we see the Count watching *The Vampire Lovers*, which was only a couple of years old, on late night TV and dubbed into Spanish. The freshness and vitality of the Yorga films (and, more importantly, the money they made) prompted Warner Brothers to ask Hammer for a contemporary Dracula. The resulting project, which started life with the striking title 'Dracula Today', can be regarded as a major turkey or a neglected cult item. Truth be told, it's both.

Dracula AD 1972, which in West Germany was given the far groovier title of *Dracula jagt Mini-Mädchen/Dracula Hunts the Mini-Girls*, starts conventionally enough in 1872 with an exciting, blue-tinged clash between Van Helsing and Dracula atop a carriage going through Hyde Park (in reality the ubiquitous Black Park) which ends with the Count impaled on a wooden wheel. After this startling opening – as good as anything else in the series – and the impressive credit sequence, all traffic jams, office blocks and motorway flyovers, the film soon starts to come unstuck. A group of deeply unconvincing jaded Chelsea hipsters (including one who for some unspecified reason is dressed as a monk) led by the hokey Johnny Alucard (geddit?) perform a faintly silly black mass in a deconsecrated church where Dracula's ashes have been buried.

Unlike Stoker and Kelljan, screenwriter Don Houghton makes no effort to have Dracula experience modern life and instead keeps him confined him to the church, snarling and sending the hapless Johnny off to procure a series of nubile chicks. The film could be dismissed as just one of the more boring entries in the Dracula saga but the painfully outdated grooviness and ill-judged youthsploitation elements turn the whole thing into a bizarre curio. The Kings Road kids are played by a disparate bunch of vaguely culty names: Marsha Hunt, singer, one of the stars of the stage show Hair and mother to one of Mick Jagger's kids, Caroline Munro, model and 'scream queen', fresh from her cameo as the dead wife of *The Abominable Dr. Phibes*, Christopher Neame as Johnny Alucard, Michael Kitchen, who would go on to play a creepy 70s Satan in *Brimstone and Treacle* (1976) and a pre-*Dynasty* Stephanie Beacham as Jessica Van Helsing. Neame, who was being lined up along with Shane Briant and Ralph Bates, as a new Hammer star is pretty awful and the oft-derided sequence when poor old Van Helsing has to use a pen to work out that Alucard is Dracula backwards is deeply silly. There are a couple of moments which suggest how interesting a contemporary Hammer vampire film could have been – Van Helsing running through the gaudy Chelsea night looking for his granddaughter or wandering disconsolate past walls sprayed with football graffiti, Johnny Alucard stalking a woman doing her washing in a late night launderette and the eerie scene when a bunch of kids find a blood-drained body underneath the rubble on a building site. But these moments are outweighed by the ridiculous would-be hip milieu, the coffee bar kids drinking coke through straws and talking about the forthcoming 'jazz spectacular at the Albert Hall'. Or the death of Alucard when, hot on the heels of Van Helsing's suggestion that clear running water may kill a vampire, the unfortunate Johnny stumbles into his bathroom, accidentally opens the blinds, flooding the room with daylight, tumbles into the bath and manages to turn on that fatal shower, a scene closer to *Some Mothers Do 'Ave 'Em* than Fisher's *Dracula*. Oddly enough in recent years the film's cult status has grown (see for example the loving tributes in issue 22 of the American magazine *Little Shoppe of Horrors* [2009]) largely down to this faux-groovy setting and terrible dialogue, a very middle-aged version of youthspeak which managed to be both ridiculous and, even in 1972, woefully dated.

Given the obvious shortcomings of Hammer's first contemporary Dracula, it's hard to see what is the bigger surprise – the fact that Hammer let director Alan Gibson and writer Houghton have another crack at a contemporary Dracula the following year or the fact that this time, they succeeded. Lee certainly had his doubts. The star, who had in the past been increasingly reluctant to revisit what had become his most famous role, was openly contemptuous of the project which was developed with the extremely unwieldy, very 70s title 'Dracula is Dead...But Well and Living in London'. Indeed, for anyone tired of actors on the PR circuit enthusiastically plugging a worthless product, Lee's candour in a 1972 interview is startling, refreshing and well worth quoting in full:

> I'm doing the next one under protest. I just think it's fatuous. I can think of twenty adjectives – fatuous, pointless, absurd. It's not a comedy. At least with me it's not a comedy. But it's a comic title. I don't see the point. I don't see what they hope to achieve. I think it's playing down to people. I don't think people like it. I don't think people appreciate it either, because people who go to see a character like this go to see him seriously. They don't laugh at him. That I know. They may laugh at some of the things in the pictures but they'll never laugh at me to my knowledge. (Hallenbeck 2009: 68)

THE SATANIC RITES OF DRACULA (1973)

Sporting an eye-catching title, this was not only a radical departure from the Kings Road kids of *Dracula AD 1972* but it also abandoned graveyards and gothic trappings. Instead, the whole thing has a kind of fast-moving, chilly, hi-tech quality that is equally indebted to the spy film, apocalyptic sci-fi and a lot of TV thrillers (from *The Prisoner* [1967-8] and *Department S* [1969–70] to, notably, *The Avengers* – a series whose imaginative generic playfulness had a considerable influence on British horror).

From the start, it's clear this is a modish spin on the familiar, with the credits played out over a series of touristy London locales shot with a wide-angle lens, the Count's shadow superimposed at the edge of the frame, growing larger throughout the sequence. The first scene is of one of the eponymous rites, some Wheatley-esque shenanigans with a

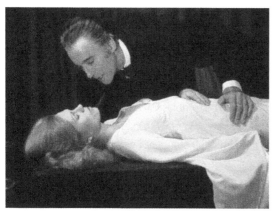

pentacle, robed figures, a naked woman and a nervous chicken.

In a sign of the times, the satanic goings-on both here and elsewhere are more graphic than the slightly-embarrassed, semi-clothed fumblings of *The Devil Rides Out*. There follows a jarring cut to a man wearing a sheepskin waistcoat listening to the ceremony in a bland, anonymous room while he makes a cup of tea. It's equally telling that

The end of the line: *The Satanic Rites of Dracula*

although Gibson's film features a large country house, that beloved staple of British genre film-makers, it is far from a gothic pile, resembling instead an upmarket hotel, albeit a hotel fitted with motion detector beams and a basement full of shackled vampire women. The convoluted story is concerned with a satanic cult made up of the elite – a politician, an industrialist, a soldier and a landowner – who are involved with a reclusive, Howard Hughes-style businessman D.D. Denham, who is actually Dracula.

While the cult believe they are plotting a coup, Dracula is actually trying to bring about the end of the world, which will then lead to his own death through starvation. The whole thing moves at such a pace and there are enough striking set-pieces to paper over some of the illogicalities, as well as a weird blend of styles and generic borrowings (Houghton even manages to draft in some biker minders, who wear a uniform of sunglasses and Afghan waistcoats and who are there presumably to capitalise on both US biker films and concerns over anti-social subcultures). The potent blend of satanic ritual and apocalyptic fantasy casts a gloomy pall over the whole enterprise, a atmosphere of decay and unrest best summed-up by the rambling of germ warfare expert Keeley (a sweaty Freddie Jones): 'Evil rules, you know, it really does... Nothing is too vile, too dreadful, too awful.' The paranoid conceit – a secret society made up of men of influence who use dark forces to wield destructive power – is a familiar one, although watching the film now it's hard not to see some bizarre parallels with the stories about right-wing industrialists and military men who were planning to seize power if Harold Wilson was elected (he was and they didn't).

The main weakness in the film is Lee, who seems bored by the whole thing (as he was by this time). Indeed, the scenes where Van Helsing goes to confront Denham are by some way the worst in the film. It has been stressed a number of times that Denham is a recluse who doesn't allow himself to be photographed (itself a neat explanation for the fact that vampires don't show up on film). But when Cushing turns up at the tycoon's imposing lair, Pelham House, security consists of one guy in a uniform sat behind a desk who doesn't even bother to search this stranger, although he does ask if he is carrying a camera (which he isn't, just a gun loaded with silver bullets). Once in the office, Denham sits behind a desk shining a light into Van Helsing's eyes and speaking in a weird, very unconvincing accent (which is apparently supposed to be Transylvanian but sounds more Dutch/South African). This attempt at disguise, as well as being daft, is also a waste of time – Lee's distinctive baritone can clearly be discerned under the wobbly accent. It's fitting for a film so suffused with a sense of the final – a plot to end the world in what was to be the last Hammer Dracula – that the end is so effective, if extremely contrived.

Pursued by Dracula, Van Helsing flees the burning house and ends up in the overgrown grounds. After he snags his jacket on the thorn of a hawthorn tree, an earlier snatch of dialogue is replayed, which relates the little-known fact that hawthorn, the tree used to make Christ's crown, can kill a vampire. Van Helsing calls out to Dracula, luring him into the bushes, where he becomes entangled, his cloak ripping, his face and hands gashed and his flesh smoking. The Count collapses, lying with arms outstretched and thorns wrapped around his head (a reminder that the symbolism of Hammer was rarely subtle) and Van Helsing runs him through with a fence post. The by-now familiar disintegration scene follows, with the flesh dissolving in wreaths of smoke, at one point leaving a very creepy looking fanged skull, until the skeleton too crumbles to dust. It wasn't released at all in the US until it sneaked out in 1978 under the far more prosiac title *Dracula and his Vampire Bride*.

END TIMES

Hammer's last horror film was another Wheatley adaptation. *To the Devil a Daughter* (1975), directed by Peter Sykes from a script by Chris Wicking and John Peacock is a strange mix of the creepy, the nasty and the silly. Wheatley hated it – the grim, brooding tone is far from the rip-roaring thrills of *The Devil Rides Out* – but there is a lot to enjoy: some good (and very un-Hammer) location footage, a strong supporting cast (Honor Blackman, Denholm Elliott, Anthony Valentine), a very young Nastassja Kinski as a nun and a very nasty Lee as the satanic priest, Father Michael. After so many films where the actor turned up and said his lines as if under duress, it's striking just how chilling and vicious he is here. But Richard Widmark is miscast in the lead and his unhappiness in the part doesn't help (according to the DVD documentary *To the Devil…the Death of Hammer*, Widmark not only dismissed the film as a 'Mickey Mouse production' but also kicked over a wind machine in a fit of rage). There are some grim scenes of childbirth, demonic babies and some fairly explicit debauchery but the whole thing is fatally wounded by the oft-ridiculed finale, Widmark killing Father Michael by throwing a stone at him in a deeply anti-climactic ending cobbled together when the money ran out.

The Hammer story didn't end there, although you could be forgiven for thinking it had. They went on to produce two series for television, *Hammer House of Horror* and the later *Hammer House of Mystery and Suspense*, which have been largely ignored by critics (the latter perhaps with good reason). When they have been written about, they're often unfavourably compared to Hammer's cinematic outings and it's true they lack the lush period settings and the familiar 'country house gothic' atmosphere. But the best episodes not only represent some interesting excursions into domestic gothic but also offer an interesting coda to the Hammer story.

HAMMER HOUSE OF HORROR

As the gothic was dying in the cinema, it experienced a burst of life on the small screen. From the vantage point of today, with the schedules awash with 'cops 'n' docs' dramas and reality shows, the late 70s and early 80s seems like a golden age for horror and fantasy on British TV. A whole generation was turned on to the genre with a series of horror double-bills screened every summer on BBC2, starting in 1975 (*The Cabinet of Dr. Caligari* and *Quatermass II*) and running through to 1981 (*The Body Snatcher* and *Theatre of Blood*). These double-bills served to spawn a British version of the 'Monster Kid', that generation of youngsters in the US who got bit by the horror bug through a combination of old movies on TV and magazines such as Famous Monsters of Filmland.

The family sci-fi show *Dr. Who* produced a number of stories that borrowed heavily from Hammer and fittingly drew the attention of the morality campaigner Mary Whitehouse. *The Seeds of Doom* (1976) was about killer alien plants, *Horror of Fang Rock* (1977) dealt with a shapeshifting alien on a remote lighthouse and *The Talons of Weng Chiang* (1977) offered a bizarre tale set in Victorian Limehouse involving Fu Manchu-style Oriental villainy, a deadly homunculus and a giant rat.

The creator of *Quatermass*, Nigel Kneale, a key figure in the Hammer story, moved from the BBC to the independent channel ATV and came up with a series of six hour-long dramas based on man's relationship to animals. *Beasts* (1976) was interesting and unusual, occasionally brilliant. Much attention has been focused on the story of 'The Dummy', largely because of the jaundiced insights it offers into the last days at Hammer. The parallels are blantant, a horror studio which churns out endless entries in a popular period horror saga, a cameo-ing knight of the theatre (played by Hammer regular Thorley Walters) and a leading man who seems to be channelling Richard Wordsworth in the first Hammer/Kneale collaboration, *The Quatermass Experiment*. While a couple of the *Beasts* stories don't work – the daft 'What Big Eyes' wastes Patrick Magee and despite a nice atmosphere, 'Buddy Boy' fizzles out – there are a couple of stand-out episodes. 'During Barty's Party' is a reworking of *The Birds* (1963) with hordes of (never seen) rats trapping a well-do-do couple in their home while the titular chirpy radio show is playing throughout while 'Baby' features a young couple who find a hideous mummified creature hidden in their old country cottage.

From September to December 1980, ITV transmitted the series, *Hammer House of Horror*. This consisted of 12 hour-long episodes transmitted in a prime-time slot (9:15 on a Saturday evening). The series featured a number of Hammer alumni: directors such as Peter Sasdy, Robert Young, Don Sharp and Alan Gibson, writer Anthony Hinds (reviving his John Elder pseudonym) and actors including John Carson, Denholm Elliot and Jon Finch. One episode even had a lead role for Peter Cushing.

The series is often spooky and of particular interest for the way it revisits the studio's former glories and put a modish spin on them, giving them contemporary settings – suburban streets, factories, shops as well as the familiar country manors. Ironically, their seedy ambience and humdrum backdrops suggest nothing so much as Amicus.

'The Carpathian Eagle' offers the kind of sexploitation the studio resorted to in the early 70s (alebit in a diluted form) while 'Visitor from the Grave', written by Hinds/Elder is yet another reworking of the mini-Hitchcock/woman in peril story. There were outings for a mad scientist (Cushing) in 'Silent Scream', country house cannibals ('The Thirteenth Reunion') and the Dennis Wheatley-style satanic thriller 'Guardian of the Abyss'. This last episode is an elaborate riff on *The Devil Rides Out*, not only in terms of plot but also in the casting of Rosalyn Landor, who appeared in the earlier film aged 7. Significantly, this time round the devil wins. This kind of very un-Fisheresque downer ending was a trademark. So 'Children of the Full Moon' ends with the heroine dying giving birth to a lycanthropic baby conceived through rape while her husband is killed off by the axe-wielding patriarch of the rural werewolf clan. Other episodes – 'Rude Awakening' and 'Mark of Satan' – offer a fragmented nightmare narrative. The former is a 'dream within a dream' story with a typically harassed Denholm Elliott as an estate agent having elaborate fantasies about his mousy secretary and dreaming of killing his wife. The scenes where Eliott imagines himself having sex with the object of his desire in a telephone box in broad daylight owe more to Dennis Potter than it does to Hammer.

'Mark of Satan' may be the best episode, a strikingly gloomy take on mental illness wherein a sadsack hospital porter becomes gradually unhinged. It's very grim – squalid suburban misery in cramped rooms – and slightly queasy – we see a plunger used to unblock a clogged morgue sink – and erupts into some hallucinatory Polanski-style suburban satanism. Except here an unfortunate baby is set up not as the spawn of the devil but as a meal to be roasted and eaten. Two episodes in particular seem to have scarred impressionable viewers of a certain age. 'Two Faces of Evil' is a creepy doppelganger story which plays like a supernatural take on *Invasion of the Bodysnatchers* (1956). The series' regular intro – enigmatic scene followed by a moody credit sequence, all gothic font, looming mansion and full-blooded theme by Roger Webb – is used to disturbing effect here as a nervy Anna Calder-Marshall, on a day out with her family glimpses an eerily still figure by the road dressed in yellow waterproofs. An unspecified time later, the figure suddenly steps out in front of the family's car. They offer the man a lift only to have him attack the husband, clawing at his face with an unpleasantly overgrown fingernail. One measure of just what an alarming effect this opening had is the fact that when one types *Hammer House of Horror* into a well-known internet search engine, one of the options that comes up is 'long fingernail'.

'The House That Bled to Death' is a British suburban take on the Amityville phenomenon. It features another unsettling pre-credit sequence, this one completely wordless and offering up a shabby version of one of Orwell's English murders. White powder is poured into a dainty china tea cup by a middle-aged man in a tank top while his unsuspecting wife is knitting. He reads his newspaper until she dies, reaching out for the tablets he callously moves out of reach. Then he takes down one of the kukri hanging on the wall and starts to sharpen it… The fact that the titular house is not the kind of gothic pile we see in the credit sequence but rather a perfectly pleasant semi in High Wycombe is indicative of the low-key approach. One scene may be the best remembered of the whole series, a splendidly excessive *Grand Guignol* moment as a broken pipe sprays gouts of blood all over the guests at a kid's birthday party. A second series was planned, featuring such evocatively-titled treats as 'Half a Pound of Tuppenny Cyanide' and 'The Lady is for Burning' but it never happened. The US-funded *Hammer House of Mystery and Suspense* proved disappointing, excising almost all of the nastiness and nudity while adding some second-rate American stars and elongating the episodes to feature-length.

After a series of false starts, Hammer returned in 2007 after a long period where the brand changed hands but no-one produced any films. This return appears to be essentially in name-only – how could it not be? – but there are some tantalising and off-the-wall proposals that suggest the possibility of a new genre empire under that name. To date, there has been a lot of handsome merchandise adorned with a glitzy new logo and a series of tie-in projects – proposed TV, radio and theatre pieces as well as a series of novels, some of which are novelisations of previous Hammer films – *Kronos* by Guy Adams and *Twins of Evil* by Shaun Hutson – and some refreshingly left-field original fiction by Helen Dunmore and Jeanette Winterson, amongst others.

The first film project wasn't a film at all but a web-series (twenty four-minute parts) which premiered on MySpace. *Beyond the Rave* was a tale of techno and vampires which, appearing as it did 20 years after 'the 2nd Summer of Love' gives it a certain *Dracula AD 1972* quality, which is nothing if not traditional. The films since have been an eclectic mix. *Let Me In* (2010) was a remake of the acclaimed Swedish film *Låt den rätte komma in /Let the Right One In* (2008), which relocates the action to 1980s New Mexico. *The Resident* (2011) was an underwhelming, anonymous thriller starring Hilary Swank and also shot partially in New Mexico (the new Bray?) while *Wake Wood* (2011) was a moody, unusual tale of the undead shot in Ireland and Sweden.

The new Hammer's biggest film to date is the 2012 adaptation of Susan Hill's *The Woman in Black*, starring Daniel Radcliffe. He isn't bad at all but the presence of Harry Potter prompted the decision to remove certain shots and darken others in order to attain a 12A certificate to cash in on his appeal to children, a decision which sits oddly with the gloomy pall hanging over the film. Hopes were high for The Quiet Ones (2014), a ghost story set in the 1970s, but it underperformed compared to *The Woman in Black*. Oddly enough, Hammer's great rival Amicus was also relaunched in 2005, although there was far less fanfare and, as it turned out, far less success. To date they have produced one film, Stuart Gordon's off-beat *Stuck* (2007).

They could be lazy and formulaic, were certainly too slow to take chances on zealous newcomers and sometimes displayed an extremely cavalier attitude to their own creative endavours. But Hammer's supreme achievement is surely a successfully realised fictional universe carried over from film to film, which managed to completely reinvent – it's tempting to say gave new blood to – the hoary old gothic tropes of terrorised women, cruel aristocrats and haunted castles – a strange netherworld of mittel Europa where everyone speaks English and carries on with a wild sexual intensity against vibrant Eastmancolor backdrops. Hammer exemplifies the notion of the studio as auteur as much if not more than Warner Bros. in the 1930s or even Ealing. British horror still hasn't recovered from the loss.

CHAPTER 3: THE AMERICAN INVASION – CAMP AND CRUELTY

British cinema has often had a problematic 'special relationship' with Hollywood. The temptations of regular, high-profile work, lots of money and sunshine have traditionally proved too tempting for successive generations of British film-making talent. As discussed earlier, the first wave of American horror in the 1930s was made possible to a large degree by the input of British writers, actors and directors. Inversely, there have always been Americans heading the other way – *The Ghoul* director T. Hayes Hunter was an ex-pat. But the horror boom of the 1950s and 60s initiated by Hammer led to an influx of enterprising American companies. This influx was also encouraged by the Eady Levy, which came into effect in 1950 and became statutory in the Cinematograph Act of 1957.

Like the 1927 quota, the Levy imposed a tax on box office receipts in an attempt to boost film production and led to a number of American companies and film-makers relocating. This influx continued until the 1970s, when the money started to run out and the British film industry went into decline. Indeed, it's notable just how many of the landmark, ostensibly British films of the late 1960s and early 70s – *Women in Love* (1969), *Performance* (1971), *Straw Dogs* (1971), *The Devils* (1971), *A Clockwork Orange* – were made by big US studios.

As we have seen, Herman Cohen was one of the first American producers to come and cash-in on the new teen market and their taste for graphic gore with his *Horrors of the Black Museum* while Rosenberg and Subotsky's Amicus films proved to be Hammer's only serious rival. But the contribution of American International Pictures to British horror is considerable and their series of Vincent Price vehicles would bring a very different sensibility and star persona to British horror. This playful semi-seriousness resulted in a series of stylised and gruesome black comedies which differed wildly from anything Hammer had to offer. Indeed, if they resembled anything in British genre history it was the films of an earlier era, the 1930s shockers which added humour to their scares and foregrounded their own theatricality. The often-baffled response to AIP's campy semi-parody of the British horror tradition is perhaps best summed-up by David Pirie's opinion of the first *Dr. Phibes* film as 'the worst horror film made in Britain since 1945' (2007: 165).

AMERICAN INTERNATIONAL PICTURES (AIP)

AIP was started in 1956 by James H. Nicholson and Samuel Z. Arkoff. From the outset, they specialised in the production and distribution of low-budget projects targeted at the newly-emergent teenage audience. This meant lurid titles (such as *The Brain Eaters* [1958] and *How to Stuff a Wild Bikini* [1965]) and a reliance on genres: principally horror and sci-fi but also race-car, 'juvenile delinquent' and beach party films. Always keen to exploit trends, AIP would adjust their product with the times, so as the *zeitgeist* shifted from giant radioactive bugs and drag-racing to LSD and motorcycles, the company came up with the likes of *The Trip* (1967) and *Hell's Angels on Wheels* (1967). AIP's best-known producer-director was the aforementioned Roger Corman.

CORMAN

What with an honorary Oscar in 2009 and the release of the documentary *Corman's World* in 2012, Corman is finally getting his due after decades as cult icon and frequently under-rated director who has perhaps been best-known for his remarkable ability to spot emerging talent. The list of Corman alumni is extremely impressive – actors such as Jack Nicholson and Robert DeNiro, screenwriters like Robert Towne and John Sayles, directors such as Scorsese, Coppola, Jonathan Demme, Monte Hellman and James Cameron – and it's debatable as to whether the American New Wave of the 1960s/70s would have happened without him. Aside from his role as mentor to the Movie Brats, consider how many of the major hits of this period resemble the kind of stylish genre films he was knocking out at AIP. *The Godfather* (1971), *The Exorcist* and *Jaws* are essentially Cormanesque reworkings of established genres (gangster movie, horror/monster movie) made under the kind of auteur-friendly conditions AIP could never afford – big budgets, name actors and longer shooting schedules. From 1955, the year of his debut *Swamp Women*, Corman's output was daunting – he would direct another 3 films in that same year and 9 in 1957. The typical Corman product from this period is fast-paced, cheap and easily exploitable, sensational, often in an action/fantasy genre (Western, sci-fi, horror) and sporting some fantastic titles (*Attack of the Crab Monsters* [1957], *She Gods of Shark Reef* [1958], *Teenage Cave Man* [1958] and the extremely poetic *The Saga of the Viking Women and their Voyage to the Waters of the Great Sea Serpent* [1957]). Corman's early work was, in Ethan Mordern's words:

> a mash of genre and cliche and shock material and your budget is three cents and the shooting schedule is already over – *The Little Shop of Horrors*, Corman himself admitted, was made in two days and a night. This is wildcat stuff. However, necessity breeding invention, wildcat stuff can concoct its peculiar fancies. Do it enough and it becomes a style. (1990: 222)

While often regarded as camp or silly, a lot of these early films display real energy and wit, such as the social problem film *Sorority Girl* (1957), the aforementioned killer plant movie *Little Shop of Horrors* and *A Bucket of Blood* (1959) which blends *Mystery of the Wax Museum* with some sharp satire of the Beats. The inventive quality of Corman's early work is more than evident when compared to the slipshod output of Troma, who seem to put more effort into their titles than their films. As well as (depending on your point of view) giving chances to/exploiting the talents of a series of ambitious Film School grads, Corman recognised the value of good writers, working with the likes of the aforementioned Towne, Charles B. Griffith, Charles Beaumont and Richard Matheson.

In 1959, tired of making black and white cheapies, he approached Arkoff and Nicholson and suggested making a bigger picture in colour for the price of a black and white double feature. They agreed to adapt Edgar Allan Poe's short story 'The Fall of the House of Usher', although Corman is fond of telling how Arkoff balked at this:

> 'There's no monster in this movie' he announced. I didn't want to lose the project so I did a bit of quick thinking. 'The *house*,' I said, 'The *house* is the monster.' I suppose he bought that line because we made the movie. (qtd. in Naha 1982: 28; emphasis in original)

Arkoff disputes this (see Naha 1982) but it isn't hard to imagine AIP having doubts. Although Poe's influence on the horror genre is immeasurable, the company made films for the youth crowd and for generations of American schoolkids, the writer was an old dead guy whose often-impenetrable poetry was taught in High School English classes. The success of the film led to a series of Poe adaptations (as Matheson quipped 'It was like making shoes or something' [in Naha 1982: 26]). Corman, both cinephile and showman, was always on the look out for name actors he could afford; throughout the 60s he worked with most of the legendary figures in the genre including Karloff, Barbara Steele, Peter Lorre and Basil Rathbone. But his most fruitful collaboration started with *Usher* and would help turn a veteran character actor who was nearing 50 into a genre icon.

THE PRICE OF FEAR

Vincent Price was born in St. Louis, Missouri in 1911, studied art history at Yale and attended The Courtauld Institute in London before starting to act. He appeared in a couple of striking films noir *Laura* (1944) and *Leave Her to Heaven* (1945) and in *Dragonwyck* (1946) he first demonstrated the brooding gothic persona that was to make him famous. In the 1950s, he appeared in *House of Wax* (1953) and *The Fly*, displaying a distinctive performance style, an appealing blend of sinister and camp. This style was exactly what Corman was looking for in his atmospheric but hip productions and Price, with one of the most distinctive voices in cinema and a string of stylised turns that hinted he was in on the joke, became to the Poe series what Cushing and Lee were to Hammer.

The Poe films are loose adaptations of the stories, frequently owing little to their source material except a title, sometimes even being based on work by other authors (*The Haunted Palace* [1963] takes the title from a Poe poem but is actually an adaptation of 'The Case of Charles Dexter Ward' by HP Lovecraft. Similarly, *Witchfinder General* was released in the US as *The Conqueror Worm* – another Poe-derived title – and brief snatches of Price reading Poe were added as a prologue and epilogue). They didn't always star Price (Ray Milland played the lead in *The Premature Burial* [1962]) while *The Raven* (1963) is as much comedy as it is horror. But they remain a striking achievement, belying their B-movie status with the lush sets of Daniel Haller, Floyd Crosby's rich colour-saturated photography and witty, literate scripts. Their semi-satirical humour, lurid (though often bloodless) action and hallucinatory, psychedelic touches caught the mood of the times and appealed to the cine-literate youth crowd: Tony Rayns has written of the 'secret kinship' that exists between Corman's gothic horrors and the counter-culture (2006: 179). Corman eschewed the dynamism and gore of Terence Fisher in favour of a stately, atmospheric quality which owes more to Italian contemporaries like Mario Bava – mist-wreathed exteriors and ruined castles.

But by 1964 it seemed as though Corman's interest in the gothic was waning. He reportedly (apocryphally?) shot *The Terror* (1963), a horror film which owes nothing to Poe but has that vibe about it in a weekend and any disillusionment can only have been exacerbated by the box-office failure of *The Intruder* (1961), an unusually downbeat tale of a stranger who travels round the South inciting racial strife. This film, which contains a truly remarkable performance from the young William Shatner, is often cited as the director's 'personal' film – not least by Corman himself, who 'decided... that I would never again make a movie that would be so obviously a personal statement' (in Naha 1982: 50). But the idea that a gothic horror film or an acid movie can't be as personal or as heartfelt as a message movie is a deeply flawed one. The decision to make two more Poe films in England, co-productions between AIP and Anglo-Amalgamated, seems to have revitalised the director. Indeed, *The Masque of the Red Death* (1964) and *The Tomb of Ligeia* (1965) would arguably be the best films of the whole cycle.

THE MASQUE OF THE RED DEATH (1964)

Julianna in the aftermath of a demonic falcon attack

Poe's stories, with their unreliable narrators, fixation on extreme pyschological states and disturbing ambiguity, have been adapted, reworked, bastardised and ripped-off, not only by film-makers but also by musicians, authors and theatre companies. The chaos, madness and all-pervading sense of impending catastrophe which permeate his work are still relevant today, maybe even more than when they were written. As the musician Lou Reed, who adapted Poe for the weird but effective concept album *The Raven*, put it:

> Poe is that most classical of American writers – a writer more peculiarly attuned to our new century's heartbeat than he was even to his own. Obsessions, paranoia, wilful acts of self-destruction surround us. (Dansby 2002)

The stories are full of striking imagery – pits and pendulums, talking ravens and melting men: as Neil Gaiman writes 'Poe's stories will always cry out to be illustrated. They contain central and primary images, blasts of color [sic.] and maddening visual shapes (2004: xii). An additional factor behind these endless adaptations is undoubtedly the brevity of the stories, encouraging interpretation and reinvention. The scope this provides for an enterprising film-maker is immense; one need only look at the versions of 'The Black Cat' (a story less than 10 pages in length) directed by four talented directors – Edgar G. Ulmer's 1935 version, Sergio Martino's loose adaptation, *Your Vice is a Locked Room and Only I Have the Key* (1972), Lucio Fulci's 1981 adaptation and the Dario Argento version which makes up half of the oddball *Two Evil Eyes* (1990) – to see how a Poe story can be reworked, opened out and transformed to taste.

'The Masque of the Red Death', published in 1824, is one of Poe's most evocative stories, the tale of the decadent Prince Prospero who throws a masked ball for visiting nobles while outside, a virulent plague is laying waste to the population. A mysterious guest at the revels is confronted by the Prince and revealed to be the Red Death, after which the inhabitants of the castle all die. The simplicity of this scenario invites numerous different readings – a story about mortality, a class war revenge fantasy, even perhaps autobiography (see Rein 1960). This ambiguity, coupled with Poe's remarkable imagery, is what gives the story such a haunting power which has led to numerous adaptations, from computer games (*Under a Killing Moon* [1994]) and an erotic webcomic (Wendy Pini's *Masque of the Red Death* [2007–10]) to a whole host of songs, mostly by heavy/death metal bands, as well as being referenced in works by Stephen King, Tom Wolfe, Terry Pratchett and Chuck Palahniuk. As Arthur Hobson Quinn puts it a tad effusively:

> With a restraint that is one of the surest marks of genius, Poe gives no hint of the great moral the tale tells to those who can think. For the others, he had no message. (1941: 331)

Corman took a while to find the right screenplay for the first of his British Poe films, turning down drafts by, amongst others, Towne. He settled for a script from R. Wright Campbell and Charles Beaumont. Campbell wrote a handful of other Corman films (including *Teenage Caveman* [1958]) as well as the screenplay for the Lon Chaney biopic *Man of a Thousand Faces* (1957). He also coined the phrase La La Land for Los Angeles. Beaumont was a gifted writer of short stories who wrote some of the best-known episodes of *The Twilight Zone* (1959–64) including 'The Howling Man'. His screenwriting credits included *The Intruder, Night of the Eagle* and an earlier Poe film, *The Premature Burial*. Beaumont died aged 38 from a horrible, undiagnosed illness (possibly a combination of early on-set Alzheimer's and Pick's Disease) which left him unable to work and prematurely aged him. Campbell and Beaumont take the basic outline of the short story, which Poe sets out in simple terms:

> There were buffoons, there were improvisatori, there were ballet-dancers, there were musicians, there was Beauty, there was wine. All these and security were within. Without was the 'Red Death'. (2004: 41)

They shorten the duration of events – in the story the guests are enclosed in the castle for months with the doors welded shut – and they also use the very visual device of Prospero's colour-coded rooms. They end up throwing another Poe story into the mix, 'Hop Frog', the tale of vengeful dwarf who persuades his enemies to attend a masked ball dressed as apes before burning them alive. They also introduce two contrasting female characters, the pulchritudinous, decadent yet needy Juliana, Prospero's lover and the innocent teenage peasant Francesca.

A number of factors helped make *Red Death* the most visually accomplished of the Poe films. The comparatively lower costs allowed a longer shooting schedule at Elstree Studios, five weeks rather than the usual three. The production was also able to borrow and recycle costumes and sets from the recently-wrapped historical epic *Becket* (1964). In place of his regular cinematographer Floyd Crosby, who was adept at disguising budgetary shortcomings, Corman used Nicolas Roeg, on his way to becoming one of British cinema's most innovative directors. Roeg's dazzlingly unreal use of colour is a world away from the inky gothic of, say, *The Pit and the Pendulum* (1962). It also features an unusually heavyweight cast: in addition to Price's star turn as the jaded and cruel aesthete Prospero, there's Patrick Magee as the creepy aristocrat Alfredo, Nigel Green as a rebellious peasant, Hazel Court as Julianna and Jane Asher as Francesca.

The fantastical opening sets the tone for the rest of the film: howling wind, skeletal tree branches, mist. An old woman collecting firewood encounters a figure sitting at the foot of a tree, hooded and robed in red. He holds up a white flower and turns it red with a wave of his hand before handing it to the woman, telling her to take it back to the village and tell the occupants that 'the day of their deliverance is nigh'. The vivid reds of the robe and the flower amidst the muted greys and blacks of this defiantly studio-bound forest anticipate the ending of the film and the inevitable triumph of the Red Death.

The Prince's entourage discovers (via an alarming crash zoom) the old woman dying of the Red Death, blood oozing from her pores. Before having the village razed to the ground, Prospero has Francesca taken to his castle, along with the man she loves and her truculent father. Campbell and Beaumont's script uses the Red Death as a kind of wraparound device, a means to start the film and end it with their real interest lying in a number of sub-plots. Chief among these is the lengthy pseudo-courtship of Francesca by Prospero. He is clearly fascinated with the girl from their first meeting, bewitched by her innocence yet keen to get rid of it. When the lecherous Alfredo breathlessly wonders 'Can such eyes ever have know sin?'; Prospero assures him 'They will.' Francesca's deep-seated devout faith mirrors that of the Prince but while she is god-fearing, the Prince is a Satanist and proto-fascist, explaining how

the world lives in pain and despair but it is at least kept alive by a few dedicated men. If we lost our power, chaos would engulf everything. Sometimes that power must be used to teach harsh lessons.

There are a number of similar discussions about the nature of evil and belief, reflecting Prospero's fascination with pain and torture. Far from a one-dimensional bad guy, he is vain and decadent but also a keen student of human suffering descended from a long line of sadists. When he shows Francesca the yellow room, he relates how his father had a man locked up in there for three years who afterwards couldn't bear to look at the sun or a daffodil. Later, in an oft-quoted speech, the Prince waxes philosophical:

> If you look around this world and believe in the goodness of a god who rules it… Famine, pestilence, disease, war and death, they rule this world. If a god of love and life ever did exist, he is long since dead. Someone, some thing rules in his place.

The excesses of Prospero and his revolting guests are mirrored by the opulent *mise-en-scene*. As the Prince descends a staircase, the frame is crowded with detail – ladies-in-waiting, rows of boar heads mounted on the wall, candelabras full of carefully selected coloured candles. At a banquet Prospero appears hemmed in by the trappings of his life, food and drink and violence, silver bowls overflowing with green and purple grapes, an ornate wine jug and the handles of the daggers which have been stuck in the table. The shooting style is expansive, with the director clearly liberated by the vast sets. Scenes are shot from on high, there are prowling tracking shots and one slow 360° pan.

The dazzling series of connected rooms – each painted and decorated in one colour, white, yellow, purple – are exploited for maximum effect, with Prospero guiding Francesca through them and later Julianna running from one room to another filmed by a stationary camera. The sub-plot concerning Julianna is, in fact, full of such deliriously heightened moments. She burns her breast with an inverted cross and feeling peeved by Prospero's fascination with Francesca, decides to marry herself to Satan in a bizarre stylised ritual sequence. After drinking a hallucinogenic potion, she imagines herself laid out in a diaphanous gown and repeatedly sacrificed by a series of costumed characters, including a leaping African warrior in a feathered headdress and a Kabuki-faced Japanese. The image shimmers and distorts, there are a series of slow dissolves, the lens is fogged and the whole thing is bathed in a sickly green light, reaching a hysterical climax (no pun intended). (This astonishing sequence, with its multiple penetrations of a nubile semi-clothed woman unsurprisingly proved too much for the BBFC, who insisted it be removed.) The following scene, with Julianna bloodily offed by a falcon, can only come as something of an understatement. The hallucinatory visuals and distorted imagery, along with the wild splashes of colour elsewhere, can be seen as anticipating the likes of *The Trip*, written by Jack Nicholson and itself banned in the UK for 35 years. Corman's background in the horror genre can't help but influence the 'bad trip' sequences in the latter film with Peter Fonda being pursued by black-clad horsemen in what could be an outtake from one of the Poe films. *The Trip* represents Corman's move from the psychedelic gothic of *Red Death* to gothic psychedelia.

The story of Hop Frog is woven in as another sub-plot. The eponymous dwarf is employed as Prospero's in-house clown-cum-jester. He is in love with the 'tiny dancer'

Esmeralda, who becomes yet another object of lustful fascination for the incorrigible Alfredo. The fact that she is clearly played by a child dubbed with the voice of a woman, gives Alfredo's fixation an even creepier paedophiliac inflection. After he humiliates her, Hop Frog persuades him to don an orangutan suit for the masque before, as in the story, tying him to a chandelier, hoisting him up into the air, soaking him in brandy and setting fire to him.

Given the striking set-pieces contained in the sub-plots, the comings-and-goings of the assorted nobles leading up to the masque can't help but seem a bit anaemic in comparison. Like a lot of onscreen 60s decadence (the tepid orgiastic goings-on in films as varied as *Corruption, The Curse of the Crimson Altar* and *The Devil Rides Out*), what we see is severely curtailed by censorship. So we see Prospero's guests limit their perversions to acting like farm animals and some noisy mastication. There is an effective sequence where the two men in Francesca's life are forced to play a version of Russian roulette for the amusement of the court with a series of daggers, one of which is covered in a fast-acting poison, each man forced to cut himself in turn. This is played out before the swinish guests, who are alternately aroused and semi-bored by the whole thing.

The climax, with the Red Death appearing as uninvited guest at the masque is well-staged, even if Corman felt it could've been better if he had been willing to pay for an extra day's shooting over Christmas (see Del Valle and Dietrich undated) A much bigger flaw is the appearance of several guests wearing red, despite Prospero's clear warning not to wear the colour, suggesting a degree of carelessness in the costume department. The heavily-stylised 'Dance of Death' as the Red Death passes amongst the revellers, infecting them as he goes, sails close to silliness but the imaginative direction and the hysterical reveal – Prospero unmasking the figure to find the face is his own – is startling.

There are a number of images which seem to be direct lifts from *The Seventh Seal* (1957), Ingmar Bergman's oft-parodied stark medieval fable inspired by the threat of nuclear war. These are not only found in the portrayal of the Red Death but also in the Dance of Death, with Bergman's film ending on a similar note of ghoulish glee. Corman denies any obvious influence, telling Steve Biodrowski that he considered adapting *Red Death* earlier as his second Poe film but turned it down as he felt there were similarities with Bergman's film:

> Finally, I had run out of what I thought were the best Edgar Allan Poe stories, so I said, 'I don't care if they think I'm copying Ingmar Bergman; I'm going back to "Masque of the Red Death," because I think that and "Usher" are really his two greatest stories.' (2007)

Apart from the vague resemblance the Red Death has to Bergman's Death (they both wear robes), there is actually very little in Poe's story to back up Corman's assertions. Also, the director's Red Death (and his blue, yellow and black comrades we see in the last scene) shares more than a look with the Bergman character, with Corman even pinching one of the Swedish director's editing devices (a robed character gliding past the camera used as a cut). The ending of the film can't help but feel a bit diluted. Given that Campbell and Beaumont brought in some sympathetic characters – not just Francesca and her intended but Hop Frog and Esmeralda – they need to be saved. This is in marked contrast to the apocalyptic ending of the story. As usual for the Poe cycle, the last (on-screen) word is given to the author, with a caption that reads: 'And Darkness and Decay and the Red Death held illimitable dominion over all.'

There are a couple of subtle hints that Prospero's seduction of Francesca has worked. Yes, he begs the Red Death to spare her, suggesting that his feelings for her are those of love but she watches Alfredo burn not with horror but with something like studied blankness and is reluctant to leave the Prince at the end (the fact that the man she is betrothed to is dull and his character barely sketched-in may be intentional on the part of Campbell and Beaumont). The fact that *Masque* pushed the stylised, studio-bound Poe series as far as it could go is evidenced by the next, and final Corman adaptation, *The Tomb of Ligeia*.

The film uses locations – notably a ruined Norfolk Abbey – and the cinematographer was Arthur Grant, whose work for Hammer (including *The Plague of the Zombies* and *The Devil Rides Out*) employed a kind of heightened naturalism. His work for *Ligeia* is of a very different order to Roeg's vivid colours and the whole film is unusually restrained. Price's cold, obsessive Verdin Fell, who wears some groovy mirror shades for his photosensitivity, is a marked contrast to his flamboyant Prospero and points the way to his even more contained performance as the titular *Witchfinder General*.

In 1967, AIP opened a London office for their overseas operation, American International International. Louis 'Deke' Hayward was the man in charge, a controversial character who earned a reputation for being perennially meddlesome. He is credited as a writer on the AIP/Tigon co-production *Witchfinder General*, for example despite contributing nothing to the screenplay and scotched Michael Armstrong's choice of David Bowie as the lead in *Haunted House of Horror* – although he did request Armstrong write a part for the 30 year-old Frankie Avalon (!). As a result of this London base, the company's involvement in British horror increased considerably.

In 1969, AIP teamed up with Amicus for the aforementioned *Scream and Scream Again*, a bizarre sci-fi horror film which teamed Price with Lee and a cameoing Cushing. The pairing of director Gordon Hessler and screenwriter Chris Wicking could produce work which was flawed (their strange *Murders in the Rue Morgue* [1971], made worse by studio tampering) or just dull (*Cry of the Banshee*) but *Scream and Scream Again* is something else. It's a startling blend of Swinging London, mad science and totalitarianism which feels remarkably fresh, especially when compared to the late 60s gothics, from the ambitious structure to the breathless pace, emphasised by hand-held camera, rapid zooms and whip-pan edits. The fragmented plot is appropriately Frankensteinian, stitched together to make something which is exciting and often startling, if not entirely coherent.

A jogger collapses in a park and wakes up in a hospital bed missing a leg. A cop (a memorable Alfred Marks) is trying to catch a hippyish sex murderer (an energetic and beautiful Michael Gothard) who picks up a series of glam chicks in nightclubs before whisking them up to Hampstead Heath in his red sports car, slaughtering them and drinking their blood. In an un-named East European totalitarian state, a uniformed official tortures dissidents and when questioned has no qualms about killing his superiors. The stories all lead back to the country house surgery of the urbane Dr. Browning (played by Price – and just in case anyone didn't get that he shares a surname with the director of *Freaks*, Wicking would go one better in the script for *Blood from the Mummy's Tomb* and call the hero Tod Browning!). For all its confusion (perhaps because of it) Hessler's film plays out like a nightmare, a nightmare containing some memorably vivid imagery. As well as the unfortunate jogger who sheds limbs throughout the film, we see the killer sprinting up the side of a cliff like a mountain goat, a ripped-off hand left hanging in handcuffs and a cupboard full of body parts.

Browning's house is a world away from the gothic castle of traditional Frankenstein fare, a cavernous, brightly-lit interior with walls painted lilac while his laboratory may have the requisite acid bath but also a bank of flickering TV monitors. Wicking and Hessler were admirers of Don Siegel, the American director of tough, innovative films in a variety of genres, including sci-fi (*Invasion of the Bodysnatchers*), war films (*Hell is for Heroes* [1962]) and thrillers (*The Killers* [1965]). *Scream and Scream Again* comes on like a mutant blend of British horror and Siegel riffs. Wicking apparently wanted to combine the hard-edged sci-fi of *Bodysnatchers* with the counterculture milieu of *Coogan's Bluff* (see Rigby 2000) but there is also a worldweary cynicism which would not feel out of place in *The Killers* while Gothard's groovy sex killer anticipates the long-haired sociopath Scorpio in Siegel's *Dirty Harry* (1971). The American director's most notable disciple – and certainly the most devoted – in British horror was Michael Reeves, who began his career as dialogue director for his hero (a position which had earlier been held by the young Sam Peckinpah – Siegel was as astute a mentor as he was a film-maker). Reeves' *The Sorcerers* seems to have been a largely unacknowledged influence on Hessler's film, being another gritty, fast-paced 'low-fi sci-fi' tale with a Swinging London backdrop while both films feature hip young murderers who are revealed to be merely puppets of their perverted elders. Wicking went on to Hammer while Hessler's career would fizzle out with a series of negligible or odd films, the oddest of which is probably the TV movie *Kiss Meets the Phantom in the Park* (1978), which to date is the only sci-fi comedy starring a popular rock band set in a theme park.

THE ABOMINABLE DR. PHIBES (1970)

The Poe films had helped turn Price into a genre icon and from *Phibes* onwards, he was going to start acting like one. The role of the disfigured, vengeful organist Anton Phibes is

The Curse of Frogs: *The Abominable Dr Phibes*

to some degree built around the actor's by now familiar persona, not only his theatrical blend of sadism but also his oft-reported interests in art and food (he published a couple of cook books). As well as referencing his extra-generic hobbies, the role of Phibes consciously evokes his tragic Corman protagonists, often in mourning for a lost love along with his 'mad genius' roles such as *The Mad Magician* (1954) and *House of Wax*, as well as a series of scientists (*The Tingler* [1959], *Dr. Goldfoot and the Bikini Machines* [1964]), eccentric millionaires (*The House on Haunted Hill* [1958]) and inventors (*Master of the World* [1960]).

But there are also a number of other generic touchstones thrown into the mix, including Gaston Leroux's much-filmed *Phantom of the Opera*, a back catalogue of ingenious yet refined sadists including Lionel Atwill in *Murder in the Zoo*, the masks and weird inventions of the German *krimis* and the very English notion of the artistic psycho. While the final film was unusually stylised and tonally ambitious, the plot was ingeniously simple (and would prove to be extremely influential). London, 1925 and a series of bizarre murders are committed against medical professionals, with one man killed in his bed by bats, another having his head crushed by a mask and another manually drained of blood. The detectives in charge of the case discover that all of the victims operated on Victoria Phibes, the late wife of a famous musician who is himself believed to have died. But although hideously burned, Phibes is not dead and along with his mysterious and beautiful assistant Vulnavia, plans to wreak revenge on the medical team he blames for his wife's death, using the Ten Biblical Curses visited upon Pharaoe as inspiration.

Given that this is a typically cost-conscious AIP production, it looks ravishing, a fact that even its many detractors seem to agree on. The oft-remarked upon production design by Brian Eatwell is disorientating, mixing and matching the 1920s and early 70s with scant regard for anything as square as versimilitude. Vesalius's flat is a good example of this, with its decorative ethnic masks and enormous pot plants, metal and glass furniture, a shaggy throw and some very 70s beige and brown wallpaper. The Phibes house is an astounding creation, the elevating organ, the large dance-floor, the clockwork orchestra. Here, too, there are some glaringly anachronistic choices; note the haunting scene where the house closes for the night, chairs stacked on tables while Vulnavia sweeps the floor as the Clockwork Wizards play a very Sinatra-esque version of 'One for the Road' (a song not written until 1943).

The odd tone and visual style seems to have been brought over from *The Avengers*, in particular an episode directed by Robert Fuest called 'Game' (which starred Inspector Trout himself, Peter Jeffrey). The film also veers between two extremes, which it sometimes struggles to reconcile, a lot of arch, often silly, humour and extremely sadistic murders. The jokes are at their weakest when they rely on (frequently repeated) puns and word-play: Trout is referred to, in one scene alone, as Pike, Bream and Perch while more laboured humour centres on pronunciation of the name Kitaj. This kind of stuff is presumably what critics have in mind when they talk of 'flip, undergraduate humour' (Rigby 2000: 209) and 'crassly undergraduate approach' (Hardy 1985: 228). There are also some script weaknesses. One initial idea had the aforementioned Dr. Kitaj (Peter Gilmore) attacked by rats on a boat but the location was changed to a plane, as it was feared audiences would just wonder why the victim didn't just jump into the water. But it's equally hard to see why the man killed by artifical hail generated by a clockwork device placed in his car, didn't just get out of the car. Or at least change seats.

But for all the word-play and improbability, Fuest manages to invest the film with so many striking moments: our first glimpse of Phibes, face hidden beneath the hood of a long shiny cape, playing an organ that rises out of the floor, Phibes melting the faces of a series of wax busts after every killing, his applause after he watches Kitaj's plane crash. The cast seem to be enjoying themselves, sometimes a little too much. Joseph Cotten as Vesalius is fine, if a bit out of place (he replaced Peter Cushing, whose wife was gravely ill and who would've been a more fitting adversary for Phibes), Peter Jeffrey and Norman Jones are OK as the comedy cops, at least in comparison to the mugging of John Cater who plays their superior and, among the victims, Terry-Thomas is given more to do before he is killed off (by slow exsanguination), as befits his starrier status.

Virginia North as Vulnavia stands out amongst all the heightened performances, in part because she just has to look impassive while wearing some striking costumes. The scenes where she accompanies Phibes as he kills – playing a melancholy violin, walking a greyhound – are very effective, all the more so because screenwriters James Whiton and William Goldstein resist the temptation to clarify who she is and what exactly is her relationship to Phibes. Like the Amicus films of this period, there are a host of cameos, some so brief as to be distracting: Hugh Griffith is fine as a Rabbi but it's jarring to see John Laurie appear for a couple of minutes with just the one line of dialogue.

But this is Price's show. Phibes disguises his disfigured head with a wig and what amounts to a Vincent Price mask, impassive, chalk-white with red-rimmed eyes. The scene where he attaches his face in front of a mirror, picking ears off a tray, emphasises the performative aspects of the character. He also has a hole in his neck which serves as a mouth, pouring wine and spooning food into it and speaking by means of a device he plugs into the hole which is attached to an amplifier. A review in *The Aurum Encyclopedia of Horror* complains about the actor 'being deprived of his most characteristic instrument, his voice' (ibid.) but this is misleading; it's stilted and crackly but clearly Price, both familiar yet strange. In many ways, the Phibes films, along with the similar Price vehicles that followed (*Theatre of Blood, Madhouse* [1974]) simply embellish the persona the actor developed in the Corman series – semi-serious yet affecting performances in stories which are both atmospheric and grimly funny. Yet, there is an emotional undercurrent to the picture, one which the daft jokes and mugging can't entirely alleviate, Fuest creating a strong sense of both the Doctor's grief and rage.

While Price's sexuality has long been a source of speculation, his camp appeal is undeniable, the extension of his 'artistic aesthete' persona. Harry Benshoff in his book *Monsters in the Closet: Homosexuality and the Horror Film* (1997) sees Phibes, along with the actor's later turn as Lionheart in *Theatre of Blood*, as 'monster queers', complete with female 'beard' (Vulnavia and daughter Edwina respectively), arguing persuasively how:

> For some spectators, Vincent Price's queer avengers provide an empowering fantasy-figure, a cunning trickster who could turn society's holiest texts [The Bible and Shakespeare] into vehicles for spectacular (and stylish) revenge – and get away with it. Like Blaxploitation heroes from *Sweetback* to *Blacula*, Price's queer avengers were violent killers but according to the films' logic they were wholly within their rights to be so, deserving of respect and even admiration. (1997: 217)

MURDER AS ART

'I thought he was one of them performance artists.' (*Se7en*, 1995)

The representation of murder as performance art/artistic expression is a remarkably enduring one. The elaborate killings of the Phibes films look forward to *Se7en* (1995) which also has a string of murders linked by a religious theme and the many imitators that followed, such as the BBC crime series *Messiah* and its sequels (2001-8), the elaborate killing cycles of *Copycat* (1995) and *The Bone Collector* (1999). While the most blatant Phibes imitation can be found in the *Saw* series, the murder-as-art sub-genre also takes in *Mysteries of the Wax Museum* and the remake *House of Wax* (which starred Price), Corman's *A Bucket of Blood, Peeping Tom* and *White of the Eye* (1986). Common themes in these disparate examples include the murder-as-spectacle, the killer as artist and killings which are frequently linked thematically: the ten Biblical plagues (*Dr. Phibes*), Shakespeare plays (*Theatre of Blood*), the Seven Deadly Sins (*Se7en*), infamous murders (*Copycat*) or the fates of the Apostles (*Messiah*). This desire to impose an overarching, explanatory narrative on the phenomenon of serial murder, with clearly-defined motives and methods employed by an almost supernaturally efficient *uber*-villain enables us to slot the serial killer – surely *the* twenty-first-century monster – into the pantheon of cinematic horrors while at the same time, satisfying what Richard Dyer identifies as our desire for seriality (see Dyer 1997).

The notion of the 'artist killer' draws on a long tradition of the 'cultured monster', which includes characters such as the intellectual strangler of *They Drive by Night*, the Beethoven-loving rapist and murderer Alex DeLarge of *A Clockwork Orange*, the 'snuff' auteur Mark Lewis and Dr. Hannibal Lector nee Lecktor, who combines art appreciation and erudition with cannibalism. (Indeed, this tendency is parodied in the Brett Easton Ellis novel *American Psycho*, with its boorish central character performing his murders to the depressingly dreary M.O.R. sounds of Huey Lewis and Phil Collins). However, the figure of the 'artist killer' does not reside solely in fiction.

A number of murderers seem to treat their crimes as a form of self-expression – the aforementioned selection of a name and the grim poetry of their letters along with those who displayed the bodies of their victims (the Ripper, The Boston Strangler [whoever he may have been] and the Hillside Strangler[s]) and the list of killers with artistic pretentions is a long one; Charles Manson the folk singer, John Wayne Gacy the painter (and clown), Ian Brady the author. Cop-turned-author Steve Hodel has compiled a moderately compelling case (in Hodel 2006) that his father was the Black Dahlia Avenger, the killer of Elizabeth Short in LA in 1947 who regarded his crime as a work of art intended to outdo the photographs of his celebrated friend, Man Ray (and it's surely this 'artistic' aspect of the Short murder that has led writers to theorise that Orson Welles or John Huston may have been responsible!). [5]

Although the 'mad artist' is an archetype almost as old as cinema itself, the character has become inextricably linked to the figure of the serial killer who, in fiction if rarely in fact, is shown as possessing intellect, charisma and an almost-philosophical intent. Perhaps, as with the *auteur* theory, where a film-makers authorial concerns are assessed by the study of a body of work, the artist/killer needs a number of victims. There may also be an identification of sorts between male killer and male filmmaker. Interestingly, *Gebroken Speigels* (1984) by Marleen Gorris, one of the few serial killer films directed by a woman, offers us a faceless killer commiting squalid, nasty and prolonged murders stripped of any baroque flourishes and pointedly lacking an authorial signature.

As far as *Phibes* goes, a similar blend of hip camp and horror conventions would appear in Brian De Palma's dazzling *Phantom of the Paradise* (1974). A scene where the disfigured Winslow, wearing a bird mask (not unlike Phibes' fancy dress mask), manages to speak in a crackly synthesised voice with the aid of recording technology seems to be a direct reference to Fuest's film (one of many regurgitated images in De Palma's wildly imaginative and still unfairly-neglected film). However, for all its modish camp and tongue-in-cheek grooviness, *Phibes*, with its mixture of stylised performance, black humour and sadistic cruelty looks back to the work of barnstorming ham Tod Slaughter.

The inevitable sequel, *Dr. Phibes Rises Again* followed a year later and it turned out to be disappointing, with the emphasis on laughter from the outset. It opens with a montage of clips from the first film, accompanied by a clumsily overdone American-accented voiceover:

The fiendish Dr. Phibes was prepared for such an emergency and preparing his face anew, he entered the crypt where he had entombed his beloved wife, neither alive nor completely dead.

Unlike the first film, where we have to wait to hear Phibes' voice, here he doesn't shut up from the outset, delivering reams of exposition. In an attempt to resurrect his wife, Phibes and Vulnavia travel to Egypt to find the River of Life, which can grant immortality. But another group, led by the mysterious American Bieberbeck, is also trying to locate the river, so Phibes has to kill them off. There is so much wrong here it's hard to know where to start. Opening out the film with scenes of an ocean liner and the deserts of Egypt (actually Spain) is a big mistake, sacrificing the weird, timeless artificiality – Phibes and Vulnavia dancing on the deck of an ocean liner out at sea doesn't have anything like the same poignancy as similar scenes in the original film.

Also, with the revenge plot and an overarching theme for the murders both done away with, it just becomes a series of killings, the majority of which are neither as ingenious or as nasty as in the first film. The 'murder-by-falcon' is a rehash of the bats and rats from the first film (even down the quick cutting and bloodied face make-up), the 'sandstorm in a car' echoes the hail murder and the man crushed concertina-style in his bed is just daft (the daftness only emphasised by the lack of blood and the fact he is reading *The Turn of the Screw* moments before). Whereas the final punishment in the original film, with Vesalius forced to operate on his own son in order to retrieve a swallowed key makes a kind of hideous sense (with Phibes blaming the surgeon for his wife's death on the operating table), the climactic scene here, with Biederbeck struggling to free his wife from a descending ceiling of sharp-tongued metal snakes, is like something from a malign version of 'It's a Knockout'.

The only memorable murder is the death by scorpions, with one unfortunate having his arms trapped in the spike-lined claws of a gold scorpion. Phibes pointedly places the key inside a statue (the fact that the statue is a likeness of the HMV dog, Nipper, which is placed next to a gramophone is a nice touch, and when the victim manages to smash open the statue, he releases a lot of scorpions which, over a period of time, sting him to death. Scenes of scorpions crawling over a face, inside a shirt, into trousers intercut with Phibes, dressed up in a black Sheikh outfit, lying back eating fruit while Vulnavia plays the violin over the screams are the most potent images in the film, being as nasty, cruel and smart as anything that came before. But elsewhere the sequel has a rushed, perfunctory feeling to it. Vulnavia is now played by Valli Kemp (Virginia North had retired after marrying into money). Robert Quarry, being groomed as a possible successor to Price after his impressive turn as Count Yorga is lacklustre here – he was startlingly effective as the undead Bulgarian but pretty unconvincing playing anybody else. The fact that Terry-Thomas and Hugh Griffith turn up again in different roles is another indicator that the film aims to be taken much less seriously.

In 1973, Fuest wrote, directed and designed *The Final Programme*, a self-consciously groovy take on a Michael Moorcock novel about a Byronic action man scientist (Jon Finch) and a looming apocalypse. Like *Phibes*, the casting is striking (Jenny Runacre, Sterling Hayden, Hugh Griffith, Patrick Magee) and it looks gorgeous but the script is all over the place and it ends up as an achingly hip mess. Fuest followed this with the off-beat US satanic horror film, *The Devil's Rain* (1975) with its memorable climax of a cult gloopily melting in the titular shower. Sadly, Fuest did nothing of note after, ending his career with the soft porn film *Aphrodite* (1982). He died in 2012.

Price went on to *Theatre of Blood*, another intoxicating blend of camp and gore. The character of Edward Lionheart, a Donald Wolfit-style Shakespearian ham who slaughters his critics in a series of murders inspired by the work of the Bard is perhaps Price's signature role. Certainly, he has a lot of fun impaling, drowning and decapitating in a series of outlandish disguises – bearded Scottish masseur, ultra-camp afroed hairdresser. The critics are a grotesque bunch of vain and foolish monsters and the likes of Michael Hordern, Dennis Price and Harry Andrews are reliably unpleasant, the script leaving little room for subtlety – Andrews, for example plays (ahem) Dickman, whose lechery seals his fate.

The screenwriter Anthony Greville-Bell is an intriguing character, an Australian who served in the SAS in World War II before becoming a sculptor and screenwriter (he wrote the neglected Jack Starret film *The Strange Vengeance of Rosalie* [1972]). Unlike Fuest, whose background was in the pop-arty camp of *The Avengers*, director Douglas Hickox was used to grittier fare. His films include the Joe Orton adaptation *Entertaining Mr. Sloane* (1970) and *Sitting Target* (1972), with a psychotic Oliver Reed breaking out of prison to kill his unfaithful wife, which exemplifies a certain kind of grim British crime thriller. He would go on to the John Wayne-in-London cop romp *Brannigan* (1975). Accordingly *Theatre…* eschews stylised sets for location footage of Chelsea, Kensal Rise and Hammersmith. The dilapidated theatre where Lionheart performs to his disinterested wino henchmen was the Putney Hippodrome, which had closed in 1961 (it also turns up in *Sitting Target*).

Yet for all its arch humour and scenery-chewing, the film is very nasty: Arthur Lowe having his head sawn off as he sleeps accompanied by the sound of gurgling blood or Robert Morley's camp dog-owner being fed his pets in a pie. Sure, the latter is particularly grotesque, with his ridiculous silver quiff and pink suit and Lionheart is disguised as a terribly-accented TV chef but the sight of a funnel being jammed into the victim's mouth as he is force-fed poodle pie, slowly choking to death on the revolting slop is still strong stuff. But even more than *Phibes*, there is a genuinely affecting undertone of melancholy to the proceedings. Lionheart is clearly no ham – his performances are often spellbinding but like the actor playing him, he appears to be a man out of time – note his complaint that the critics award has gone to 'a mumbling boy', i.e. a method actor. As Leon Hunt has pointed out, this is a story of old versus new in the manner of much British horror of

Lionheart serves up a poodle pie: *Theatre of Blood*

this period but 'how can one side with modernity when the 'past' is embodied in such persuasively flamboyant and wittily elegant form?' (Hunt 1998:144). Phibes, Lionheart, Price. The era of the horror star, an element of the genre since its inception was coming to an end. While actors would still become known for genre roles – Robert Englund's Freddy Kruger, Tobin Bell's Jigsaw – they would fail to carry that over in any meaningful way to other roles in other films in the way that earlier performers, from Conrad Veidt to Lee, Cushing and Price managed to do. Price would go on to other gothic roles – including playing a horror star in the underwhelming AIP film *Madhouse*. But it's hard to shake the feeling that as Lionheart, engulfed in flames falls off the roof, something is being lost and it won't be coming back.

CHAPTER 4: SOFT SEX, HARD GORE AND THE 'SAVAGE SEVENTIES'

The shift from the hippy utopia of the 1960s to the grim dystopic 1970s has been well-documented. Indeed, the grim touchstones of the late 60s – the Altamont gig, the Manson Murders, My Lai – have become as familiar as Make Love Not War banners, tie-dyed t-shirts and stoned teens handing flowers to riot police. The popular notion of this swift transition from the loved-up Flower Children to the tooled-up likes of the Baader-Meinhof, the Weathermen and the Angry Brigade is a simplistic one but it's undeniable that police brutality, acid and the Viet-Nam War helped idealism to sour into gloom, disillusionment and, yes, violence.

As Leon Hunt has observed (1996), while the American horror of this period is often seen as being grounded in a specific social context, British genre films are often overlooked in this regard. Hunt quotes the Aurum Encyclopedia of Horror which sees no contradiction in lionising *Night of the Living Dead* and the social grounding of 'the body in pieces fantasy' while dismissing the films of Pete Walker as 'cynically trying to cash in on the phenomenon' (1996:163). But with terrorist bombings and strikes, power cuts, rising crime and the growth of the far right, it's not hard to see 70s Britain as a breeding ground for violent horror fantasies. Piers Haggard, the director of *Blood on Satan's Claw*, a Victorian bad trip into orgiastic Manson-style cults was blunt in Screen International:

> We are mostly all chest-deep in blood. I think our society is probably about to shatter. (in Sweet 2005: 271)[6]

In Britain, a number of the major films of the early 1970s reflected this grim climate, helped to a large degree by the death of the Hollywood Production Code and a (comparatively) liberal incoming regime at the BBFC (John Trevelyan left in 1971, leaving his short-lived predecessor Stephen Murphy to tackle a number of extremely contentious titles). These included *Straw Dogs*, *The Devils*, *Get Carter* (1971), *Clockwork Orange* and *Performance* (while the latter was shot in 1968 it was only released in 1971) with the International Times warning potential viewers that the latter was 'a heavy evil film…Don't see it on acid' (in Umland 2006:146).

While the costume gothic was still popular – in the years 1970 – 1,22 of the 45 British horror films released were period films – the tradition was getting tired with Hammer's output, as noted earlier growing more and more decadent and 'unruly'. Meanwhile Amicus were overproducing and becoming increasingly reliant on their anthologies. There were still some gems being released (*Blood on Satan's Claw*, *The Creeping Flesh* [1972]) but also a lot of dull stuff, such as the silly *The Asphyx* ([1971], the lone directorial outing for Hartford-Davis collaborator Peter Newbrook), the boring *Cry of the Banshee* and the rare Amicus period outing, *And Now The Screaming Starts*.

The period gothic was also a comparatively expensive tradition and this was undoubtedly one of the reasons behind the proliferation of contemporary gothic horrors, a number of which dealt with groovy youth preyed on by the relics of less-enlightened times that dwelt in isolated pockets of rural England. These relics may be monstrous creatures or geriatric throwbacks to simpler, crueller times but they often shared a marked desire to lash out at permissive and wanton youth. This was the theme of a number of important American films from the same period, not all of them horror pictures: *Easy Rider* (1969), *Deliverance* (1971) and *Straw Dogs* dealt with the same kind of collision between old and new that ends in violence and this same idea would inspire *The Texas Chainsaw Massacre* (1974) and *The Hills Have Eyes* (1976). The silliest of these is *Trog*, directed by Freddie Francis and starring a washed-up Joan Crawford alongside an unconvincingly-masked caveman escaped from a cavern in the Peak District.

A similar idea is expressed far more effectively in the stylish and nasty *Death Line* aka *Raw Meat*, which locates its monster not in some bucolic back of beyond but rather in the heart of a London which has definitely stopped swinging. The monstrous subterranean hulk (credited as The Man and played – extremely well – by Hugh Armstrong) is the last in a line of cannibals descended from a group of nineteenth-century workers trapped underground by a cave-in. The Man is a tremendous creation, a shambling, straggly-haired brute who kidnaps late night tube travellers for food and snacks on rats but is also capable of great tenderness and grief (the scene where he mourns his female partner and her unborn baby are genuinely affecting). The decision to limit his vocabulary to three words – 'Mind the Doors' – is a masterstroke and Armstrong does a lot with this one phrase, using it as a howl of pain, wail of grief or imploring plea. *Death Line* was the directorial debut of the American Gary Sherman and it appears that he also wrote the screenplay (although it's credited to a Ceri Jones). He handles both the very graphic gore and the pathos with considerable skill. The seemingly devoted Man and Woman have their above-ground counterparts in the appealing Patricia (Sharon Gurney) and the deeply unappealing Alex (a wooden David Ladd, brother of the producer and son of Alan). After his mate dies, the Man kidnaps Patricia and takes her back to his lair.

His clumsy attempts at seduction (such as trying to feed her a dead rat) leave her understandably revolted but her rejection of him still comes across as painful, a generic trope that goes back to *Bride of Frankenstein* and is perhaps best demonstrated in *King Kong* (1933) while the presence of an old brass bell in shot as he tries to woo her may be a reference to another 'beauty and the beast' story, Victor Hugo's oft-filmed *The Hunchback of Notre Dame*. The extremes of the world below ground are vividly expressed in a lengthy tracking shot around the subterranean chamber, maggoty body parts and feeding rats alongside the carefully laid-out rotting bodies of the Man's relatives. There is also a generous amount of black humour, most of which comes from Donald Pleasence as the tea-swilling copper Calhoun, shabby, sarcastic and cynical. Like a grindhouse Joseph Losey, Sherman takes some pointed swipes at the British class system.

The investigation only gets started after James Manford O.B.E disappears from the tube platform and his involvement attracts the attention of MI5, in the form of a cameo-ing Christopher Lee as the sinister Stratton-Villiers who pops up to warn Calhoun off, even going so far as to refer dismissively to his 'working class virility'. (This device of a monster unknowingly killing off a VIP would reappear in *Wolfen* [1981].)

Sherman's horrors are very British, the director having acknowledged the influence of the Sawney Beane legend which tells of an interbreeding cannibal clan in the sixteenth-century Scottish Highlands. The Beane story is also the clear inspiration for the flesh-eating mutant family in *The Hills Have Eyes* and was at one stage earmarked as a late Hammer project. Michael Weldon has suggested that the film 'would be scarier if set in New York City, where thousands of homeless people live in subway tunnels' (1983: 578) but this is a point acknowledged in the script, when Alex says of the down-and-out Manford, 'in New York we step over these guys'. But we don't in London. At least we didn't in the early 1970s. Whereas the NY subway system had been portrayed as a terrifying place in any number of cops shows and thrillers, London Underground were keen to preserve a reassuring image, frequently rejecting requests to shoot violent or horrific films on the tube (a hurdle the canny Sherman got round by submitting a non-horror script for consideration).

Death Line depicts the would-be genteel, civilised heart of London as a scary, seedy place, where the pervy Manford can approach a woman on a tube station, proffering money and asking 'how much?' only to be kneed in the groin and his money nicked. This idea is presented in the film's memorable opening scene, Manford, the bowler-hatted epitome of Englishness, swimming in and out of focus, surrounded by the neon lights and lurid window displays of Soho sex shops soundtracked by the weirdly upbeat, eminently hummable score by Jeremy Rose and Wil Malone. In one later, seemingly inconsequential scene, Sherman depicts the startling shift taking place at this time, from the idealism of the old decade to the cold, hard brutality of the new. Patricia and Alex are sitting in a café and he is looking at the cinema listings in a newspaper. He asks her if she wants to see *The French Connection* and she declines, because it's 'too violent'. The story on the front page of the paper is a shock horror expose about Michael X, the would-be black revolutionary turned murderer. William Friedkin's 1971 cop thriller features a violent reactionary protagonist, Popeye Doyle, whose misanthropic philosophy ('never trust a nigger...never trust anyone') is as far from hippy idealism as it gets, while Michael X, whose supporters included John Lennon and Yoko Ono, went from involvement in the utopian London Free School to a double murder rap (he was hanged in Port of Spain in 1975).

We are left in no doubt that events above ground are no less savage and cruel than the cannibalistic goings-on below. This transition is one the director knew all too well, having gone from directing the insipid, hippy-lite Coca Cola ads with the New Seekers ('I'd like to give the world a coke') to graphically-depicted gore in a nightmare world beneath

London. The initial reviews were, perhaps predictably, poisonous. For Cecil Watson in the *Daily Mail*, November 1972, we the viewer:

> Spend an inordinate time in the madman's dark, dank and bloody lair peering through the murk at the most revolting sights imaginable and wondering how such a sick and sick-making film came to be made. (qtd. in Perks 2002:146)

Yet Sherman's film is one of the great achievements of British horror. Sadly, the director has yet to match it, although he has made a couple of interesting exploitation pics (*Dead and Buried* [1981], which was classified as a Video Nasty in the UK and *Vice Squad* [1982]) as well as the second sequel to *Poltergeist*.

Tower of Evil shares some similarities with Sherman's film but is much more formulaic and much less resonant. Jim O'Connolly's film is a youth-oriented proto-slasher film based on a story by the prolific George Baxt (*Circus of Horrors, Vampire Circus*). A group of archaeologists travel to the desolate Snape Island after a group of American teens are slaughtered with an ancient Phoenician sword, only to find the killing starts again. The plot is unnecessarily convoluted and poorly written, with a lot of red herrings and showcases the least-convincing bunch of would-be hipsters this side of *Dracula AD 1972*, one of whom is the future sex comedy star Robin Askwith with a dubbed American accent. On their way back from visiting 'a jazz festival in the West Country', they end up on the grimly uninviting island, announcing 'we have sounds, food and some great grass. This place is really far-out', while one would-be lothario is dismayed to end up with 'the only chick in Europe who doesn't want to get laid'. As well as some terrible performances and some more awfully dated dialogue the film has a an unusual amount of nudity and gore – lopped-off hands and rotting corpses covered in crabs, a severed head bouncing down stairs (an image cribbed from *Hush, Hush, Sweet Charlotte* [1965]) and poor old George Colouris – a long way from *Citizen Kane* – stabbed to death by a hysterical naked woman. The film also utilises the double-ending which would become commonplace in later slashers where two killers are unmasked, an insane father, bearded and babbling and his monstrous son, both fairly pathetic figures who just happen to be murderous, a device echoed in *Death Line*. But in contrast to the brilliantly-realised setting of Sherman's film, the charnel-house cannibal lair just feet away from platforms teeming with commuters, *Tower of Evil*'s mist-shrouded setting is very old-fashioned, harking back to the 'mysterious island' films of the 1930s (*The Most Dangerous Game* and *White Zombie*).

HORROR HOSPITAL (1973)

At first glance, this appears to be another generic teens-in-peril gothic, even down to the familiar setting (a country house) and the stars (Askwith and another pissed Dennis Price cameo). But *Horror Hospital*, saddled with the meaningless title *Computer Killers* in the US, is a genuine oddity, not least for the wildly uneven tone and the affectionately irreverent eye it casts on the tradition that spawned it. The film was co-written and directed by

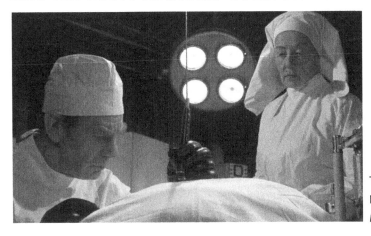

The Abominable
Doctor Storm:
Horror Hospital

Antony Balch, who had form in two seemingly contrasting traditions, avant-garde experimentation and hucksterish exploitation. Balch collaborated on a couple of short films with the feted literary outlaw William Burroughs and had attempted to adapt the author's *Naked Lunch* as a starring vehicle for Mick Jagger. He distributed films by the likes of Kenneth Anger and Russ Meyer and brought *Freaks* to British screens after a 3 decade BBFC ban, as well as running two London cinemas, *The Times* in Baker Street and The Jacey in Piccadilly Circus (it's entirely appropriate that the Jacey's neon sign can be glimpsed in a montage scene from *Corruption*).

Balch was a great showman, buying the rights to a series of arthouse and sexploitation pictures, giving them new titles and promotional campaigns that heavily played up the sex and gore quotient. Balch applied this commercial nous to his first feature, a strange, almost uncategorisable mixture of silliness, satire and menace given the eye-catching title, *Secrets of Sex* aka *Bizarre* (1970). His showman's instincts proved correct and the film ran for 6 months at the Jacey. *Secrets of Sex* was produced by Richard Gordon, a veteran distributor turned producer whose past credits included Karloff's *Grip of the Strangler* and *Fiend without a Face*. His work in British horror would stretch from monochrome period gothics through to the gory excesses of Balch and Norman J. Warren.

Horror Hospital, the second Gordon/Balch collaboration, offers a characteristic blend of the arty and the sleazy – the suggestion in *Time Out* that one should 'search no longer for the missing link between William Burroughs and Confessions of a Taxi Driver' (in Hunt 1998:13) is apt, even though the latter film doesn't actually exist (the author is mixing up *Adventures of a Taxi Driver* with the Askwith-starring *Confessions...* series, which to be fair is easily done). The end result is strikingly unusual, being too daft to work as a straight horror film but way too off-beat and disturbing to work as a spoof.

Jason (Askwith), a burned-out young songwriter answers an ad in an underground magazine offering Hairy Holidays in the country for young hipsters (the wolfish hippy type who encourages him is played by Balch, and co-writer Alan Watson appears as the cross-dressing rock singer who punches our unfortunate hero). After a meeting with a sweaty, lecherous travel agent (Price) Jason heads out to Brittlehurst Manor, a stately home/health farm run by Dr. Storm (Michael Gough in a wheelchair and black furry hat) and policed by a gang of leather-clad bikers. It transpires that Storm is actually a hideously burned mad scientist and is performing experimental brain surgery on his charges, turning them into white-faced zombies and using the women as sex slaves.

The film would be worthy of cult status on the basis of the cast alone. Askwith is an unlikely icon of 70s British cinema, appearing in comedies such as *Carry On Girls* (1973) and *Bless This House* (1972) before becoming well-known as the star of the ribald *Confessions* series (he made 4 films from 1973 – 7). But he also appeared in a couple of Lindsay Anderson films (*If…*[1968]) and *Britannia Hospital* [1982]) and Pasolini's *Canterbury Tales* (1972) as well as playing one of the leads in Pete Walker's *Cool It Carol* (1970). The same qualities of youth and roguish charm that Askwith brought to his comedy roles also made him good victim material in 70s horror – as well as being impaled in *Tower of Evil*, he was killed off in *The Flesh and Blood Show*. Dennis Price's performance as the sinister travel agent is a very weird one, shifty, sweaty and a long way from *Kind Hearts and Coronets*. This was one of the many roles he took in low-budget horror films as his alcoholism got worse and his mainstream career floundered. As Storm, Michael Gough gives his best performance. He had a great face for horror films – handsome but cruel – but could be wildly hammy (*Horrors of the Black Museum* and the giant ape movie *Konga* [1961] being a couple of cases in point) but in Balch's world, heightened to the point of hysteria, even Gough seems fairly naturalistic. The film's tone - shifting from parodic comedy to surreal nastiness and back again – is established in the opening scene. A couple of young people, disorientated and bloodied, their heads swathed in bandages, make their way through a forest. We see Storm, wearing that very fancy fur hat, and his dwarf assistant Frederick in their limo. They start the car and long blades emerge from each side as it bears down on the couple, decapitating them, Boudicca-style, their severed heads captured in matching nets.

The film is full of this kind of arresting image: the dinner scene where the zombified guests sit in silence in front of plates of sludge and wine glasses full of green liquid or the startling moment when the newly-arrived Jason catches sight of a bed saturated in blood ('we all have our little accidents', Frederick says drolly). There is also an extremely creepy flashback sequence where we see two of Storm's victims having joyless, robotic and eerily silent sex in a harshly-lit sandpit. So many of the elements in the film are jarringly odd but by design rather than accident – the extremely eclectic, sometimes completely inappropriate score courtesy of the De Wolfe music library or the strange dialogue. When Jason meets the heroine Judy (Vanessa Shaw) on a train, he tries to approach her only to be fobbed off and responds with 'There's no need to get uptight, I'm not going to rape you'. She replies 'I'm sorry, I'm always a bit timid with people on trains. Would you like a bit of cheese as well?' Storm's over-ripe dialogue could have been lifted from *Black Museum* and in one very funny moment, he tells Jason his back-story. 'In the late

20s, before Stalin came to power, I was a disciple of academician Pavlov' to which Jason responds with a seemingly sincere 'Wow!'. So many familiar generic elements are thrown into the mix, including a country house and a mad scientist, a 'freaky little dwarf' and a disfigured monster but Balch and Watson also exploit the contemporary generational divide which preoccupied so many genre directors of this period while at the same time parodying it. Storm hates the young, a feeling which seems to stem largely from his envy of their opportunities for sexual expression, opportunities which have been ruled out for him after a fire has left him looking hideous *a la House of Wax* and *Dr. Phibes*. Storm actually describes himself at one point as 'a puppetmaster', adding himself to a long line of creepy, manipulative elders which includes Dr. Caligari, Gough's Bancroft from *Black Museum* and *Witchfinder General*'s Matthew Hopkins, an idea which would go on to be reworked a number of times in the films of Pete Walker. The contemporary echoes don't stop there: notice just how many times Jason is beaten up by the baton-wielding, leather-clad bikers with one scene where he is battered in the woods seeming to go on forever. These images of a long-haired youngster being beaten by thugs in uniform could have come from any one of a number of student protests of the period. Balch's film has such wildness and verve, it's a real pity that he never had the chance to make more, dying of stomach cancer in 1980 aged only 42.

1970S 'SHOCKERS'

In contrast to the monsters lurking in caverns, lighthouses and tube tunnels, there were also a number of excessive thrillers made in late 60s/early 70s which aimed to bring murder back into the home, where Hitchcock argued 'it belongs'. Like the shockers of the 1930s, these films included horrific elements and sought to locate the bloody excess of the gothic in the houses, pubs, lay-bys and parks of a recognisably contemporary Britain (or at least London and the home counties). They can be regarded as a kind of British gialli, the stylishly violent Italian murder mysteries which emerged in the 1960s, a tradition which itself owed much to Hitchcock's thrillers.

While these films lack the often glamorous settings, delirious style and strikingly-shot death scenes of their Italian counterparts (the fashion house slasher *Blood and Black Lace* [1964], for example) they do have a seductively seedy ambience which appears to have been lifted from the kitchen-sink social realism of the previous decade and just like the wider British horror tradition, the cycle attracted both hacks and respected auteurs. They also share the giallo's fixation on eroticised violence. Indeed, a recurring factor in these 70s shockers is their obsessive focus on terrorised women and girls.

Assault (1971) about a rapist stalking sexy schoolgirls is blatant in its blend of violence and titillation but the likes of *Revenge* (1971), *And Soon the Darkness, Fright and Blind Terror* (1972) are also concerned with maniacs terrorising attractive women. Peter Hutchings, taking his cue from Hammer's ad campaign for the *Straight on 'Till Morning/*

Fear in the Night double bill, has dubbed this cycle Women in Peril thrillers – adding the aforementioned Brian Clemens' TV series *Thriller* into the mix (see Hutchings 2009). These films offer up the kind of lurid tales which made the pages of the Penny Bloods and are still popular fodder for tabloid newspapers and true crime publications, innocent maidens stalked, ravished and dispatched by beastly, rapacious men.

In particular, the frequent depictions in these shockers of seedy men pursuing nubile teenagers kitted out in mini-skirts and knee socks fits a narrative of predation which has been revived post-Savile and Operation Yewtree, the 1970s being retrospectively cast as not just a time of freedom and liberation but also of sleaze and lechery. The loosening of traditional moral codes and the coming of the pill led to what Paul Jackson, a BBC director in the 70s described as 'a suddenly sexualised society' (Halliday and Brown 2013: 4) and these films reflect that, superficially condemning this new frankness and lack of restraint while hoping to make money off of it.

The most interesting contribution to this cycle is *I Start Counting* (1969), starring Jenny Agutter and directed by David Greene. Greene was a former child actor who graduated to directing a number of flashy very 60s pictures including the atmospheric *The Shuttered Room* (1967) and the spy spoof *Sebastian* (1968). Adapted by Richard Harris (not that one) from the novel by Audrey Erskine Lindop, this story of sexual awakening and murder with a side order of catholic guilt could easily lend itself to a breathless, overheated treatment but Greene imbues the whole thing with a dream-like quality, elliptical and hazy. Wynne (Agutter) is a 15 year old who has a crush on her older stepbrother George (Bryan Marshall), even though – maybe even because – she suspects he may be the murderer of a string of young women. The film doesn't shy away from the titillating potential in this story of a schoolgirl's sexual awakening; indeed, the first shot is of a bedroom littered with open textbooks, cuddly toys, a crucifix hanging on the wall and a school uniform hanging on a chair.

Moments later we see Wynne dressing, putting on her navy blue knickers and fastening her white bra. Agutter would go on to become an iconic sex symbol in the 1970s but in both Greene's film and the later *Walkabout* (1971) she combines her undeniable allure with an appealing awkwardness and confusion. The focus here is less on terrorised nubile teens but more on the the dark fascination of violent crime, repellent and terrifying yet dangerously seductive. And not just for Wynne. As her shaggy haired brother Len muses over a family breakfast, 'You'd think if he was gonna kill 'em he'd at least rape 'em. It seems such a waste'. Greene's film is really about the desire for escape from the stultifying everyday humdrum, whether in the form of forbidden desire (for semi-incestuous sex or murder) or any of the other ways out on offer – the whisky and suicide attempts of George's older lover, the pills Len scores off long-haired space case Jim (Michael Feast)[7] or the TV which is always on in the family flat.

It's tempting to see Sidney Lumet's 1973 film *The Offence* as a variant on this cycle. It starts off as an English version of the police dramas the director kept returning to throughout his career (*Serpico* [1973]), *Prince of the City* [1981], *Q & A* [1990]) but moves slowly into the realm of nightmare. A predatory paedophile is raping schoolgirls and unlike the reliably salacious images of saucy mini-skirted schoolgirls elsewhere on screens at this time, the victims here are children (the one victim we see is supposed to be 12 but she looks younger). When drunken businessman Baxter (Ian Bannen) is brought in on little more than circumstantial evidence, Detective Sergeant Johnson (Sean Connery) becomes convinced that he is the man they're looking for.

The screenplay was written by John Hopkins, based on his 1967 play, *This Story of Yours*. Hopkins worked on *Z Cars* (1962–78) and did some rewriting on *Thunderball* (1965). He also wrote an episode of the *Play for Today* strand, A Story to Frighten the Children about a rape/murder on a housing estate which could serve as a fitting sub-title here. The film was a pet project for Connery. He had seen Hopkins' play and suggested an adaptation to United Artists when they agreed to back two projects of his choosing in return for his participation in *Diamonds are Forever* (1971). *The Offence* flopped and Connery's second project, an adaptation of *Macbeth*, didn't happen as Polanski got there first.

Baxter and Johnson
face off: *The Offence*

Lumet was always good at claustrophobia (consider his *Twelve Angry Men* [1957]) and the majority of *The Offence* takes place in a series of drab interview rooms. The whole thing is a gruelling, alienating experience – muted colours, pale greens, blues, greys, blinding lights, the cracks, pops and drones of the score by the avant-garde composer Harrison Birtwistle. Lumet was also a skilled director of actors and *The Offence* is anchored by powerhouse performances from a rumpled Vivien Merchant, dessicated Trevor Howard and Ian Bannen, in between his babysitter-terrorising lunatic in *Fright* and his pathetic worm-struggling-to-turn in *From Beyond the Grave*.

Connery's performance is startlingly free of vanity. He looks awful, knackered and hollow-eyed, spending most of the film in a deeply unglamorous sheepskin coat and trilby, at one point pestering a shifty suspect with the startlingly prosaic 'Give us a chip, I've been on the go all day'. Even his wife describes him as 'no oil painting'. He peels away the hard man exterior and reveals what Baxter refers to as 'the sad little man' beneath, neurotic, vicious and on the verge of mental collapse, his head full of horrors. We get nightmare flashes of the terrible things he can't unsee, naked dead women strapped to beds, battered pensioners, dangling corpses, a kid's arm hanging limp out of a cot, images he sums up as 'the bodies…stinking, swollen, black, putrid'. The Offence isn't a horror film in any kind of traditional sense but it's certainly a horrible film – both Bannen and Connery are rumpled, loathsome and fucked-up, prone to violent, impotent displays of self-loathing which is barely kept in check by drink – but it's also terribly hard not to empathise with both of them.

Lumet's film would make a great double-bill with I Start Counting, not only having some thematic similarities but also sharing a setting in Bracknell. Connery's character even lives in the same block as Wynne's family, Point Royal, a Grade 2 listed modernist tower-block monstrosity which looms over the town. And what a hideous vision of the town Lumet creates, a grim place of housing estates, forbidding concrete underpasses and predatory kid-fiddlers. In one scene, all the more chilling in how underplayed it is, anxious parents crowd together outside a school to meet their kids at the gate and bundle them into waiting cars. It's a deeply unpleasant trip and it's also one that we can't get off – we never find out if Baxter is guilty. It could be Johnson. It could be anyone.

The settings of the 70s shockers are superficially attractive, suburban streets, new-fangled concrete shopping centres and local beauty spots, ponds, copses of trees but they are transformed into places where bad things happen, places as threatening as the gothic castles of Hammer but without the dashing romance. The sleepy backwaters of Middle England become hunting grounds for rapists and sex-killers, a vision that evokes memories of Stranger Danger campaigns and Public Information films where all manner of rural horrors abound. (Even when fimmakers stray further afield, such as the French setting of And Soon the Darkness, the horrific events take place against a familiar generic backdrop of country lanes and rolling fields). The thrillers of this period also encompassed a handful of generation gap psycho films which, in sharp contrast to the geriatric villains of Reeves and Walker, featured baby-faced, vaguely-hippyish psychos – Twisted Nerve (1968), Straight On Till Morning, Deadly Strangers (1974). Kim Newman (2002) identifies the influence of the 'angry young men' cycle of the late 1950s and early 1960s – Laurence Harvey in Room at the Top (1959) and Albert Finney in Saturday Night and Sunday Morning (1960). The two strands were merged as early as 1963 when Karel Reisz cast Finney as the young head-in-a-hatbox psycho in a remake of Night Must Fall (1963), advertised with the dramatic tagline 'the lusty brawling star of "Tom Jones" goes psycho' but the early 70s saw a host of such characters.

In John Mackenzie's Unman, Wittering and Zigo (1971), there is a whole class of murderers and would-be gang rapists. David Hemmings plays a new teacher at a rural school whose students – clean-cut, eerily polite (they end every sentence with sir, a habit that becomes increasingly sinister) and eager to share with him the fact they killed his predecessor. Form

5b are the creepy cousins of the schoolboy anarchists of *If* and it's entirely appropriate than one of the class, Michael Kitchen would go on to play Satan himself in Dennis Potter's aforementioned suburban nightmare for the BBC, *Brimstone and Treacle*. These films not only reflect the template of deeply un-innocent children seen in *The Bad Seed* (1956) and *Lord of the Flies* (filmed in 1963) but also a very contemporary anxiety about the young, who seemed to be transformed in the public imagining into foul-mouthed, long haired stoners chucking Molotov cocktails at the police, running riot on the streets and university campuses, the Flower Children having been replaced by acid casualties, Jesus Freaks and terrorists. There was the alarming case of Mary Bell, aka The Tyneside Strangler, an 11 year-old from the north of England convicted of the manslaughter of two young boys (one of whom she killed when she was only ten). Mackenzie's strange, oddly-muted film seems today like the mid-way point between *Village of the Damned* and *Die Weisse Band/The White Ribbon* (2009). Given just how many of these clean-cut cinematic killers there were, it really doesn't come as a surprise when, at the end of *I Start Counting*, the murderer is revealed to be Simon Ward's boyish, sweet-munching bus conductor, motivated by his disgust at the 'dirty' modern woman.

The odd, stagey Amicus thriller, *What Became of Jack and Jill?* (1972), a co-production with the US company Palomar Pictures, deals explicitly with this generational clash. Feckless longhair John (Paul Nicholas) and his foxy sociopathic girlfriend Jill (Vanessa Howard) try to frighten his house-bound grandmother (Mona Washbourne) to death by convincing her that a radical youth group are out to generationally cleanse their elders. On first sight, the film appears to be a very British – and very un-Amicus! – take on hip US youthsploitation films like *Wild in the Streets* (1968) and there's some attempt to be topical (at one point John shows his grandmother news footage of campus riots in the US and tells her it's happening in Yorkshire). But it becomes increasingly reactionary – as well as being murderous, these youngsters are materialistic, stupid, even fascistic (with John fantasising about leading a Nazi firing squad gunning down a group of OAPs). The young may inherit the earth, we are told, but they won't know what to do with it and it all ends with Jill dead in the street and a terrified John crawling up the stairs calling for his granny.

As well as Howard, who played another sexy psycho in *Mumsy, Nanny, Sonny and Girly* (1970), another female equivalent of these seductive boy sociopaths was undoubtedly Linda Hayden, who was only 15 when she appeared in *Baby Love* (1968), a horror-tinged kitchen sink reworking of Pasolini's *Teorema* (1968). She combined a jail bait kind of minxy sex appeal with blank-faced sadism. In *Taste the Blood of Dracula*, she is one of the respectable Victorian kids induced by the Count to kill off their hypocritical fathers while in *Blood on Satan's Claw* she is the ironically-named Angel Blake, leader of a murderous sex cult. Indeed, the screenwriter, Robert Wynne-Simmons in a talk given at the Bloodlines Conference in Leicester in 2010 was emphatic that the queasy echoes of both The Family and the Bell case were no coincidence.

There was also a series of graphic films inspired by real crimes. These ranged from the respectable (*10 Rillington Place*, with its clearly-stated argument against capital punishment) to the salacious (*The Fiend*) and Hitchcock's *Frenzy*, which managed to be both respectable and sleazy. Clearly one of the reasons for this kind of true crime story is the relaxation of censorship; for a long time even mentioning real criminals was frowned on, for fear this would lead to glamourisation (as is evidenced by the renaming of Burke and Hare for *The Greed of William Hart*). According to John Trevelyan, the policy of both the BBFC and BBC was 'for a long time' to refuse reconstructions of any murder which happened less than 50 years earlier. In 1960, this period was changed to 30 years, then modified so each case was looked at individually (see Trevelyan 1973).

While noting how he was 'firmly opposed to the making of a film based on the 'Moors Murder' case (1973:161), Trevelyan tells how the director, the American Richard Fleischer persuaded him that his examination of the Christie case would focus mainly on the element of miscarriage of justice – but in practice, the director seems far more interested in the murderer. While it had long been possible for film-makers to skirt round the revolting reality of the Ripper murders by employing the familiar oddly comforting imagery of the Victorian era – a thick peasouper and pub singalongs, a mysterious stranger in a top hat and cape – portraying the crimes of slum landlord and necrophiliac serial sex killer John Reginald Halliday Christie was a more daunting prospect. Bryan Marriner has written that:

> it is Reginald Christie rather than Jack the Ripper whom we should claim as the man who truly ushered in the modern age of the sex killer, the era when the sex killer emerged as a social reality…though no one doubted that he was evil, talk of the devil was never mentioned. Christie's motives were too transparent for that. His crimes were neither frenzied nor manic. Instead the killer employed a cool, twisted logic to satisfy his gruesome predilections…His crimes were as passionless as they were perverted and…the Christie case still has the power to horrify and shock. (1992: 25)

Making a mainstream film about such an unpleasant, squalid character – about as far from De Quincey's 'Miltonic ruined god' as it gets – was a daunting prospect, one taken up by the veteran Fleischer. Fleischer, in addition to a string of exciting genre films (*Narrow Margin* [1952], *The Vikings* [1958]) had directed a couple of true crime films which combined a sober, journalistic approach with some stylish directorial flourishes. *Compulsion* (1959) dealt with the thrill killers Leopold and Loeb (who also inspired the murderous couple in Hitchcock's *Rope* [1948]) and *The Boston Strangler* (1968) featuring a lot of very 60s split-screen and a startling turn from Tony Curtis.

Rillington Place is based on the book by Ludovic Kennedy and tells the story of Christie's decade-long killing spree, including the murder of one of his tenants, Beryl Evans and her baby daughter, a crime for which her husband Timothy was hanged. The Evans story was of particular interest to Kennedy, who was a long-time campaigner against miscarriages of justice but Richard Attenborough's Christie dominates the film. With his bald head, shiny

Attenborough's extremely unsettling turn as Christie: *10 Rillington Place*

glasses and soft voice, Christie is a chilling creation, a loathsome mixture of the would-be superior and the self-pitying loser. The acting throughout is excellent, particularly Judy Geeson as Beryl, justifiably creeped-out by Christie but desperate to procure an illegal abortion and John Hurt as the doomed illiterate fantasist Evans.

The film has an overpowering sense of claustrophobic squalor, helped immeasurably by the hideous settings, some of which were actually in Rillington Place, then renamed Bartle Close (Fleischer had to settle for the then-empty number 7 as a location after the tenants in number 10 were reluctant to temporarily vacate the premises). This blend of naturalism and gothic is evident from the start, the text that tells us This Is A True Story, the sound of air-raid sirens and John Dankworth's unsettling score, the shot of the street sign. In a subtle reference to the way the address would, like 25 Cromwell Street, become notorious, Christie warns Evans against getting into debt, telling him how he doesn't want 'this house getting a name'.

The film captures with a queasy skill the squalid, twilight world of cramped rented rooms in this delapidated house next to an overground stretch of the Metropolitan Line in what was then a forbidding corner of West London, the ugly wallpaper, the outside toilet, the tiny garden where bodies are buried while another is stuffed in a cupboard under the stairs and the door papered over. The kitchen, complete with incongruous deckchair where Christie makes endless cups of tea and convinces Beryl that he knows how to perform 'a termination, as we call it', reassuring her that he's seen hundreds of them performed. Everyday domestic details fill out the time between the horrendous murders – Christie and his wife sitting in their drab and dingy living room, listening to light music on the wireless or the darkly funny bit where Christie, trying to convince a woman to inhale gas, says 'put the mask over your face...have you finished with your cup of tea?'

In a moment that would be echoed in *Henry: Portrait of a Serial Killer*, Christie catches sight of his reflection in a mirror as he prepares to go and kill Beryl, staring at himself for a long moment. Christie, who as a young man earned the nickname 'Reggie No Dick' was a classic 'little man' with pretensions to intellectual superiority and Attenborough captures this perfectly (his whimpers of lust are particularly distressing). There is no hint of the demonic charisma he displayed playing another psychotic, Pinky in *Brighton Rock* (1947) although there is a hint of his put-upon husband from *Séance on a Wet Afternoon* (1964) but far more wheedling and malign here. *10 Rillington Place* is a deeply disturbing film which, for all its noble intentions, is clearly part of a line which stretches back to the Newgate Calendar and productions of Maria Marten, while also serving as a perfect example of early 70s home-grown grim and grot which makes you want to take a shower after watching it. But in a good way...

THE FIEND (1972): GOSPEL SOUNDS AND SEX MURDERS

The Fiend aka *Beware the Brethren* aka *Beware my Brethren* is the last – and best – horror film from Robert Hartford-Davis and offers an excellent showcase for his wayward talents. This odd, extremely effective serial killer story covers similar ground to Fleischer's film but with a wildy different tone. *The Fiend* has been summarily dismissed – The Aurum Enyclopedia illustrates their damning review of it with a still from a later film of the same name – or omitted entirely – neither David Pirie or Andy Boot mention it. *The Fiend* is the story of Kenny Wemys, played by a very intense Tony Beckley (intense even by Beckley's usual standards). He is a swimming pool attendant, security guard and serial killer who is dominated by his sick mother (played by former Gainsborough star Ann Todd, here looking vaguely lost – and who can blame her?) who belongs to an evangelical cult called The Brotherhood and is in thrall to the charismatic Minister (Patrick Magee).

The plot is clearly indebted to *Psycho*, Kenny the twisted yet sympathetic mother's boy who can only respond to the women who turn him on by killing them. But screenwriter Brian Comport (a Pete Walker collaborator and writer of the very odd *Mumsy, Sonny, Nannny and Girly*) actually offers up a thinly-disguised treatment of the 'Jack the Stripper' killings. Six prostitutes were murdered in West London between 1964 and 1965, a number of them found in the Thames. In 1970, the detective in charge of the case had given a TV interview in which he stated that the killer was a security guard who had evaded capture by committing suicide. (Brian McConnell's 1974 book about the Stripper or Nude Murders was called Found Naked and Dead, which would be a fitting subtitle for Hartford-Davis's film or its [slightly] more respectable cousin, *Frenzy*).

Comport's script lifts elements from the case – violent sex murders, a security guard killer, trophies taken from the victims and corpses stripped and left on display, while also throwing in elements of the Moors Murders – Kenny makes tape-recordings of his crimes and plays them back later in his basement room surrounded by the jewellery and underwear of his victims. He goes one step further than Brady and Hindley, however, using multiple tape recorders to blend the screams with sermons from the founder of the Brethren (based in – where else? – California), creating an early example of the remix. This use of real murders as reference points turn *The Fiend* into a story, in Steve

Chibnalls'words 'ripped from the headlines' (2002:163) and both he and Rigby (2000) identify the connection the film has to Pete Walker's later issue-oriented exploitation vehicles.

Indeed, Hartford-Davis here anticipates the attacks on religion in *House of Whipcord* and *House of Mortal Sin* (1975). The Brethren are a grotesque bunch of whey-faced misfits, wearing ill-fitting suits, lank-haired and glassy-eyed. While Kenny is sympathetic, cringing and cowering before his victims, the Minister is an authoritarian with no redeeming features; when Kenny begs him to allow Birdy her insulin injection, we can see who the real monster is. Unlike the moral certainties of early Hammer, *The Fiend* is one of a number of genre films which followed in the wake of *Witchfinder General* that regard religion not as a bulwark against evil but rather a symptom of that evil. The point is made in a fantastic opening sequence which is probably the best thing Hartford-Davis ever shot.

Kenny stalking a lone woman is intercut with a sermon, the highlight of which is Wash Me in his Blood, a gospel song belted out by Maxine Barry (later to achieve a measure of fame as the Grand Final Winner on the TV show Stars in their Eyes, impersonating Shirley Bassey). Taken at face value, the scenes in the church stretch credibility to near-breaking point – it's hard to believe a group such as the Brethren, who shun all forms of entertainment would be getting their groove on to these *Godspell*-style tunes and it's even harder to believe that these sounds are produced entirely by Birdy bashing away on an organ (wildy inappropriate and/or intrusive music is a Hartford-Davis trademark, such as the m-o-r jazz noodlings of *Corruption*). But the scenes of baptism intercut with the woman being strangled and dropped into the Thames as the music reaches a crescendo pack a real charge and effectively convey the point that, as the detective in *Frenzy* says, 'religious and sexual manias are often related'.

Like *The Sorcerers* and later Walker films, *The Fiend* dramatises the culture wars of the late 1960s, with its min-skirted groovy young things (including the chain-smoking, hard-drinking Paddy played by Suzanna Leigh) set against Magee's joyless, sexless congregation and graphically depicting the violence meted out by repressed squares against the young and hip. Although his hair is perhaps too fashionably long for the role, Beckley is excellent as Kenny, wandering around gaunt and sullen in his motheaten brown dressing gown with his soft, flat voice (slightly reminiscent of John Major).

A talented actor in some high-profile films of the period (*The Italian Job*, *Get Carter*) and some offbeat cult items (*The Penthouse*, *The Lost Continent*), Beckley went to the US in the late 70s but made only one film there (playing another sad pyscho in the creepy *When A Stranger Calls* [1980]) before he died of cancer. No matter what worthy targets the film lashes out at, however, it is is still a sensational shocker which exploits as much as it entertains, in much the same manner as *The Yellow Teddybears*. The murders are very graphic and frequently sexualised, leading to the film only being made available in its uncut form as late as 2011 (although the BBC transmitted a complete version in error in the early 2000s). There is an interesting tension at play between our disgust at the actions of the misogynist protagonist and the palpable thrill we are supposed to feel as we see a parade of women terrorised, abused and dead. Naked victims are shown falling out of cement mixers and hanging from meathooks in freezers, while in one startling scene, a woman is choked when Kenny shoves a torch into her mouth (this scene presumably inspired by the frequently-repeated tale [now discounted] that Jack the Stripper choked his victims through fellatio). A contemporary feature in the magazine *Cinema X* quoted the film's press-pack alongside a photo-spread of the naked victims:

> One thing Robert Hartford-Davis can do. He can sure make a corpse look sexy… But – man! – those corpses. They were so good and aroused such interest in the audience…If these three girls can be so sexy dead, just think what effect they would have alive. (anon c. 1972)

The vicious, blatantly sexed-up murders of Hartford-Davis's film are about as far from Orwell's English murder as any could be – motivated by a toxic mixture of sexual repression and religious mania and filmed in unflinchingly lurid detail. Like so much of the horror of this period, which either rejected the trappings of period gothic or couldn't afford them, *The Fiend* juxtaposes the horrific with the humdrum. The settings are really ugly, a West London of gloomy back alleys and dimly-lit riverside paths, industrial estates and building sites, a milieu which is undeniably grim but with a certain sleazy charm, a world away from the mittel Europa of Hammer or the home counties suburbia of Amicus.

There is a notable scene where Kenny picks up one victim at a cinema showing a Hammer double bill (*Scars of Dracula* and *Horror of Frankenstein*). This, Hartford-Davis seems to say, is the real horror. Hammer were often used a yardstick for the genre in this period. As well as the scene noted earlier where Count Yorga watches *The Vampire Lovers* on TV there is also the moment in *Fright* where Susan George's nervous babysitter is made much more nervous after glimpsing the hallucinogenic dream sequence from *Plague of the Zombies* on TV.

The world of *The Fiend* is that of *Up the Junction* (1968) and *Poor Cow* (1968), familiar and yet staggeringly ugly. Indeed, it's often as though we see the film through the eyes of tragic, demented Kenny, a grim place of seedy delights offering fleeting pleasure and eternal damnation.

HITCH AND HORROR

I am particularly keen to put Hitchcock back where he belongs, firmly in the home-grown horror tradition. This most-discussed of all film directors is rightly celebrated as a prodigiously talented maker of highly personal, innovative genre films but this seems to frequently necessitate sidelining his enthusiasm for the sleazy and the lurid.

So many elements of British horror come from Hitchcock, both in terms of theme (dominating mothers, sympathetic killers) and tone (black humour, graphic violence). But Hitch also owed much to the British gothic tradition, from his 'English gentleman as fairground showman' persona through to his very British fascination with murder, kinky sex and sleaze.

Indeed, Hitchcock as much as any film-maker sums up the importance of the aforementioned long-standing English notion of horror, found in sensational newspapers and at the end of the pier as well as in gothic literature. His films are full of killers, murderous spies and assassins, anarchist bombers and saboteurs, charming, amoral rogues and a whole slew of wife-killers. But Hitchcock is particularly, perhaps even obsessively, interested in the sociopath (a term which has replaced psychopath, in part due to the stigma around the latter term, a stigma which largely springs from horror films). Murderers who kill not for profit or revenge but for the thrill of it crop up regularly in Hitch's cinema, from the Ripper in *The Lodger* onwards: the Leopold and Loeb-ian duo of *Rope*, the charismatic, funny and completely crazy Bruno in *Strangers on a Train* (1950), Uncle Charlie, 'The Merry Widow Murderer' in *Shadow of a Doubt* (1943), sweet, sad Norman Bates.

Hitchcock had a particular fascination for the very English kind of sex killer highlighted in the Introduction, the tweed-jacketed vampire killer Haigh, the nerdy necrophiliac Christie, the Ripper. Did Hitchcock see himself in these respectable gentlemen within whom lurked perversion and violence? Certainly, the director seems to have taken little interest in such frenzied American spree killers as Richard Speck and the Manson Family, perhaps because they lacked a mask of respectability and this sense of a double life. Ever the sensationalist, controversial Hitchcock biographer Donald Spoto suggests a connection between the director and a nerdy sex murderer:

> While Hitchcock chose to sublimate in art whatever dark impulses may have lurked in his mind, Christie ultimately lived out his own. (1983: 34)

Hitchcock had a particular interest in Neville Heath, a charismatic womaniser and sadistic sex murderer who killed and mutilated two women in London in 1946 (one of them was found in a hotel in Notting Hill, also Christie's hunting ground). Heath appeared to be a charming well-to-do gentlemen – he used the alias Group Captain Rupert Brooke – although he was in actuality a not-particularly-successful con artist. Hitchcock also doubtless appreciated Heath's dark wit. When he was offered a whisky just before his execution on the 16th October 1946, he accepted, adding 'Considering the circumstances, best make it a double'.

It's often been pointed out how Hitchcock used James Stewart as his alter-ego in the likes of *Rear Window* (1954) and *Vertigo* (1958) – weak, flawed, attempting to dominate – while Cary Grant (in, say, *North by Northwest* [1959]) is his idealised self-projection. In much the same way, we can see Christie or Haigh as a James Stewart-esque sex murderer while Neville Heath, dashing, impeccably-dressed and possessing a dry sense of humour, is a Cary Grant.

FRENZY (1972): 'DISGUSTING GRATIFICATIONS'

The wrongest of Hitchcock´s wrong men: *Frenzy*

Frenzy was Hitchcock's penultimate film and both a comeback and farewell to the city of his birth but it started out in the early 60s as a very different kind of project. Irked by the critical attention garnered by arthouse icons such as Antonioni and Godard (and perhaps envious of the creative freedom they enjoyed), Hitchcock began planning an experimental film, variously titled *Frenzy*, the much more 60s *Kaleidoscope* or *Kaleidoscope Frenzy*, a graphic murder story with a contemporary backdrop featuring a cast of young unknowns.

After all, the last time he tried something different and followed the glossy *North by Northwest* with the monochrome brutality of *Psycho* it had paid off both critically and commercially. But *Kaleidoscope Frenzy* proved a big turn-off to Universal, now owned by MCA who found the whole project distasteful, especially the 'impossibly ugly villain' (Jeffries 1999) and they killed the film.[8]

The next *Frenzy* would be different again, riffing on the director's ouevre rather than radically departing from it but the idea of a modern take on the sex killer remained intact. It was based on Arthur La Bern's novel *Goodbye Piccadilly, Farewell Leicester Square*, written in 1969 and like *The Fiend*, inspired in part by the Jack the Stripper murders. The novel also contains a number of themes and motifs from Hitchcock's films – a psycho killer, the wrong man and a chase narrative. This notion of a director 'cannibalising' himself by adapting a book which feeds off his previous work is a fitting one. *Frenzy* is a film about appetite (for sex, food, murder) but it also works as a reflexive comment on the Hitchcock back catalogue. More than any of his previous films, it reflects his abiding fascination with the English murder. The stereotypical notion of the city as a playground for serial killers is explicitly referenced in the dialogue, with the Ripper namechecked twice while one character laments the fact - over a lunchtime pint - that 'we haven't had a series of good juicy sex murders since Christie'. He goes on to explain how 'in a way' he hopes the Necktie Killer isn't caught:

> It's good for the tourist trade. Foreigners somehow expect the squares of
> London to be fog-wreathed, full of hansom cabs and littered with ripped
> whores, don't you think?

The film is reminiscent of contemporary British shockers and indeed Hitchcock and Shaffer watched *10 Rillington Place* and *Twisted Nerve* as part of their preparation (and the director would use Billie Whitelaw and Barry Foster from the latter film). Hitchcock undoubtedly noticed Foster's strong resemblance to Heath – even getting him to copy the murderer's hairstyle and lending him a book about the case before shooting started.

The lead role was played by Jon Finch, who had graduated from small parts in Hammer films to playing the title role in Polanski's *Macbeth* (1971) and the rest of the cast contains a lot of familiar faces but no stars – a decision doubtless inspired by the failure of *Torn Curtain* (1965), a vaguely soulless spy thriller starring A-listers Paul Newman and Julie Andrews. Anna Massey had been in *Peeping Tom* while Alec McCowen, Barabara Leigh-Hunt and Vivian Merchant were all noted stage performers. The screenwriter was Anthony Shaffer, who was no stranger to weird genre pieces having written the hit play *Sleuth* (filmed twice). He would go on to write the screenplay for *The Wicker Man* (1973).

The plot is very straightforward, stripped-down and fast-paced and sticks closely to the novel. Dick Blaney is an ex-RAF man turned self-loathing failed barman who drinks too much and has a violent temper. After his ex-wife, Brenda (Leigh-Hunt) is murdered by the serial killer known as the Necktie Murderer, Blaney goes on the run with his girlfriend Babs (Massey). When she is found murdered, Blaney turns to his friend Bob Rusk (Foster), for help, not suspecting that Rusk is in fact the killer. Rusk frames Blaney for the crimes and he is convicted. The detective in charge of the case, Chief Inspector Oxford (McCowen) doubts Blaney's guilt and starts to suspect Rusk. Blaney escapes from the prison hospital and goes to Rusk's flat to kill him. When Oxford goes to the flat he finds Blaney there, along with the corpse of Rusk's latest victim. Rusk arrives and is arrested.

Hitchcock's films are full of sympathetic killers and unpleasant protagonists (handsome and appealing Anthony Perkins versus lumpen John Gavin in *Psycho*) and *Frenzy* is perhaps the most extreme example of this. Rusk is a charming Jack-the-Lad who is close to his 'old mum' and always willing to help out his old friend Dick while Blaney is the wrongest of the director's many wrong men, volatile, self-pitying, often drunk and seemingly devoid of charm.

It's easy to see how the police come to suspect Blaney as we can't help but do the same, Hitchcock fingering him as the murderer in a couple of early scenes, cutting from the necktie on a corpse to Blaney tying his own (before his breakfast of stolen gin) while later, he is in shot all the time as two characters discuss how psychopaths can appear normal. A mention of the psychopath's anger at thwarted desires is immediately followed by Blaney taking a barman to task for giving him short measures.

There is a distinctly unwholesome view of sex and the film underlines the fundamental incompatibility between men and women (whether it be divorced Brenda and her marriage bureau or her briefly glimpsed Donald McGill-ian clients, a scary Australian woman and her wimpy beau). Instead, food replaces sex (as it seems to have done for

Hitch) and the film is stuffed with it. The main setting is the Covent Garden fruit and veg market (which the young Hitch would often visit with his grocer father). The seemingly-celibate Oxfords discuss the Necktie Murders over their evening meal – much as Hitch and Alma would thrash out screenplay ideas – as she serves up a series of increasingly revolting 'European' dishes. Rusk hides the body of Babs in a sack of potatoes and potato dust provides the final clue that traps him. When Blaney loses his temper, he stamps on a bag of grapes and later, crushes a wine glass with his hand. There are references to people starving and a significant number of characters are shown eating: one of the first times we meet Oxford he is attacking an enormous English breakfast with relish.

The murders of Brenda and Babs are dealt with very differently but food plays a notable part in both. Brenda is eating her 'frugal' meal and her secretary is on a lunch break when Rusk enters the office. He picks an apple up from her desk, takes a bite in what seems to be a grotesque parody of the Biblical story of Adam and Eve: is Brenda 'tempting' Rusk with her obvious fear? Or by being female, attractive and alone? He asks her to go for lunch with him, talks about fruit, telling her how 'you don't squeeze the goods until they're yours'. This echoes an earlier, slightly weird, comment he makes when he tries to reassure her, that he 'likes flowers, fruit'. After the murder, he leaves the corpse but remembers to take the half-eaten apple. The murder of Babs takes place off-screen (although it is shown briefly in a rapidly-edited flashback) but here again, there is food. A long tracking shot through the market follows Rusk taking Babs to his flat (where we know she'll die) as lots of workers cross their path carrying boxes. Bob tells Babs how she should go and see the world, adding how he'd like to go to 'the Cape, California, Jaffa, where the fruit comes from'. As the camera pulls away in an oft-remarked upon bravura tracking shot as they enter Rusk's flat, it ends up back in the street, back to other box-carrying workers walking past. When Rusk dumps the sack of potatoes containing the body of the unfortunate Babs, he disguises himself as one of these workers wearing a flat-cap, her body in a barrow. Later, relaxing post-kill, he nibbles a pork pie. In a particularly nasty touch, we are told earlier that the potatoes are unwanted and being sent back to Lincolnshire, 'to be ploughed back in'.

And wherever there is food, there is waste. Hitchcock, whose girth testified to his love of eating, told Truffaut of his idea of making 'an anthology on food', showing how it is distributed, bought cooked, consumed and ending with shots of the sewers (see Spoto 1983: 512). This idea is echoed at the start of *Frenzy*. A minister standing on the banks of the Thames is making a speech about river pollution, watched by a group which includes the bowler-hatted director. He talks of brown trout (a fish, yes but also a euphemism for excrement), effluent and the foreign bodies, the 'waste products of our society with which we have for so long poisoned our river', only to be interrupted as the body of naked woman floats into view, a tie wrapped round her neck (an image which echoes a scene in *The Lodger* as well as the opening of *Young and Innocent* [1937]). This equation of women with waste is not only fuel for critics who regarded the director as a misogynist but it also conflates food and murder – when appetites are satisfied, all that is left are shit and corpses.

Frenzy is the most controversial film made by this most-discussed of directors. Although its critical stock has risen in recent years (as evidenced by the title of the recent book by Raymond Foery, *Alfred Hitchcock's Frenzy: The Last Masterpiece*) it is still disliked by many. But it's clearly no aberration. Hitchcock had always pushed the envelope when it came to sex and violence (and sexual violence). In much the same way as the once-vilified Hammer films of the 1950s became rehabilitated and held up as examples of restraint in comparison to the likes of *Witchfinder General,* so the shocking excesses of *Psycho* – and many other censor-baiting elements such as Marnie's wedding night rape – were forgotten as the director became respectable, leading *Frenzy* to be seen as a mistake, an unfortunate blot on a distinguished career.

The liberalised climate meant Hitch could show more than he ever had before, including some voguish tasteful nudity as Babs (or at least Massey's body double) gets out of bed naked and puts on her socks before going to the bathroom. In much the same way as he felt in competition with auteurs like Antonioni in terms of technique, Hitchcock may have felt left behind when it came to depicting violence. In *Straw Dogs* and *Clockwork Orange,* Peckinpah and Kubrick had featured graphic rapes.

However, even when compared to those other films, *Frenzy* is a gruelling, singularly unpleasant experience. In large part this is a question not so much of content – a lot of women are raped and killed in a lot of films, especially in the early 70s – but rather one of technique. Charles Barr wrote an incisive article for *Movie* magazine in 1972 which attempted to pin down why Peckinpah's film was the subject of such vitriol (including an outraged letter to *The Times* in December 1971 from thirteen leading critics) while many of the same voices praised Kubrick's film barely a year later. For Barr the answer lay in a fear of 'contamination; the director is involved: if we respond we become involved too. Violence is a vampire bite' (1972: 26).

Unlike Peckinpah, Kubrick employs a number of distancing devices – fast motion, heightened performances – but compared to Hitchcock's unflinching gaze at the murder of Brenda even *Straw Dogs* appears stylised. The infamous lengthy murder is perhaps the most unpleasant scene in the director's filmography, protracted, unflinching and designed to heighten our sense of powerlessness – Brenda attempts so many thwarted escapes (agreeing to lunch, offering to take Rusk home, lying about her secretary's return, playing dead before kicking him) and later we get a shot of her outstretched arm, her flailing legs, the camera uncomfortably close to their faces. Rusk slurs his words, elongating them, drunk on the anticipation of what is to come. This idea of murder as intoxicant is revisited later when we see Rusk after the murder of Babs, laughing and jaunty, sated and relaxed, his mood reflected by the upbeat score.

The rape scene is unsurprisingly grim – her praying while Rusk, out of shot, mutters 'lovely' over and over again. Except it's hard to tell if the act actually takes place or whether Rusk suffers from a Christie-style inability to perform. Certainly his rage moments later ('women…you're all the same') suggests the latter. The murder scene is the most graphic strangling of the many the director staged – the close-ups of Rusk's hand holding the tie, the knot at her throat, her hands grasping at it. The lack of music heightens the sounds, her pleading, his gasping (Hitchcock had originally planned to shoot the *Psycho* shower scene without sound).

Rusk certainly seems more sated after the murder than he does after the what-might-be-rape, sweaty and breathless. The music comes back in on the grotesque shot of dead Brenda, blouse and eyes open, tongue sticking out. In Spoto (1983), Shaffer claims to have talked Hitch out of including a planned close-up of Brenda's tongue but it's hard to know why he bothered – how could it leave us any more sullied than we already are?

A later scene rivals the murder for sheer prolonged nastiness. Upon returning to his flat after dumping Babs' body, Rusk realises his tie pin is missing and we see a quick montage of the murder – a sharp contrast to the drawn-out staging of Brenda's death. When Rusk climbs into the back of the truck to find the potentially incriminating jewellery, it drives away. The ensuing scene is essentially a prolonged variant on the moment in *Psycho* when Norman dumps Marion's car in the swamp and for a second, it seems it won't sink. We are forced to sympathise with Rusk in his plight, trapped, panicking, tossed around by the movement of the truck. It's a relief when he finally finds the pin – but a temporary one, as rigor mortis has set in and it's clasped tightly in her fist. He uses a penknife to snap open her fingers, but the blade snaps and he resorts to breaking them manually. It's grotesque, a painfully extended bit of ghoulish slapstick and audience manipulation. He manages to escape when the truck stops at a transport cafe straight out of *They Drive By Night* while Babs ends up dumped naked on the road, her white face frozen in terror, surrounded by rotten potatoes.

Frenzy reflects that strange moment in the early 1970s when the liberalising forces of the 1960s had entered the mainstream but were untempered by the concerns around issues such as race and gender which would kick in towards the end of the decade. So the jaw-dropping moment in Hitchcock's film when a barmaid brings up the Necktie Murderer's M.O of 'raping them before he kills them' only to be told by a customer that 'every cloud has a silver lining' should be seen as another product of this joyously unreconstructed time, along with Peter Wyngarde's jaunty song Rape, *the Black and White Minstrel Show* (1958–78) and the sit-com *Love Thy Neighbour* (1972–6).

Hitchcock was conscious of the gothic nature of *Frenzy*, telling director of photography, Gil Taylor 'that he had no desire to make a 'Hammer horror'' (in McGilligan 2003: 703). Certainly, the end result looks far from both the ravishing home counties horror or the cold, gloomy mansion settings of the 'mini-Hitchcocks'.

In addition to the violence, the anachronistic depiction of London is often considered one of the central flaws of the film. Spoto writes how 'the British Press found the film wildly anachronistic, locked emotionally into a long-gone British reality and providing merely a tourist's view of modern London' (Spoto 1983: 518). McGilligan gets closer to what Hitch intended when he writes 'In subtle and unsubtle ways, Hitchcock was determined to make the film deliberately archaic' (McGilligan 2003: 701). Even Shaffer seems to have not got it, suggesting changes during the shoot (in Spoto 1983). La Bern hated the finished film, even going as far as to write to *The Times* to complain about it, calling the film 'distasteful' and 'a painful experience', describing the dialogue as 'a curious amalgam of an old Aldwych farce, *Dixon of Dock Green* and that almost forgotten *No Hiding Place'* (La Bern 1972) before lamenting the loss of his 'authentic London characters'.

But recently this idea of the film as hopelessly out of touch has been challenged. For Jonathan Jones in a perceptive essay for *The Guardian* entitled 'The Body in the River' (1999), Hitchcock's penultimate film is

a gory autopsy of his childhood, his early career and the metropolis that spawned him…London is the city of Hitchcock's imagination, and *Frenzy* is his last visit. (Jones 1999)

John Orr has suggested that Hitchcock's achievement

was similar to what David Lynch would achieve with *Blue Velvet* (1986) in the following decade. Lynch had made a film that was simultaneously past and present, blending two different American time zones, the 1950s and the 1980s. Hitchcock did the same with a film that simultaneously evoked the London to which he returned in 1972 and the London he had left in 1939 within a single film. (Orr 2005: 68)

Blaney is a walking example of this collision between then and now – longish, shaggy hair and sideburns worn with a ratty tweed jacket with leather elbow patches! Ironically, it's Spoto – a critic of the director's approach – who puts it best, saying the film presents 'Hitchcock's attitude, Hitchcock's London, Hitchcock's Covent Garden and Hitchcock's tone' (1983: 518).

In a sense, *Frenzy* can be regarded as a kind of savage self-parody, awash with authorial motifs, chock-full of references, puns and regurgitated ideas and parodying through grotesque excess, father to the equally-misunderstood likes of *Bring Me the Head of Alfredo Garcia* (1974) and Brian De Palma's *Raising Cain* (1992). *Frenzy* is both a classic Hitchcock film and a startling addition to the increasingly grim and grimy ranks of the seedy 70s shockers. And things were about to get a lot seedier…

PETE WALKER: SEX, SADISM AND SOCIAL COMMENT

Walker is a fascinating director who is still underrated, even by perceptive critics. Kim

Newman has described his films as 'highly derivative and distinctively the work of their director at the same time' while also suggesting he 'has yet to make an entirely satisfactory film' (1988: 21). His films are strikingly, fiercely individual with the best of them managing to update the gothic tradition with energy, nihilism and a grisly wit. Born in Brighton in 1939, Walker was the son of the comic Syd Walker and a chorus girl. He worked as a stand-up and actor before becoming a director of sexploitation films with the self-financed *School for Sex* (1969). A couple of off-beat exploitation films followed, the vaguely Hitchcockian thriller, *Die Screaming Marianne*, which boasts star Susan George go-go dancing her way through an impossibly groovy credit sequence and *Cool It Carol* aka *The Dirtiest Girl I Ever Met*, the surprisingly involving tale of a couple of innocents who travel to the metropolis and end up in a twilight world of porn and prostitution, both of which hinted Walker was a director of some talent.

Walker made the move into horror with *The Flesh and Blood Show* (1972), a strange film which is relatively light on gore (despite the excellent, lurid title) but in what is perhaps a sign of his reluctance to leave sexploitation completely, very heavy on nudity. Indeed, there are a fair few user comments on The Internet Movie Database which make this point (numerous variations on 'a lot of flesh and not enough blood') and the director has acknowledged that the sex may have helped dissipate the tension (see Chibnall 1998). The story (by the veteran screenwriter Alfred O'Shaughnessy, who would go on to write episodes of *Upstairs, Downstairs* [1971-5]), is another in the mould of *Tower of Evil* and a handful of Mario Bava films, which anticipates the slasher sub-genre that would emerge following the success of *Halloween* (1978).

A group of vaguely-hippyish kids are rehearsing a play in an out-of-season coastal town (actually Cromer in Norfolk) only to be killed off one by one. The use of 3D at the end of the film stands out (it was a device Walker would also use in his biggest hit, the sex film *The Four Dimensions of Greta* [1972]) and, in a suggestion of what was to come, the killer of all these groovy young kids is revealed to be an elderly actor, whose motives stem in part from puritanism. This theme of the old preying on the young is, as we have seen an enduring one in British horror but the turbulent events of the 1960s gave it a renewed urgency and Walker would rework this theme obsessively.

MISCHIEF

Walker's films have been consistently under-appreciated, not least by the director himself. He takes a perverse pride in telling interviewers how he 'doesn't like any of the films I've made' (in Chibnall 1998), explaining how he revisited the films for their DVD release 'and you know what? They're not as bad as I thought' (Hodgkinson 2005) and in a quote that inspired the title of Steve Chibnall's book-length study of the director's work, 'all I wanted to do was create a bit of mischief' (ibid.). He has always been blunt about his reasons for making genre pictures:

I would prefer to make sentimental love stories. But I used my own money and I have to give the public what it wants. (in Rigby 2000: 258)

But for all his disingenuous comments and self-deprecation, Walker's work offers a striking illustration of the D.H. Lawrence maxim, 'Never trust the teller, trust the tale' (in Jacobson 2008). In 1974 Walker teamed up with a young actor and critic turned screenwriter David McGillivray and the collaboration would be a fruitful one. The three Walker/ McGillivray films – *House of Whipcord, Frightmare* (1974) and *House of Mortal Sin* – are a remarkable achievement, squalid, disturbing and nasty with a strong dose of snarky wit. The level of excess owes much to contemporary US horror yet in their condemnation of hypocrisy and the potent blend of cruelty and satire, the films can be seen as throwbacks to the work of Tod Slaughter. In the BBC film *Magic, Murder and Monsters* (2007), part of the British Film Forever series celebrating a century of home-grown cinema, the Slaughter/Walker connection is explicitly acknowledged, with the director described as 'the man who put the strong meat back into British horror' and star Sheila Keith dubbed 'the Tod Slaughter of the seventies'. Certainly the incredibly low-budgets have something of Slaughter about them. *House of Whipcord* cost 60,000 pounds and as Pirie points out, 'without making any adjustments, it is stil far less than Hammer's lowest budget horrors cost sixteen years earlier' (2007:199). He regards this as proof as of the 'downscaling of UK horror' but it also stands as testament to Walker's thriftiness.

Whipcord is, at first glance, one of the few British examples of the 'women in prison' sub-genre, which offers a perfect setting for the exploitation of both violence and sex eg. Jess Franco's *Barbed Wire Dolls* (1975) and Jonathan Demme's *Caged Heat* (1974). Certainly, the film features many of the familiar WIP staples – a nubile teenage protagonist, a predatory lesbian warder (called Walker and played by Sheila Keith in the first of her many appearances for the director), a shower scene and inmates being stripped and flogged. As if to underline the film's impeccable exploitation credentials, the poster – featuring a screaming woman and a noose – was designed before the script was written. A French model, Anne Marie (the wobbly-accented glamour model Penny Irving) is courted by an enigmatic man who calls himself Mark E. Dessart (McGillivray was never subtle when it came to naming his characters). She accepts Mark's offer of a weekend away but ends up imprisoned in a private prison in the Forest of Dean run by his mother, Mrs. Wakehurst and her partner, the elderly blind judge Bailey (yet another example of the less than subtle approach to character names). The prison was set up to punish 'wayward women' and offers a kind of 'three strikes and you're dead' approach to punishment: solitary confinement, flogging, hanging. *Whipcord* sums up the contradictions in Walker's work, being both surprisingly restrained (most of the flogging is heard not seen) and deeply nihilistic, discreet yet sleazy, cynically exploitative yet structurally ambitious; as Jonathan Rigby puts it, 'the film is structured with the mesmeric circularity of a nightmare' (2000: 255). It also displays Walker's trademark pessimism, with Anne-Marie managing to escape only to be rescued by a lorry driver (called Mr. Kind!) who delivers her back to the prison in the belief that it's a hospital. At the end of the film, Anne-Marie's sister arrives to rescue her only to find she was hanged moments before.

Walker's use of locations, which springs primarily from his not being able to afford to shoot in a studio, is one of the things that gives his work such power. The backdrop to his catalogue of horrors is a recognisable one, sleepy suburbs, creepy corners of rural England and the grim yet stylish London of the period. As Christopher Fowler notes:

> His films captured London at a unique moment in time. They feel oddly real, but also portray the city as a desolate, dangerous and lonely place, where bad things can happen to good people simply because they talk to the wrong strangers. (2013)

Walker once dismissed a later McGillivray script (for what would go on be *House of Mortal Sin*) as 'a Play For Today with murders' (in Chibnall 1998: 152) but this is actually one of the most effective things about these films, the scenes of people drinking wine and chatting in would-be modish apartments or posing at Kensington parties contrasted with the *Grand Guignol* brutality and horror which follows in old houses, private prisons and isolated farmhouses. The importance of one or two central locations – prison, farmhouse, country manor – lends the films a cramped, confined quality which creates a creeping claustrophobia which can't help but makes Hammer's films seem expansive and sweeping in comparison.

While Walker has talked of his nakedly commercial motives ('when we sat down to do *House of Whipcord*, we said "What turns them on? Sadism and flagellation"' [in Chibnall 1998: 119]), there is clearly more going on here than a parade of strippings and whippings. Following the advice of Alfred O'Shaugnessy to 'do it so they don't know what side you're on' (in Chibnall 1998: 132), Walker added a title card dedicating the film to

> those who are offended by today's lax moral codes and who eagerly await the return of corporal and capital punishment.

The BBFC's Stephen Murphy regarded the film as an allegory of the on-going culture wars then taking place in Britain, with the so-called permissive society under attack from the forces of reaction such as the high-profile evangelical Christian group, the Nationwide Festival of Light. Murphy saw Mrs. Wakehurst and Judge Bailey as thinly-disguised versions of the religious reformers Mary Whitehouse and Lord Longford. Walker and McGillivray have frequently suggested that any such satirical intent was unintended (indeed, the screenwriter has recalled that when he was informed that the film was regarded by many as social critique, 'this was news to me' [in Chibnall 1998:124]). It is, however very hard to avoid the point being driven home when one considers Wikipedia's description of the lobby group's stated aim, 'to protest against "sexploitation" in the media and the arts, and to offer the teaching of Christ as the key to recovering moral stability in the nation' (Nationwide Festival of Light: Wikipedia) and then looks at *Whipcord*, where the aged moral crusaders quote the Old Testament and a nude model is stripped then flogged on an altar beneath a banner than reads The World For Christ.

Leon Hunt (1996) offers a persuasive reading of *Whipcord*, casting Judge Bailey, reactionary but ineffectual, unaware that no-one ever leaves the prison in the role of Edward Heath (Prime Minister from 1970-4) while Mrs. Wakehurst, a nastier, sadistic matriarch becomes Mrs. Thatcher. Of course, in some ways Walker makes an unlikely radical: a Rolls Royce-driving, blazer-sporting resident of Esher in Surrey who concedes that Mrs. Whitehouse 'had got a point' (in Chibnall 2008: 132). Indeed, biographer Chibnall is almost euphemistic when he says Walker 'is no Bunuel or Godard' (2002: 158). It may well be that Walker, aided by the cinephile McGillivray, was as keen to exploit critical favour with the same zeal as he exploited sex and violence.

FRIGHTMARE (1974)

An everyday story of country folk: *Frightmare*

Walker, post-*Whipcord* and keen to find new taboos to tackle, reportedly received a late night one-word telephone call from McGillivray: 'cannibalism'. The subject was to become a recurring motif in 1970s horror. In the US, there was *The Hills Have Eyes* and *The Texas Chainsaw Massacre*, the latter, like *Psycho* and the later *Silence of the Lambs* (1991) a twisted homage to the crimes of Ed Gein while in Italy there was a series of extremely graphic (and luridly-titled) cannibal films (*Cannibal Holocaust* [1980], *Cannibal Ferox* aka *Make Them Die Slowly* [1981]). While most of these appeared after Walker's film, the cannibals-on-the-underground romp *Death Line* had been released in 1972. *Frightmare* was inspired by events far more recent than the Gein murders – the Chilean aeroplane which crashed in the Andes, leading the survivors to eat the corpses of their fellow passengers. (The crash and its aftermath would later be the subject of the Mexican exploitation film *Survive* [1976] and the starrier *Alive* [1993], a dreary po-faced Hollywood attempt to render the whole grim story tasteful, if you'll pardon the pun.)

Like *House of Whipcord*, the plot of *Frightmare* is deceptively simple. In a black and white prologue set in 1957, we see a man visiting a nondescript caravan in a deserted funfair. From the first frames, Walker's characteristic miserabilism is in evidence – the bleak setting, the cramped interior, a dripping tap. After a series of shots of grim, shuttered-up fairground attractions and a dissolve-heavy series of tracking shots around the drab interior, we discover the man slumped against the wall with half of his head gone. Watching it today, there is a strange, unintended frisson in recognising the actor as Andrew Sachs, in one of his last roles before *Fawlty Towers* [1975–9] where he played the Spanish chef, Manuel. Younger viewers may know him as the unwitting star of 'Sachsgate', a brief media firestorm that arose when the radio performers Jonathan Ross and Russell Brand left a ribald message on the actor's answerphone. We then cut to an establishing shot of the Old Bailey, where a couple, Edmund and Dorothy Yates, are being committed to a mental hospital for their 'sickening, disturbing' crimes. The slightly hokey credit sequence which follows, shots of red candles and tumbling Tarot cards, gets a real boost from Stanley Myers' eerie, brooding score. Myers worked regularly with Walker and his low-key work is far from the bombastic scores of Hammer's James Bernard.

Jackie (Deborah Fairfax) is an attractive upwardly-mobile twentysomething who works at the BBC. Her 15 year-old half-sister Debbie (the aptly-named Kim Butcher) is a sulky, sexy delinquent who hangs out with a motorcycle gang. As well as trying to act as guardian to the wayward Debbie and starting a relationship with geeky pyschiatrist Graham, Jackie pays regular night-time visits to a forbidding isolated cottage in Haslemere. This is the home of her father and stepmother, the couple we saw sentenced in the prologue and now released. Edmund (a stunningly pathetic Rupert Davies, far from his TV role as French cop *Maigret*) is scared that his wife is in danger of relapsing into cannibalism. Jackie, who has tried to shelter Debbie from the truth about their parents, reluctantly agrees to bring animal brains for Dorothy to eat. But Dorothy (Sheila Keith again) has fallen off the wagon in dramatic fashion, advertising her services as a Tarot reader in *Time Out* and killing the lonely women who call at the cottage before eating their brains. And not only does Debbie know all about her parents, she is also a willing accomplice in her mother's crimes...In many ways, this is pretty generic stuff and the characters are familiar types. We first see Jackie at a dinner party, where she meets Graham, perhaps the most ineffectual of Walker's parade of useless heroes (played by another future sit-com star, Paul Greenwood, the eponymous copper in *Rosie* [1977–81]). In contrast, our first glimpse of Debbie is at a deeply ungroovy disco, where she gets involved in the brutal beating of a barman who won't serve her a drink.

As with good girl Jackie/bad girl Debbie, there is weak dad Edmund/evil mum Dorothy. Keith is always entertaining in Walker's films and although she overplays it a bit on occasion, her portrayal of the cannibal granny is deeply disturbing. The soft Scottish burr to her voice, her extraordinarily expressive face (which goes from confused to menacing in an instant) and her creepily childlike manner (note her look of shame when Edmund discovers a mutilated corpse in the barn) – she's like something out of Grimm. Indeed, there are a number of fairytale echoes in the film – the seemingly-welcoming cottage in the woods, the Tarot cards that imbue Dorothy with a witchy, almost-supernatural quality.

Leon Hunt describes the narrative as being 'like a violent fairy story' (1996:166). Keith is almost as disturbing as the twinkly-eyed wise old woman as she is power-drill-wielding psycho. There is a very weird scene where she reads the Tarot for a woman called Delia. When there is a noise, Dorothy attempts to reassure her with:

> Sometimes the little animals come in and go all over the place. They're awfully naughty. Do you like little animals? Little squirrels and things? There's one peeping at you down there. (Pause) Not really.

Her demeanour changes dramatically as she becomes mocking and sneery before snatching a red-hot poker from the fire and impaling the unfortunate Delia through the belly. After tasting her blood, she clubs her to death. In a very eerie nightmare sequence, Jackie is in a train carriage when Dorothy appears, looking even more terrifying with a chalk-white face and black eyes, carrying a package which oozes blood. It was this image that was used on the film's poster and I vividly remember being very disturbed after seeing it on the Tube as a kid. As is clear from a short synopsis, *Frightmare* deals with the subject of family, a theme which is explored in so many of the American horror films of the 1970s (*The Last House on the Left, The Exorcist, It's Alive* [1974] and most devastatingly, the aforementioned *The Texas Chainsaw Massacre*, made the same year as Walker's film and another black comic study of a flesh-eating family). When Graham is trying to understand Debbie's wild ways, he tells Jackie that her half-sister has 'no background, no roots'. But he's completely wrong – Debbie is very much her mother's daughter, wild, violent and murderous. In the dream, Dorothy tries, unsuccessfully to hand the bloody parcel over to Jackie, who recoils in horror whereas in reality, Debbie is only too happy to accept her birthright. This notion of the hereditary taint, of inherited evil, is a familiar generic device.

The relationship between the violent, dominant Dorothy and the compliant, submissive Edmund is vividly evoked – he is so often seen pleading, sweaty, straggly-haired and sad. It's very revealing when he tries to hide his bruised face from Jackie, the way he is both embarrassed and oddly accepting. The strange co-dependent criminal relationship has a disturbing real-life counterpart: as Leon Hunt has observed:

> the film invites memories of ther Moors murderers (if Jack the Ripper is recuperable for English tourism, Brady and, in particular, Hindley surely aren't; killing women is British, killing children isn't). (1996: 166)

Like Hindley, whose 'monstrousness has never been questioned, whose recuperation is utterly out of the question' (ibid.) Dorothy is a bad mother figure – one who doesn't even shrink from consuming her own offspring.[9]

The film also launches a blistering attack on the arrogance and stupidity of the psychiatric profession. Well-meaning Graham is wrong about everything, along with his fellow psychiatrist Dr. Lytell (another revealing name!). Indeed, it's a mark of the iconoclasm of McGillivray/Walker (as well as their desire to 'not let them know what side they're on') that they quite comfortably switch from lampooning the religious right in *House of Whipcord* to attacking the liberal intelligentsia straight after. Lytell is calm and reassuring as he explains to Graham how Dorothy was suffering from caribanthropy, pathological cannibalism (a term made up by McGillivray). Hearing Lytell report that 'She's as sane as you and I', Graham believes him. Walker has a lot of fun in having Graham explain to Jackie how her stepmother is 'going through a period of readjustment. But if there is something wrong it can easily be remedied by a course of out patient treatment, in her own home if necessary' right after we've seen Dorothy very gorily dispatch Debbie's biker boyfriend with a pitchfork to the face while the fascinated gum-chewing girl watches.

Steve Chibnall links this jaundiced view of the psychiatric profession to the 'anti-psychiatry' movement of the late 1960s and early 70s (see Chibnall 1998) but in truth, it comes over more as a *Daily Mail*-ish rant about trendy liberal thinking. The attacks on institutions in Walker's films – the family, medical profession, the judiciary and in his next film, Catholicism – seem to be as much visceral as intellectual. The rational world and its institutions are frequently under attack in horror and Walker's films are some of the most extreme examples of this 'take-no-prisoners' world view. There is also a very reactionary sub-text to *Frightmare*, the idea that mental illness can't be treated and any attempts to do so are doomed to fail (an idea which is reinforced by the later *Halloween*, where Michael Myers' shrink appears to suggest his patient was born evil). McGillivray's script also contains some nice black jokes (indeed, horror scripts aside, he is best-known for comedy, writing such splendidly-titled sexploitation as *I'm Not Feeling Myself Tonight* [1975] and the sadly unfilmed *Unzipper De Doo Dah* as well as material for the comedian Julian Clary). One character suggests Graham 'needs his head examined' and that's just what happens, when Dorothy opens his skull with her drill – *Frightmare* predates Abel Ferrara's grimy murder-by-power-tool story *Driller Killer* (1981) by the best part of a decade. Jackie and Graham's cinema date is to see *La Grande Bouffe/Blow-Out* (1973), a joyously excessive black comedy about gluttony and death (although the dialogue we hear in the auditorium is clearly from *Whipcord*).

Pirie doesn't value Walker, seeming to not even regard his work as horror but rather a precursor of the alternative comedy of the 80s (see Pirie 2007). There is certainly black humour in *Frightmare*, especially the tagline which promises 'an everyday story of country folk', borrowed from the bucolic radio soap the Archers but the effect is far more distressing than it is amusing. Even among the many downer endings that came along in the wake of *Night of the Living Dead* and *Witchfinder General*, *Frightmare* stands out as terrifyingly bleak and that final sequence is probably the best thing in Walker's filmography. Jackie enters the attic only to see (in a couple of frenzied zooms) Graham, a Tarot card still held in his hand and his head broken open. Debbie and Dorothy, standing over the dead man, stare malignantly at the hysterical Jackie before Debbie picks up a huge cleaver with a bloodied hand, which earns a nod of approval from Dorothy. Both women advance on Jackie as the score erupts into loud percussion and Debbie, ever the feisty teenager, shouts at Jackie to 'Shut up with that stupid screaming!' Edmund appears but any relief is short-lived as he locks the door behind him. As Dorothy and the cleaver-wielding Debbie close in on the hapless Jackie, the camera stays fixed on Edmund as the Judge's summing up can be heard on the soundtrack:

> … and let the members of the public be assured that you will remain in this institution until there can be no doubt whatsoever that you are fit and able to to take your place in society again.

The image freezes before turning red and finally into a negative. Leon Hunt has pointed out that two of the director's films end with a door closing, leaving the characters – and us – with no way out (see Hunt 1998). The reviews for what may be Walker's best film were poisonous (even by the director's usual standards): 'both ridiculous and nasty' (*The Guardian*), 'nasty, foolish and morally repellent' (*The Times*), 'a moral obscenity' (*The Daily Mail*) (in Chibnall 1998: 142). This critical vituperation wasn't a problem for the director, ever-conscious of the market value of controversy (the bad reviews were printed on the poster). But a threatened bombing campaign by the IRA in the West End combined with an ill-advised Christmas release date (!) helped to kill *Frightmare* at the box office.

A STAR IS DEAD

The strangest project Walker was involved with was a projected biopic for The Sex Pistols. The band's manager Malcolm McLaren wanted to make a Pistols movie, presumably because that's what bands did, whether it's The Beatles with Richard Lester, The Stones with Jean-Luc Godard and a whole host of others. McLaren clearly knew his stuff, approaching Russ Meyer and Roger Ebert who had worked together on the remarkable *Beyond the Valley of the Dolls* (1969). After a while Meyer and Ebert quit the project, which was then called *Who Killed Bambi?* and McLaren approached Walker, apparently seeing a kindred spirit with his low-budget aesthetic and a potent blend of nihilism and satire. The two men, 'united by the love of a sweet deal and their mutual talent for exploitation took to each other immediately' (Sweet 2005:281). Despite having very conservative tastes in music (his planned rock musical version of *Svengali* was to have starred Alvin Stardust!) Walker was intrigued enough to hire Michael Armstrong as screenwriter and the two of them – knowing little of punk – went to a Pistols gig in Uxbridge (the director wore a suit and tie). Walker was unimpressed by the audience ('They weren't human beings…They were a crowd of animals' [in Sweet 2005: 281]) and the band split soon after. This may have been a blessing, for truth be told, apart from the stark title, the whole thing seems dreadful and a long way from the apocalyptic art-school stylings of *Jubilee* (1978). Armstrong's story is another of his beloved film-within-a-film tales with the band appearing as the Three Musketeers and some glimpses of home life – Rotten with a dominatrix mum and flatulent sister and incestuous sex between Sid and Ma Vicious. (For more on *A Star is Dead*, see Sweet 2005 and Chibnall 1998.)

The marriage between Walker and The Pistols seems like a pretty strange one. But the anger, ugliness and nihilism of the British horror film in the mid-70s anticipated both the energy and the negativity of punk. It isn't hard to see a link between Walker's vision of Britain with its tired yet brutal older generation - senile judges, sadistic authority figures and cannibal grannies – and the Year Zero No Future proclamations of Johnny Rotten. Like British horror cinema, the punk rock notion of the 'return of the repressed' also included the sex industry and the dark glamour of home-grown crime. So visitors to SEX, the Kings Road store owned by McLaren and Vivienne Westwood could see the porno chic of fishnet tights and see-through blouses alongside Cambridge Rapist masks and Destroy T-shirts emblazoned with a swastika. There was also a short-lived band called The Moors Murderers – which included Chrissie Hynde and Steve Strange in its line-up with their song 'Free Hindley' – and the infamous visit a Rotten-less Pistols took to Rio to make a record with fugitive train robber Ronnie Biggs. Along with the Nazi flirtations (the band London SS, swastika armbands), the punk imagery of sex and crime represents, like, so much of British horror, a kind of case-study in offending middle-class mores.

At first glance, *House of Mortal Sin* aka *The Confessional Murders* could easily be regarded as another slice of Walker/McGillivray mischief-making. It´s the story of Father Meldrum (a sweaty and intense Anthony Sharp), an insane Catholic priest who surreptitiously records confessions and uses an incense burner, poisoned Communion wafer and Rosary beads as murder weapons. Yet again some groovy young things – sisters Jenny (Susan Penhaligon) and Vanessa (Stephanie Beacham) who run a Richmond antique shop – are preyed upon by decrepit and sadistic authoritarians, Meldrum and his creepy housekeeper (the ubiquitous Keith, wearing glasses with a blacked-out lens hiding a hideously bulging eye). The film is comparatively restrained, especially following the ferocious gut-munching of *Frightmare* and this may be why there was none of the expected outrage. For the director this came as a disappointment:

> 'I was really hoping to get into trouble on that one,' sighs Walker. 'I mean, he kills people with a communion wafer, which is meant to be the body of Christ in Catholicism. I made that film because I went to a Catholic school where hellfire and damnation were rammed down my throat. I was waiting for a blasphemy charge from the Vatican. But it never came.' (Hodgkinson 2005)

Meldrum is certainly a terrifying figure, initially cold and reptilian and becoming more gibbering and bug-eyed throughout the film. In places, however, he is oddly sympathetic – the victim of that generic standby, an overbearing mother – and the issue of what one character (played by *Dead of Night*'s Melvyn Johns) calls 'the life sentence' of enforced celibacy is referenced throughout, not least in the character of Father Cutler (Norman Eshley), who plans to give up the Church for the comely Vanessa. The fact that Meldrum's first name is Xavier (i.e. Saviour) is a characteristic McGillivray joke and there is a very effective scene of Vanessa skulking around the presbytery and finding the priest's mute and bed-bound mother who hands her a note which reads, 'Help me my son is mad'. The unhappy ending is par for the bleak, clammy course; Meldrum blames his many murders on the recently-deceased house-keeper and convinces Cutler to return to the Church (what with Vanessa being strangled to death) before leaving to kill the only surviving witness to his crimes, the sound of a choir on the soundtrack as he puts on his cape and black leather gloves. Watching the film today in the knowledge of the cover up of serial abuse by Catholic clergy unearthed in recent years, there is a chill of recognition when Meldrum tells Cutler, 'The Lord will forgive us for preserving the honour of his church.'

Walker's later work is not without interest. Both *Schizo* (1976) and *The Comeback* (1977) are glossier and more conventional than his usual fare. The former was a giallo-inflected Hitchcock rip-off (the title and the credits underline this) with Lynne Frederick being stalked by the man who killed her mother. It was based on an idea by Murray Smith (who had written *Die Screaming Marianne*) and written by McGillivray, although the latter wasn't convinced it would work, believing – rightly as it turned out – that the identity of the killer was too obvious (see Chibnall 1998). A different title would've helped a little in this regard, while the film is overlong and also relies to some extent on the fanciful notion that an adult male can't or won't disarm a knife-wielding six-year-old. There are some stylish murders, including a knitting needle through the head and a hammer attack which leads to the victim falling under a bus but then even the most pedestrian of the director's films perk up when it comes to the violence. *Schizo* was marketed with the staggeringly tasteless tagline 'when the left-hand doesn't know who the right hand is killing'.

The Comeback feels even more like Walker-lite. The casting of the crooner Jack Jones (!) as a libidinous rockstar is weird, although his performance isn't actually that bad, but he is predictably overshadowed by the one-off pairing of Bill Owen and Sheila Keith. There are some atmospheric settings – a glitzy penthouse, a country mansion – and a horrendous sickle murder. In a characteristically grim touch, we keep returning to the decomposing corpse at regular intervals, the face wriggling with maggots and later being gnawed by a rat.

After a return to his roots with *Just Before Midnight* (1978), which blends melodrama and sexploitation, Walker would make only one more film, a curiously creaky old dark house romp. *House of the Long Shadows* should have been better, teaming as it did Walker and screenwriter Michael Armstrong with a dream cast of Cushing, Price, Lee, John Carradine and Sheila Keith in the umpteenth remake of the Earl Derr Biggers novel, *Seven Keys to Baldpate*. But the result is a hoary old muddle, nowhere near atmospheric or nasty enough and fatally wounded by Desi Arnaz Jr. in the lead role. This kind of hokey haunted house stuff was handled much better by the cult porn auteur Radley Metzger in his neglected but stylish flop, *The Cat and the Canary* (1978) produced by the veteran Richard Gordon. But Walker's film is notable as a swan song not only for the director but also for the gothic and it's hard not to be moved when Price looks around at the crepuscular surroundings and laments 'the old order is gone forever and now we too must crumble into dust'. Able to see the way the tide was turning for British film-makers, Walker quit and moved into property and cinema exhibition.

The kind of nasty, sexed-up sensationalism pioneered by Hartford-Davis and Walker would become commonplace in the latter half of the 1970s as the golden age of the British horror film fizzled out. James Kenelm Clark's *Expose* (1976) aka *The House on Straw Hill* is the most notorious example, earning the dubious distinction of being the only British 'Video Nasty'. The dual titles are the perfect illustration of what Kim Newman refers to as 'marginal cinema, where double-bill-fillers can be sold either for sex or violence' (1988: 20). Here, one title underlines the presence of the soft-porn performer Fiona Richmond while the other is clearly intended to evoke *Straw Dogs*, another sexually violent story set in rural England. The origins of the project are significant, Kenelm Clark having directed an episode of the BBC documentary strand *Man Alive* titled *X-Ploitation* in 1975, which included interviews with Walker and McGillivray.

Kenelm Clark was obviously inspired enough to give it a go himself and *Expose* was the result. It's a three-hander, with author Paul (a dubbed Udo Kier), who is married to the horny Linda (Richmond) hiring a mysterious, even hornier secretary Linda (stereotypical psychotic sexpot Linda Hayden). There is a lot wrong with the film, from Kenelm Clark's flat direction to the poor performances of the admittedly-beautiful cast – Kier has been great in films by Paul Morrissey and Lars Von Trier but here he is wooden and fatally wounded by the terrible dubbing job while Hayden's enigmatic nympho is far from her spooky turn in *Blood on Satan's Claw*. Richmond is both fetching and characteristically uninhibited but she really can't act and has the distracting habit of signalling arousal by flicking her tongue in and out like a snake. But the film has a weird, stilted quality which could charitably be called dreamlike and a certain sleazy charm. The one setting – a big house in the country (actually the director's home) – creates a claustrophobic sense of isolation and there is a lot of graphic sex and violence, from Kier's manhandling a (very willing) Richmond while wearing surgical gloves to her bloody murder in the bath-tub (a scene which is still missing from the British release). Kenelm Clark's adventures in exploitation land would continue with a couple of Richmond vehicles, *Hardcore* (1977) and *Let's Get Laid* (1977), a comedy about the adventures of one Gordon Laid…

But *Expose* looks positively polished when compared to the notorious schoolgirls-in-negligees-versus-escaped-mental-patients-on-acid romp, *Killer's Moon* (1978). For Matthew Sweet, Alan Birkinshaw's film is 'almost certainly the most tasteless in British cinema history' (2005: 273) but that makes it sound much more fun than it is. The acting is truly terrible, the pace is sluggish and the promising scenario – three lunatics undergoing LSD therapy commit mayhem in the Lake District while believing that they're only dreaming – goes nowhere. The main appeal of the film is the terrible dialogue, some of it allegedly co-written by the director's sister, novelist Fay Weldon. The moment a schoolgirl comforts a rape victim with

> Look, you were only raped. As long as you don't tell anyone about it you'll be all right. You pretend it never happened. I'll pretend it never happened. I'll pretend I never saw it and if we ever get out of this alive, maybe we'll both live to be wives and mothers

is frequently cited by bemused reviewers and there's also one character's breathless summation of events:

> One of those nights, Pete. Blood on the moon, one mangled dog, one missing axe and one lost girl who's just found a body at the wrong end of the axe. How's that for the great English outdoors?

NORMAN J. WARREN

Warren became a cult favourite on the strength of a handful of films made in the latter half of the decade, a couple of which were written by the redoubtable McGillivray. Warren's work is frequently ambitious and off-beat, if often undone by tight schedules and very low-budgets but the director has an undeniably devoted fan base, in large part due to his frequent appearances at genre festivals. *Satan's Slave* (1976) is a vaguely hallucinogenic, very bleak story of occult suburbia, with Candace Glendenning menaced by Michael Gough while *Prey* (1977) is a defiantly odd low-fi sci-fi film, which reworks D.H.Lawrence's *The Fox* by way of Jose Larraz's *Vampyres* (a film discussed in the next chapter) as the rural idyll of a lesbian couple is disturbed by the arrival of a pig-nosed cannibalistic alien. There are a number of weird scenes (the women dressing the alien in drag, a slo-mo near-drowning in a swamp which seems to go on forever) as well as some very graphic gut-munching. Curiously, Warren's best film, *Terror* [1978] was also his most derivative. While the debt to *Suspiria*-era Dario Argento is obvious - not least in its story of a vengeful witch whose malevolent spirit is killing people in stylish ways – the setting is notable.

McGillivray replaces the gothic fairytale setting of southern Germany with the much less romantic London suburb of Barnes and instead of a dance academy, the backdrop is the seamier end of the flagging British film industry (a netherworld both Warren and McGillivray were all too familiar with). *Terror* is as incoherent as Argento's film but it has an appropriately downmarket vibe as well as a decapitation, some throat slashing and impalement courtey of a flying sword. *Inseminoid* (1980) saw Warren team up with veteran producer Richard Gordon for a sleazy *Alien* rip-off shot in Chiselhurst Caves in Kent. Since then, Warren has floundered a bit, making a couple of small-scale little-seen films and working on a very long-gestating remake of *Fiend without a Face* – which seems increasingly unlikely to happen.

Ian Conrich has observed how:

> The more aggressive and excessive forms of British exploitation, especially those films that emerged in the early 70s, have been deemed lacking in value and consequently banished from the critical agenda. (2009: 104)

As opposed to Hammer 'whose horror films have gradually been reclassified as worthy and acceptable' there are a number of 'sensational films' (which for Conrich includes films by Balch, Kenelm Clark and Jose Larraz) '[which] still await serious examinations'(ibid.). Or in other words, don't hold your breath waiting for Royal Mail to bring out a set of Robert Hartford-Davis stamps...

CHAPTER 5: 'BLOODY FOREIGNERS' – NEW PERSPECTIVES

In much the same way as the wider British cinema has been enriched considerably by a steady influx of foreign film-makers (Cavalcanti, Endfield, Kubrick), the horror tradition encompasses a number of expat directors with very different sensibilities. Given the common language, it should come as little surprise that many of these film-makers have been American, including directors such as Joseph Losey and Gary Sherman, producers Richard Gordon and Herman Cohen and various AIP personnel, the best-known being Roger Corman. The American auteur Andy Milligan is regarded by many as a bottom of the barrel hack, memorably written off by Michael J. Weldon with the withering and oft-cited' If you're an Andy Milligan fan there's no hope for you' (1983: 273). But Milligan's oeuvre is uniquely, ferociously individual – the stylised period settings (with costumes made by the director), the lurching hand-held camera, the over-emphatic library music, the enthusiastic bloodletting, the casual cruelties his (frequently hateful) characters visit on each other and the lengthy, over-ripe speeches that accompany them.

As the director and Milligan devotee Nicolas Winding Refn has written 'When you watch an Andy Milligan movie, you're in no doubt whose film you're watching' (Refn 2012: 2). Milligan came to London in 1970 with his trusty 16mm camera and made five films, four of which are horror. The fifth, *Nightbirds* (1970) is a very powerful chamber piece shot in East London which owes something to Pinter and Polanski and was recently rediscovered (in part due to the efforts of Refn) and released on BluRay by, of all people, the British Film Institute. But even in this story of Dink, a naïve drifter who falls in love with predatory ice queen Dee the director's love of the gothic can be seen. Stephen Thrower has highlighted the setting, Commercial Street in the East End, one-time Ripper territory and there is even a glimpse of the Ten Bells pub in one shot. The seductive, controlling and ultimately sociopathic Dee (Julie Shaw) is represented as a kind of monster (one of many monstrous women in Milligan's work) and there are a number of references to vampirism in the dialogue with Dee telling Dink how she 'feels like a vampire in the sunlight when you smile' and later suggesting 'let's make this our last trip in daylight'. It's entirely in keeping with this grim milieu shot in grainy monochrome that the infectious taint Dee is cursed with turns out to be not vampirism but syphilis and the film ends with Dink dead and her lining up her next victim.

Milligan's British gothic horrors are especially noteworthy for the way he mines home-grown subjects for inspiration. They can be seen as bargain basement reworkings of familiar tales which combine US Grindhouse aesthetics (technically primitive depictions of graphic gore, often combined with graphic sex) and gothic romance. *The Bloodthirsty Butchers* is yet another adaptation of the Sweeney Todd story, peopled with the director's usual garrulous grotesques and advertised with the lurid tagline, 'Their prime cuts were curiously erotic – but thoroughly brutal!' It's far from Milligan's best film, with the period setting amounting to costumed actors wandering round a couple of streets in Hampstead and some music hall songs on the soundtrack along with a botched ending where the action is obscured by a frenetically swinging camera. But the blend of ramshackle sets, amateurish performances, hokey plot contrivances and graphic, badly-staged gore lends the film a weird air of authenticity, as if a Penny Gaff performance of Sweeney Todd were caught on film.

Tim Lucas has noted the debt Milligan owes to Tod Slaughter and his 'strong meat' melodramas (2012: 32) and nowhere is that influence more obvious. There is little of Milligan's trademark misanthropy – a couple of the characters are even quite likeable – and there is even a (deeply unconvincing) final scene of young lovers reuniting straight out of a nineteenth-century melodrama (or rather one of Slaughter's adaptations). Samm Deighan has described the Gaffs closely resembling 'the 42nd Street grindhouse cinemas in New York in the 70s and early 80s' (Deighan 2011) so it makes sense that Milligan, the director of such sleazy offerings as *Fleshpot on 42nd Street* (1973) and *Torture Dungeon* (1970) would be drawn to the form.

The Man with Two Heads (1972) is his extremely theatrical but oddly effective version of the Jekyll and Hyde story with a fittingly exploitative title (not to be confused with another film from the same year *The Thing with Two Heads*). Milligan had a way with titles, actually. Consider *The Rats are Coming, the Werewolves are Here* (1972), a vaguely Hammer-ish period gothic about the Mooneys, a family of Victorian werewolves. As well as the traditional generic elements – a country house setting, the transformations into furry-faced beasts, great clouds of billowing mist and the inevitably fruitless search for a cure for the ancestral curse – there are some strange quirks and bizarre interludes, from the scenes with the disfigured, wobbly-accented 'rat man' Mr. McHarbor to some very unpleasant unsimulated chicken bothering and mouse skewering. In characteristic fashion, the titular rodents ('the rats of Mooney manor', as the poster puts it) were added almost as an afterthought in an attempt to cash in on the success of *Willard* [1971], the extra scenes shot back home in Staten Island. Just in case we miss the nod towards the better-known killer rat movie, a couple of Milligan's rodents are called Willard and Ben.

The Body Beneath ([1972], 'filmed in the graveyards of England!') seems to be have been inspired by contemporary accounts of the Highgate Vampire. The plot – about a vampire who masquerades as a vicar who is planning to skip the capital ('London is a police state after midnight') for New York – takes second place to talk (of which there's a lot, even for Milligan) and some memorable set-pieces. He uses some attractive North London locations as a backdrop for his gothic goings on, conjuring haunting images of blue-faced female vampires flitting through the gravestones in daylight. The climax is a hallucinogenic cannibalistic feast reminiscent both of Corman's Poe films and Kenneth Anger's voluptuous *Inauguration of the Pleasure Dome* (1954). The director's love of the topically macabre is underlined by the scene where a character is nailed to a tree, which Thrower (2012: 11) identifies as a kind of ghastly homage to the case of Joseph de Havilland, who was crucified on Hampstead Heath in July 1968, believing it would 'make the world a happier place, no more sin and racial discrimination'(anon d.1968).The Havilland case may also have inspired the throwaway line in another vampire film from the same year, *Dracula Ad 1972*, where a character mentions some 'business on Hampstead Heath, sado-masochism'. One man's altruistic crucifixion is another's footnote in British horror.

WE NEED TO TALK ABOUT ROMAN

Roman Polanski is a major figure in post-war cinema, a remarkably gifted film-maker whose technical talents are matched by a singular off-beat sensibility and a recurring fascination with voyeurism, violence and power games. He has made a series of highly-personal, innovative genre films, a number of which managed to achieve enormous critical and commercial success.The strange, sensational and disturbing details of his life – a child survivor of the Lodz ghetto in World War II, the murder of his pregnant wife by the Manson Family and his escape and subsequent exile from the US on charges of statutory rape – are often viewed through the prism of his work and vice versa. So the occult shenanigans of *Rosemary's Baby* were initially thought to have played some vague, ill-defined role in the Manson Murders and the director's decision to adapt Shakespeare's bloodiest play for his first film after the murders, *Macbeth* was seen as his public replaying of a trauma. (One staggeringly tasteless – and staggeringly stupid - example of this unwillingness/inability to separate life and art can be seen in a contemporary review of *Macbeth* in Newsweek which describes it as 'a work of art – in the grand manner of Buchenwald, Lidice and yes, the Manson murders' [in Rigby 2000: 207].)

It is undeniable however, that Polanski – who has always been, like Hitchcock, both artist and showman – obsessively reworks a number of his experiences in his films, notably a violent assault that nearly killed him when he was young. Precisely how young differs in the telling, with him claiming on one occasion to be aged 8 and another 16, while author Christopher Sandford claims he was 15. But the details of this attack are significant, Polanski recalling 'the blood running over my face and eyes. Ever since that day, whenever I'm standing under the shower, I feel the blood running over me' (in Sandford 2007: 51). His first film as a student – which was never completed due to the footage being lost by the lab - was an account of this attack and images of flowing water occur over and over again in his work. In the documentary *Roman Polanski: Wanted and Desired* (2008), the prosecutor Roger Gunson observes how:

> Every Roman Polanski movie has a theme, corruption meeting innocence over water. I said, 'Oh, well, that's sort of what we have here, corruption, Roman Polanski, meeting innocence, a 13-year-old girl, over water', meaning the Jacuzzi.

Gunson seems to suggest we should regard even Polanski's sex crimes as some kind of auteur work. Indeed, one of the most remarkable things about Polanski's work is the way so many of these recurring themes have been there right from the start. His first completed student film was a creepy moodpiece called *Murder* about a stabbing and his other shorts portray master-slave relationships (for Polanski an 'eternal riddle' [in Sandford 2007: 233]) and shunned outsiders who are the subject of violent attacks, all strikingly shot with a distinctive tone, both darkly funny and oddly detached. (There are also some delicious ironies at work, such as the end of his short *The Fat and the Lean* [1961] when the barefoot put-upon sadsack played by the director himself escapes his bondage and flees to the farway city, which is clearly Paris). As Barbara Leaming has suggested, it is precisely 'Polanski's disconcerting proximity to his material [that] gives his films their aura of personal risk' (1982: 142).

While the director has proved extraordinarily adept at making horror films, his initial foray into the genre was opportunistic. His debut feature, the three-player boat-bound psychodrama *Knife in the Water* (1962) was a critical success, garnering an Oscar nomination for Best Film in a Foreign Language and led to the director being able to leave Poland, first for Paris then London. But he found it hard to cross over from arthouse ghetto to commercial filmmaking, especially when the project he was hawking around was a moody Beckettian black comedy, *When Katelbach Comes*. Hammer found it 'rather macabre' (Sandford 2007: 102) but a meeting with Compton Films was more fruitful. They didn't want *Katelbach* but they were open to horror projects. The resourceful Roman had just the kind of project they were looking for.

KLINGER AND TENSER

Compton was run by Michael Klinger and Tony Tenser, the kind of colourful hard-nosed exploitation merchants that Matthew Street dubbed 'the wild men of Wardour Street' (2005: 264). They had initially teamed up to run the Compton Club in 1960, a private member's club in Soho. Films screened in cinema clubs don't need BBFC certificates and so the Compton could screen much stronger sex films than their competitors (indeed, one of the founder members was John Trevelyan). They moved into the distribution of foreign exploitation films before financing the racy documentary, *Naked as Nature Intended*, starring Pamela Green, fresh from *Peeping Tom*. They went on to *The Black Torment*, directed by Hartford-Davis before that fortuitous meeting with Polanski. Klinger and Tenser would go their separate ways in 1967, with Klinger going on to produce one of the classics of British cinema, *Get Carter* (according to Steve Chibnall, Klinger was inspired to make a gangster movie after seeing Pete Walker's *Man of Violence* – a film the characteristically blunt producer described as 'a load of old crap' [in Chibnall 1998: 66]). He followed that with glossy thrillers including a couple of Wilbur Smith adaptations, *Gold* (1974) and *Shout at the Devil* (1976). David McGillivray put it best when he said in 1992:

> The British film industry is gasping its last because there is no one like Tony Tenser to kick it back to life. He was the Irving Thalberg of the exploitation movie, and like the boy wonder of MGM, his career was too short. (qtd. in Sweet 2005: 264)

Tenser formed Tigon Films in 1967 and would continue to employ young zealous auteurs in the Polanski mould including Michael Reeves, who would make two films for the company. Tenser, a great raconteur who liked to play up his hard-headed approach to film-making was nevertheless a remarkable spotter of talent. As well as the work of Polanski and Reeves, Tigon would make a handful of interesting films – *The Curse of the Crimson Altar*, the Raquel Welch rape-revenge western *Hannie Caulder* (1971) and *Blood on Satan's Claw*. It wasn't all good – *The Blood Beast Terror* (1967) was a gothic horror about a woman who turned into a giant carnivorous moth and the less said about *Sauce for the Goose* (1969), a sex comedy starring Norman Wisdom (!) the better but hey, no-one's perfect. During Hammer's final years, Tenser was one of those interested in buying the company. The thought of a Tenser Hammer is certainly an intriguing proposition, although the truth is that by the mid-70s both parties were not what they were. Unhappy at the increasing violence in the exploitation field – his last credit was as executive producer on *Frightmare* – Tenser quit the film business, married a younger woman and moved to Southport to sell wicker furniture.

It's important to remember that the British exploitation market was an accepted part of the industry, albeit a slightly shady part. Unlike the American exploitation market, where oddball outlaws like Dwain Esper, Earl Owensby and Herschell Gordon Lewis existed at the furthermost frontiers of the film industry, making films for the drive-in markets and grindhouses, in Britain the two traditions were far more integrated. So the iconic star of *The Dam Busters* (1955) Richard Todd could end up in a couple of Pete Walker films, Hartford-Davis could switch from sexploitation to *The Sandwich Man*, a mainstream comedy with a starry cast and Tigon could bring out a sex comedy starring Norman Wisdom. The best example of this process would be the many reputable actors who ended up slumming it in the sex comedies of the 1970s or the way that the director of two such comedies, *The Sex Thief* (1973) and *Eskimo Nell* (1975), Martin Campbell would go on to bigger, if not better things including *GoldenEye* (1995) and *Casino Royale* (2006).

REPULSION (1965)

A close-up of an eye. After the title glides across the screen (and the eye), the rest of the credits float slowly up and across the screen. This vaguely disorientating opening is something of a Polanski trademark; *Rosemary's Baby* opens with a pan across the New York skyline going the wrong way (right to left rather than left to right). The unease begins before the credits end. Here, the director's credit glides across the eye, 'slicing it' in what may be a reference to the slashed eye in *Un Chien Andalou* (1928) while also hinting at the razor violence to come. The score by Chico Hamilton is either sombre and portentuous (the banging drum of the credits, the shimmering cymbals elsewhere) or frenzied and hysterical – Polanski films are often distinguished by their memorable music, whether it's the two films scored by the ill-fated Krystof Komeda (who died a few days short of his 38th birthday after a couple of vodka-fuelled falls), the Third Ear Band's squawking, grating, grinding music work on *Macbeth* or the woozy romance of Jerry Goldsmith's score for *Chinatown* (1974).

Carole (played by an icy Catherine Deneuve) is a young Belgian manicurist who shares a flat in London with her older sister (Yvonne Furneaux). Clearly disturbed from the outset, prone to zoning out, twitches, tics and violent sex fantasies, Carole's mental state deteriorates when her sister goes to Italy, leading her to kill two men before retreating, presumably permanently, into a catatonic state.

The UK poster for Polanski´s first British film: *Repulsion*

The screenplay, written by the director with his long-time collaborator Gerard Brach, largely eschews the melodramatic devices of horror films dealing with mental illness: unlike *Psycho* (one clear model for Polanski's film) and its many imitators (*Homicidal* [1961], *The Psychopath*), *Repulsion* is structured more like an unflinching case-study than a thriller.

Not only do Polanski and Brach leave out a 'whodunnit', there isn't really a definitive 'whydunnit' (although there is a hint). This approach is intensified considerably through the choice of locations; not only the airy flat but also the Kensington exteriors. Polanski may have been an enthusiastic participant on the Swinging London scene (a mews house in Chelsea, hanging out at the Playboy Club, friendships with various Beatles and Stones) but Carole's city is a hostile and miserable place, full of lecherous workmen and braying pub boors, crap food and bitchy, overweight women. This stark vision is underlined by the magnificent black and white photography. In one of those collisions of high and low that crop up so often in British horror cinema, when the Oscar-winning veteran Gil Taylor (fresh from *Dr. Strangelove* [1964]) had to leave the project when the perfectionist Polanski ran over schedule, he was replaced by Stanley A. Long, whose credits included *Nudes of the World* (1961) and *Take off Your Clothes and Live* (1963). Polanski's cold vision of contemporary London is a world away from the 'red double-decker and mini-skirt' view of the capital which was coming into vogue and anticipates the grim, sour visions of Hartford-Davis and Reeves.

Polanski is fond of confining locations, whether it's the boats of *Knife in the Water* and *Bitter Moon* (1992), Holy Island in *Cul-de-Sac*, the house in *Death and the Maiden* (1994) or the ghetto in *The Pianist* (2002). But the trilogy of films set largely in apartments – *Repulsion*, *Rosemary's Baby* and *The Tenant* – represent his best, and certainly most influential work, what Mark Cousins refers to as his 'claustrophobia films' (2005: 23).

All three films deal with the alienating experience of urban life and the acute sense of isolation generated by apartment living (notice how often in these films the sound from neighbouring apartments leaks in, muffled voices, TV sounds, even satanic chanting). Of course, in both *Repulsion* and *The Tenant*, the isolation is increased because the protagonists are foreigners – in the latter case, the Paris-based Polish central character is played by the director himself. Although this film – one of the best European films of the 1970s – is based on a novel by Roland Topor, it can be seen as a remake of *Repulsion*, only with the director in the Carole role. It's tempting to think this fascination with and dread of enclosed spaces was in some way inspired by screenwriter Brach's struggles with agoraphobia – in 1994, in a *Los Angeles Times* piece called 'The Man Who Wouldn't Go Out', Brach said of his screenplays 'It's true, I never go out of my flat. I stayed here, inside for seven years; I don't even go to the elevator during that time…So these help me travel visually' (in Chollet 1994). But weirdly, the condition didn't strike until the early 80s, two decades after *Repulsion*.

Instead of a refuge, Carole's home is a place of terror and Polanski imbues everyday domestic objects – a razor and shaving brush, a crack in the wall, a family photograph, rumpled bedsheets and dirty laundry – with a creeping dread. What could have been a typical psycho gothic is turned into something much more effective through Polanski's remarkable visual gifts, his eye for composition, his assured sense of space. He uses a mixture of distorting extreme close-ups and long-shots of rooms with the camera at floor level, the frame filled with furniture, divided by walls with Carole often frozen stock-still, such as the scene where she sits in the dilapidated store-room beneath the shop where she works, unmoving for a painfully long time before she reaches over to a chair and wipes off dust which may or may not be there. There is also a series of tracking shots which float around the apartment or follow Carole down the hallway which, in one of the film's most memorable images, literally comes alive, hands appearing out of the malleable wall to feel her up. The dream sequences are silent except for the ever-ticking clock (a trick Polanski would repeat in a number of his later films). The sound is used to startling effect throughout, long periods of silence punctuated by a dripping tap, buzzing flies or the sudden rumble of cracking plaster.

Even the seemingly trivial background details are heavy with dark significance – the comic news story about eels coming out of someone's tap feeds into Carole's obsession with cleansing water (she drinks glass after glass, washes her feet in the sink, overflows the bath-tub where she will later dump a corpse). The buskers she encounters on a couple of occasions (the spoon-player apparently the director himself, though it's hard to tell), one of whom plays a banjo, prefigure the frenzied music as Carole attacks the landlord. The sweet scene where one of her co-workers tells her about a scene in an un-named Chaplin film (presumably *The Gold Rush* [1925]) where a hungry man tries to eat the star after imagining he is a chicken is a story about precisely the kind of delusions which plague Carole. And if the character in the Chaplin film is driven crazy by his hunger for food, Carole's problem manifests itself, at least in part, in her obsession and disgust with sex (the titular repulsion). She lies awake at night listening to her sister's orgasmic moans (a first for British cinema incidentally) and is bewitched and grossed out by the presence of her sister's (married) lover, Michael. She stares at his shaving stuff in the bathroom before throwing it away, buries her face in his discarded vest before throwing up and has dreams/fantasies where a man breaks into her room (after symbolically breaking down her barricades) and has violent sex with her. It's little wonder she feels this way, given the sorry state of the men in the film. While Michael is just brash and insensitive, the other characters are all overtly threatening, even if it is just talk. Ostensible nice guy Colin thinks nothing of kicking her door in (so to speak) when she won't let him in, workmen leer and catcall, Colin's hideous drinking pals boast and preen and the landlord (sweaty, frog-faced Patrick Wymark on his way to becoming a British genre staple) tries to rape her. (The director made a considerable Method-style effort to keep Deneuve away from sex, only allowing her to fly back to France to see her lover, director Roger Vadim when she was menstruating [see Leaming 1982].)

This notion of man as predatory pervert and woman as victim is underlined by the repeated references to notions of femininity. Carole, gorgeous and blonde yet broken and dangerous, works in a beautician's salon as a manicurist and yet she can't stop biting her nails. Michael hurries Helen along with 'you're not going into the Miss World competition' and also refers to Carole as Cinderella and Little Miss Muffet. The fat female client who rails against men ('there's only one thing they want') as we stare at her mouth, in a disquieting inverted close-up. Bridget crying and moaning about 'bloody men'. After the murders, Carole retreats into stereotypical femaleness, embroidering and ironing (oblivious to the fact the iron is unplugged). Of course, Carole is not simply a victim but also a victimiser, clubbing the hapless Colin to death and dumping him in the tub, slashing the landlord to death with a straight razor (the nasty bit where she slits the back of his neck finds an echo in *Chinatown*'s nose slitting scene – committed by the cameoing director). Again it's hard to resist seeing this dual nature as autobiographical. Polanski clearly identifies and empathises with his many suffering female characters and yet this unreconstructed 60s man famously dished out some suffering of his own in a Beverly Hills jacuzzi scarcely more than a decade later. Of course, *Death and the Maiden*, Polanski's underrated take on Ariel Dorfman's play, takes this process of identification even further. The story of a man who may or may not be a torturer held captive by a woman who believes herself to be one of his victims while her helpless husband looks on can be read as autobiography. Polanski has played all of the roles, being not only the aforementioned victim and victimiser but also a suffering husband who, when it really mattered, proved unable to protect his wife.

The director did shoot a third murder for *Repulsion*, Carole drowning Michael's jealous wife in the tub but apparently removed it after composer Hamilton convinced him it didn't make psychological sense. The fact that Polanski, faced with an actress reluctant to dunk her head in the filthy bathwater, dragged up in a wig and dress and played the part himself can't help but add an extra layer to *The Tenant*, where he not only 'plays Carole' but also appears in drag. At the end of *Repulsion*, Michael and Helen return home to find a wrecked apartment, corpses and a catatonic Carol. The climax has been hinted at throughout — the pouring rain outside, Carole's slender, white hand emerging from under the bed, even Helen's moans of horror echoing her earlier orgasm. The neighbours who file into the apartment are old, nosey, grotesque. Carole ends up swept away, not by a handsome prince but by a concerned Michael, although she is clearly unreachable. A bravura tracking shot around the apartment ends on the family photo which features a unsmiling Carole. We zoom in closer until the film ends as it begins, with a shot of Carole's eye. This ending is also prefigured when Bridget, crying over a boyfriend, says 'Look at my eyes'. This kind of circular narrative, where little is resolved and 'the Devil prevails' (in Ciment et al 2005 [1969]: 46) is another of the director's trademarks — *Rosemary's Baby* begins and ends with shots of the New York skyline and, in an audacious touch, *Macbeth* has a downbeat coda tacked-on, the proceedings bracketed by the malevolent witches. For many commentators, the fact that Carole is looking in the direction of her father on the photo indicates child sexual abuse but this neat solution to Carole's condition is a bit reductive. Yes, she is looking at her father and certainly, many of the symptoms she exhibits — the fascination with and terror of sex, the washing, the inability to communicate — can be regarded as a result of childhood abuse. But the expression on Carole's face may say more than where she is looking — she looks haunted, remote, already withdrawn from the world. Polanski seems to regard it as an absurd place where darkness and violence can just erupt seemingly out of nowhere and the idea that there is one cut-and-dried solution to Carole's condition would be a betrayal of this, the kind of psychological cause-and-effect which we are offered in *Psycho*.

Polanski's first foray into British horror should not be regarded as simply a case of a budding auteur making a low-budget horror film as a calling card (as is the case with Francis Ford Coppola [*Dementia 13*, 1962]) Peter Bogdanovich [*Targets*, 1968]) or Oliver Stone [*Seizure*, 1976]). He would go on to make another film for Compton, his long-cherished *When Katelbach Comes*, retitled *Cul-de-Sac*, a bizarre and brilliant grim comedy, with a cult cast including Donald Pleasence, Lionel Stander and Deneuve's sister Françoise Dorléac (who would die in a burning car the following year). He followed this with *Dance of the Vampires* (1967), an affectionate and very stylish spoof on Hammer gothic. Polanski has remarked on the similarity between horror and humour, suggesting that, 'all fear that isn't accompanied by real danger should make you laugh once it's passed' (in Delahaye and Narboni 2005 [1969]: 21) and this attitude is reflected time and again in his films.

He seems unwilling (unable?) to make a comedy without chills and struggles to make a horror film without some dark humour creeping in. *Dance of the Vampires* contains some very funny moments (such as Alfie Bass's Jewish vampire shrugging off a cross with 'Oy vey, have you got the wrong vampire') but the mood is often weird rather than comical. To some degree this is due to the slightly eerie presence of the stunningly beautiful ill-fated Sharon Tate (although she is mis-cast as an East European Jew). As well as the vast sets in the UK, there is some gorgeous location footage of the snowy landscapes of the Italian Dolemite Mountains and Polanski creates an intoxicating mittel European atmosphere, which serves to emphasise just how very English Hammer's portrait of Europe is. The ending is another of the director's trademark downers and would prove extremely influential, particularly on the short cycle of American 'counterculture vampire' films (both *Count Yorga* films and *The Velvet Vampire* pinch the ending). Although it seemed to be a step-up from the penny-pinching of Compton, the experience was not a happy one for the director. For the US release, someone at MGM (maybe producer Martin Ransohoff but more likely the duo of supervising editor Margaret Booth and head of theatrical post-production Merle Chamberlain) cut the film, bolted on a woefully unfunny animated sequence and added a stupid title – *The Fearless Vampire Killers*, or *Pardon Me, But Your Teeth Are in My Neck*.

After his Hollywood sojourn, during which he had a huge hit with *Rosemary's Baby*, Polanski returned to the UK in 1971 to make his first film after the Family murders. *Macbeth* received mixed reviews upon release – doubtless inspired in part by the fact it was a Playboy production – but it is a remarkable film. Although the brutality of the production, written by the director and the critic Kenneth Tynan is carried over from Orson Welles' noirish B-movie adaptation, Polanski's vision is as absurd, nasty and stylishly shot as anything else in his ouevre. His Macbeths are younger than usual and played with some force by Jon Finch (on a bit of a roll, with *Frenzy* straight after) and Francesca Annis, who had auditioned for the lead in *Repulsion* but was dismissed in characteristically forthright style by the director, who called her 'a Cyrano De Bergerac' on account of her nose (see Sandford 2007). In addition, British viewers of a certain age may get a weird frisson from the presence of a young Keith Chegwin as Banquo's son. Much attention has been paid to the Manson echoes to be found in the film – which is unsurprising, given it's a violent story about murder and witchery wherein a man has his family slaughtered in their home – but this risks making the film into little but an autobiographical footnote. There are many scenes which achieve the oppressive power of nightmare, the opening with the hideous and very creepy witches on an extremely unwelcoming Welsh beach and the startling silent sequence where we follow Macbeth's severed head being as good as anything the director ever came up with.

Polanski's adventures in British horror may be the best home-grown examples of what can happen when arthouse stylings and genre conventions come up against each other but they are by no means unique. The influence of the heavily-authored, stylistically innovative art cinema of the late 1950s and 60s had an enormous influence on American genre films - *Bonnie and Clyde* (1967) was at various times earmarked as a project for Godard and Truffaut, *The Godfather* combined a Cormanesque mob plot with Visconti's visual style and the slow-motion violence of *The Wild Bunch* (1968) was inspired by Peckinpah's desire to 'make a Western like Kurosawa makes Westerns' (in Weddle 1994: 107). So it should come as little surprise that a number of British genre items would also adopt a kind of self-conscious gratuitous artiness along with the sex and violence – aided in part by the relaxation of censorship and the popularity of mind-expanding substances (with both film-makers and audiences).

Newman has noted how little separates some of the more outré genre offerings of this period from celebrated arty outings such as *Performance* and Losey's *Secret Ceremony* (1970). How else to explain the weird modish psychodrama *Goodbye Gemini* (1970) directed by Alan Gibson (who would direct Hammer's two contemporary Dracula films)? The story of attractive murderous twins (Martin Potter and Judy Geeson) and their teddy bear, Agamemnon, on an odyssey through a groovy Chelsea of parties, camp ageing hipsters and cross-dressers is not entirely successful but oddly memorable. Much the same can be said of *Mumsy, Sonny, Nanny and Girly*, a black comedy directed by Freddie Francis – who makes more of an effort here than usual – about an oddball family who play murderous games with strangers in their rambling mansion (the ubiquitous Oakley Court). It's even harder to know what to make of *Psychomania* (1973), Don Sharp's film about undead bikers, stone circles, evil toads and George Sanders as Beryl Reid's satanic butler (Sanders killed himself straight after finishing the film, leaving an infamous suicide note in which he described the world as 'a sweet cesspool'). *Psychomania* isn't particularly good – Sharp seems unsure how to handle the insane script by Arnaud d'Usseau and Julian Zimet, who wrote the similarly whacky but much better *Horror Express* – but there are a handful of impressive scenes, the gang member buried sitting astride his motorcycle suddenly riding it up out of the grave and the undead trashing a supermarket in Walton on Thames. There is also an excellent spooky credit sequence, with the skull-masked bike gang riding around an ancient stone circle in slow motion, a vision of arcane rites colliding with new technology worthy of Nigel Kneale.

But it's no surprise that the best examples of arty horror came from European directors. In Britain, the concerns around gore and graphic depictions of cruelty were matched by a deep-seated suspicion of the avant-garde and the experimental. It's worth noting that the same censors who prevented British audiences from seeing *Freaks* and *Island of Lost Souls* also banned surrealist films, including *Un Chien Andalou* and *The Seashell and the Clergyman* ([1928]; the latter being memorably rejected on the grounds that

> the film is so cryptic as to be almost meaningless. If there is a meaning, it is doubtless objectionable. (in Robertson 1993: 39)

European horror has always had a pronounced artistic streak and there is little in British genre history to match the disturbing poetry of, for example, *Nosferatu*, *Eyes Without A Face*, *Daughters of Darkness* and *Suspiria*. It's entirely appropriate that the Spanish emigre Jose Larraz would adopt a style which combines elements borrowed from two of his fellow expats, Losey and Polanski.

JOSE LARRAZ

Larraz was a doctor of philosophy and comic book artist from Barcelona who relocated to Britain in the late 60s, settling in (of all places) Tunbridge Wells. He made a string of horror films in Britain, which are notable for their self-conscious artiness and strange, elliptical narratives. Larraz's films have a striking consistency of style and theme – indeed, Kim Newman has remarked how the director 'obsessively tells the same story, about murderous lesbians, in practically all his films' (1988: 21), which is slightly unfair, as more than one of his films features a male killer. But other elements – limb-thrashing sex scenes, weird, often stilted dialogue and attractive locations out in the sticks – recur throughout his work. His British films blend slow, brooding atmospherics with overheated exploitation elements, lurching from the hysterical to the lyrical, lashings of sex and gore alternating with odd longeurs and some art-movie devices (long takes, dissolves, open endings). His first British film, the thriller *Whirlpool* was once thought lost and is still hard to see. The follow-up, *Deviation* - a fitting title for almost any Larraz film – is another in a long line of post-Manson hippyfied horrors with a tag-line that sums up the sub-genre 'sex, drugs and rock'n'roll was never supposed to be like this' (a tagline which could equally be applied to the Manson Murders). In 1973, Larraz made *Scream and Die* aka *The House That Vanished*, a strange giallo-inflected murder mystery. The odd, rambling, extremely implausible plot (written by the incorrigible Derek Ford) deals with a fashion model who tags along with her burglar boyfriend and witnesses a sex murder in a spooky country mansion. There are a number of strange and disturbing sequences – a cellar full of pigeons, an extended rape/murder – and some graphic sex, notably between a fresh-faced twentysomething and his fiftysomething Aunt as well as some gratuitous artiness (the fact that Ford wrote the script is presumably why there is a lack of the director's trademark weird dialogue). Like the shockers discussed in the previous chapter, the killer here (whose identity is never in any doubt) is the young, child-like Paul (played by creepy Karl Lanchbury, a Larraz regular). The tagline is also notable:

> Are You Planning an Affair? We Can Give You 7 Good Reasons Not to Have Your Next Affair at 'The House That Vanished' – And They're All DEAD!! 1. George, 2. Marsha, 3. Ted, 4. Linda, 5. Ronnie, 6. Alice, 7. Larry.

In 1974, the increasingly prolific Larraz made *Symptoms*, a psycho thriller set in another country house. The film owes a considerable debt to *Repulsion* in its story of Helen (another eerie Angela Pleasence performance), a lonely lesbian living in a rambling country mansion (in actuality Harefield Grove in Hillingdon), whose mental disintegration leads to a series of murders. From the first line of dialogue ('last night I dreamed...'), borrowed from *Rebecca* (1940), another story which deals with same-sex obsession, the film is both familiar and extremely atmospheric. Very little happens for great stretches of the film but the tension is slowly (too slowly for some) built up. The devices used here are familiar ones - photographs, strange sounds, locked doors while at one point, an unsuspecting houseguest is woken by the sounds of masturbation (female masturbation is frequently used in films as short-hand, as it were, for instability/insanity cf. *The Sentinel* [1997], *Haute Tension* [2003], *Antichrist* [2009]). It also showcases Larraz's trademark eccentric dialogue; at one point Helen comes out with, 'I can hear things nobody else can. Coffee?' Despite being selected as the British entry at Cannes (where it reportedly impressed Jack Nicholson) *Symptoms* is ultimately little more than a well-acted and stylish Polanski rip-off. But the use of the English countryside and the odd, would-be dreamlike repetition of actions (just how many times do we see Peter Vaughn rowing his boat across that pond?) would reappear in Larraz's next, and best, film.

VAMPYRES (1974)

An appropriately lurid advert for *Vampyres*

There's a telling moment in this film when one of the eponymous undead is told she 'doesn't look English'. Neither does the film, an extreme example of the director's elliptical yet visceral *faux*-arthouse horrors. The establishing shot is of yet another country mansion: the gothic exterior is Oakley Court, the long-time home of Hammer while the interiors were again shot in Harefield Grove. Two women are naked in bed when an unseen gunman enters and shoots them both repeatedly. This dramatic opening, switching from langourous sex to shocking violence, is not only typical Larraz but also sets the tone for the rest of the film. It's never explained how the women are reborn as vampires but then the script (by Larraz and credited to D. Daubeney, his English wife, for quota reasons) is full of loose ends.

The women, tall brunette Fran (Marianne Morris) and short blonde Miriam (Anulka aka Anulka Dziubinska) make quite an impression, dressed in long cloaks and standing by the side of a country road, striding purposefully through the woods at dawn or having lengthy, frequently bloody sex. Fran in particular is both creepy and very sexy with her strong bone structure and expressionless face. The alien quality of the vampyres is further emphasised by the fact that both actors were dubbed, giving their dialogue a flat, doped-up quality (according to Morris, Larraz wanted the characters to speak like the singer and actor Annie Ross, who only the year before allegedly provided the voice for Britt Ekland's Willow in *The Wicker Man*). In the DVD featurette Return of the Vampyres, Morris says that Larraz was interested in the way they moved and it's not hard to see why: they are often in motion, walking in long-shot, running into the road to stop a car, charging through the tunnels beneath the house. Andy Boot describes *Vampyres* as having 'zilch plot' (1995: 265) and while this is unfair, it's easy to see what he means.

The narrative is stripped-down, undeveloped and repetitive, events seeming to recur over and over again as if in a dream. Just as with *Scream and Die* and *Symptoms*, what could be considered a stately pace could also be dismissed as rambling. The women wait by the road and flag down men driving alone, taking them home for what starts as orgiastic sex and ends with even more orgiastic blood-drinking. One of the men, Ted (who looks like an ugly Neil Diamond and is accurately described by Rigby as 'bovine' [2000: 256]) survives his night with Fran but keeps returning to the house, his presence creating tensions between the women. There is a sub-plot about a couple staying in a caravan in the grounds of the house, the skeptical John (Brian Deacon) and his wife, Harriet, who appears to have some kind of psychic connection to the women. She is played by Sally Faulkner, who would go on to star in another horror film about a lesbian couple whose rural idyll is disrupted by a man – in this case, a carnivorous alien – in *Prey*.

Rather than going the Hammer route of using nudity and softcore sapphic sex to spice up a traditional vampire film, Larraz makes his film about sex and slaughter, pushing both to an extreme. For David Pirie, it 'takes the idea of sex vampirism about as far as it can go' (1977: 165). The sex scenes are notable for their seemingly-unchoreographed clumsiness, with a lot of tangled limbs and thrashing about. The panting and moaning is a bit affected but there is a weird erotic charge in the scene where Fran laps the blood from Ted's wounded arm, the sound of slurping amplified obscenely. The most dramatic scene is the killing of Rupert (played by Lanchbury). After Fran leaves Ted, she finds Miriam, who had gone off with Rupert, standing in the corridor, smeared with blood, seemingly drunk with it. Fran leads her back into the room where the unfortunate Rupert lies bloodied in bed, his eyes rolled-back in his head, whimpering. The women fall on him and feed, licking at the blood and biting him as his limbs contort and his head lolls. It is one of the few vampire killings in the cinema to remind us that this is a kind of sex murder. The action is made particularly dramatic through Larraz's use of hand-held camera. The way we are right in there with the women, their moaning victims and a lot of fake blood, contrasts with the exterior scenes, the camera pulled back, figures often merging into the landscape. (Indeed, the murder scenes are so blood-boltered that Anulka recalls in the aforementioned DVD featurette that her hair was pink for months after filming). In this way, the film reveals the possible influence of recent American vampire pictures, hip reworkings of hoary old gothic stories. Indeed, the film feels very like *The Return of Count*

Yorga, a weird and extremely effective combination of gloomy atmospherics and savage Mansonish murder scenes.

As sexploitation spectacle, *Vampyres* is unusually complex. On the one hand, it employs the standard generic device of gorgeous women writhing around with pretty unattractive men (it's hard to see Ted appealing physically to any but the most charitable of viewers) – indeed, the film can be seen as yet another example of that popular notion in 1970s film and TV, that glamorous young women can't wait to have sex with really ugly men (as in the TV sit-com *On the Buses* [1969–73] and most of the *Carry Ons*). On the other hand, while the film more than fulfills the requirements of the lesbian vampire film, featuring as it does two attractive, frequently naked women getting it on with each other, the men are sidelined almost to the point of exclusion. While the standard cinematic MFF threesome features lesbian sex as a kind of foreplay before the 'real thing'(penetration), here Ted just can't keep up and passes out cold, allowing Fran and Miriam to continue without him with renewed enthusiasm. Likewise, after Rupert is gorily dispatched (with a phallic knife to the back), we see a fairly lengthy scene of the two women rinsing off his blood in a shower before Miriam goes down on Fran. As in his previous film, Larraz offers a landscape which is both familiar and utterly alien, making such oft-used locations as Bray and Denham look as cold and dead as the moon. The effect of this stylised European sensibility set against a familiar English rural setting is wildly disorientating. In that sense, it is very like *The Living Dead at the Manchester Morgue* (1974), a stark tale of zombies in the Peak District which was being shot around the same time by another talented Spaniard, Jorge Grau.

Larraz also makes the most of the cluttered, would-be boho interiors, the vibe being very much hip swinger's pad. Images of predation crop up when Ted kneels down on a zebra skin rug or shares the frame with a stuffed leopard. This is contrasted with the drab surroundings of the caravan and the scenes with John and Harriet capture the often-bleak reality of what would now be called a staycation: the cramped space, Harriet wearing her mac indoors, the sound of the rain pissing down outside. It's not a perfect film by any means. As with *Symptoms*, the dialogue is often ponderous and gnomic, not helped by the dubbing:

Fran: Does this kind of thing excite you?

Ted: Sometimes. Why?

Fran: Now don't be too impatient.

In a weird scene towards the end of the film, Ted has a bizarre monologue while he is trapped in the house and hears the women arrive home with a potential victim:

Who's there? Outside? I hear voices. Met him…picked him up…on the roadside, no doubt. Just like Rupert. Just like me. Who are you? Where the hell do you come from? I must get away from here. (Shouts) I must get away from here!

Unlike Polanski and Brach, whose *Repulsion* script was given an English makeover by David Stone, Larraz's dialogue is as weird and overbaked as his visual style. (Indeed, the director's commentary track on the DVD can be a struggle, what with his heavy accent and occasionally idiosyncratic English.)

There are also a series of blind alleys in the film, which are either infuriating or intriguing, depending on your point of view. Harriet's connection to the women is never explained: she is the only one who sees them both standing by the road as they drive by while John can see only Fran, she seems both fascinated and frightened by them and when they finally meet, Fran tells her 'I always knew we'd find each other. By this sign I'll know you' before touching Harriet's forehead. But this goes nowhere. Indeed, although the nasty scene where Harriet is killed by the women is disturbingly well-done, it seems out of step with the sexed-up slaughter we've seen previously.

After she finds John dead in his car, the women attack Harriet, slapping her and dragging her to the cellar. There, Miriam strips her and holds her hands behind her back (while Sally Faulkner demonstrates her considerable screaming abilities, making the most blood-curdling sounds this side of Marilyn Burns in *Texas Chainsaw*). While she struggles, naked, Fran approaches with an ornamental dagger and cuts her throat. There is also an intriguing relationship between Ted and the women which is hinted at but never explained. When he checks into a hotel near the mansion at the start of the film an old man at reception recognises him. Ted denies ever being there but when he first meets Fran, he tells her she reminds him 'very much indeed' of someone he knew a long time ago. At the end, after Fran and Miriam have fled from the house into a churchyard, an unconscious Ted is woken up in his car by an estate agent and told he's trespassing. As he prepares to leave, the estate agent tells a couple of prospective buyers about the unsolved murder of two women which took place there, adding how 'the murderer always returns to the scene of the crime'. We are left with the suggestion that Ted killed Fran and Miriam in a jealous rage before returning to 'the scene of the crime' and passing out drunk only to dream the events of the film. There are other teasing suggestions (a bit of bloody broken glass on the bedside table after he's first been bitten, an empty wine bottle when he wakes up in his car) but this studied reluctance to reveal all is a perfect match with the strange blend of detachment and grue.

There's something refreshing about all this opacity when so often genre films are over-emphatic and exposition-heavy. It's the same kind of unease which is used to startling effect in a couple of recent British films, the hit-man/satanic cult mash-up *Kill List* (2011) and *Berberian Sound Studio* (2012), the enigmatic homage to both *The Conversation* (1974) and Italian horror of the 70s, a self-conscious refusal to tie things up neatly – or indeed at all. The subtle chill of ambiguity in *Vampyres* contrasts with all that Euro-style sex and gore. The producer Bryan Smedley-Aston would produce another bucolic sleazefest in *Expose* but without Larraz's directorial abilities, the film falls short.

As the industry in Britain began to falter, Larraz started to commute from Kent to Spain, where there was a post-Franco demand for the sleazy and the sexploitative. This was a loss to home-grown horror but Larraz seemed to lose something too. None of his films since have made much of an impression, whether it's the soft porn of *Violation of the Bitch* aka *The Coming of Sin* (1978) (indeed, its reputation is doubtless partly down to that splendidly lurid title) or the suburban satanism of *Black Candles* (1982). But *The Edge of the Axe* (aka *Axolution*), an American slasher from 1988 is pretty awful and largely devoid of any trademark directorial flourishes. It's perhaps a measure of how generic the film is that the IMDb synopsis is a bald, almost parodic 'a deranged guy in a mask kills people with an axe'...

CHAPTER 6: RISING FROM THE GRAVE – THE SLOW, PAINFUL BIRTH OF THE NEW WAVE OF BRITISH HORROR

The decline of British gothic was swift. In 1967 there were eleven British horror films released and by the early 1970s, this number had greatly increased (20 in 1970 and 25 the year after). By 1976, it had dropped to 4 and the same amount in 1979, with 3 of those – John Badham's *Dracula*, *Alien* and *Murder by Decree* – major studio films with (relatively) big budgets and stars. With considerable irony, the low-budget British gothic was dying as Hollywood horror had acquired a kind of respectability after the enormous success of *The Exorcist* and *Jaws*. *The Omen* (1976) may have been filmed largely in the home counties but it's very much an American film. There was a series of glossy, starry Hollywood gothics made at the end of the 70s and into the 80s – *Dracula* with Laurence Olivier in the Peter Cushing role, *The Awakening* (1980) an adaptation of the same Stoker story which inspired *Blood from the Mummy's Tomb* but with an out-of-place Charlton Heston and *The Bride* (1985), a terrible big-hair Frankenstein film with Sting in another of Peter Cushing's roles. Meanwhile *The Shining* and *Alien* may have been shot in Britain but there was little home-grown about either.

VIDEO NASTIES

The fact that other EU countries, with the exception of the Republic of Ireland, managed to cope with the advent of home video without imposing wholesale state censorship on the new medium makes the UK something of an anomaly in this respect and raises the obvious question of how and why this state of affairs came about.
(Petley 2012)

Still living with the English fear, waiting for the witch hunt here.
'Witch Hunt', The Mob (1980)

At first glance, the strange case of the Video Nasties is firmly rooted in a very specific set of circumstances. The new-fangled video cassette recorder was launched at a time when regional cinemas in the UK were being closed. The major studios were wary of this new development, so a number of enterprising independent distributors stepped in to satisfy the growing demand for films. The law hadn't yet caught up with video, so these films didn't have to be submitted to the BBFC. Last and perhaps most importantly, a newly-elected right-wing government pledged to put a stop to social unrest while at the same time waging a culture war on the perceived excesses of the 1970s. So far, so early 80s. But the concerns expressed by press and politicians alike echoed persistent concerns voiced by moral campaigners for more than a century, fears around new technology, the effects of violent imagery on impressionable young men and the power of horror to warp the minds of those who consume it. The Video Nasties were simply the latest manifestation of the same social anxieties which sprung up around Penny Bloods and horror comics, rock records and the drug culture, distinguished only by the ferocity of the attack and subsequent clampdown. These perennial anxieties show no sign of abating: witness recent newspaper campaigns about the sexualisation of girls and internet pornography. It's interesting – and depressing – how the same concerns around 'unsuitable' entertainment are played out time and again with little attention paid to the cyclical nature of such concerns. Every new threat to the sensibilities – be it sensational crime reportage, violent videos or internet hardcore – is regarded as unusually pernicious, uniquely damaging.

Martin Barker, one of the few commentators to stand up at the time in defence of the Nasties notes the similarities between the campaign against video horror and the campaign mounted against EC comics in the 1950s, inspired by the very same Dr. Frederic Wertham whose arguments so impressed Derek Hill. Indeed, Barker has noted how the title of Wertham's book, *The Seduction of the Innocent* was a phrase resurrected in the 1980s (see Jake West's documentary *Video Nasties: Moral Panic, Censorship & Videotape* and Barker 1984) as the headline of a *Sunday Times* article by social commentator David Holbrook.

It's instructive to remember just what an impact the coming of the VCR had, for consumers and suppliers, how ramshackle the putative industry was before the big corporations moved in. The early days of video in the UK had a sort of wild west quality which mirrored the dawn of cinema at the turn of the century. Just as the audiences for the sensational 'Cinema of Attractions' – which were screened in music halls, church halls and fairgrounds – were drawn from the working classes, so it was assumed that this new breed of film watchers was too. It wasn't so much that the middle-classes were deaf to the siren call of Italian cannibal movies and Electric Blue soft-porn compilations but more a question of distribution, videos being available for rent in petrol stations and newsagents. The first video I rented, a fairly unremarkable monster movie called *Slithis*, came from the grandly-named Market Street Video, in reality a converted spare bedroom in a flat above a grocer's shop on a residential street in Crewe.

This lack of regulation may have imbued the time with a heady outlaw quality – but it also very quickly became the subject of newspaper scrutiny. As is par for the course in a moral panic, the press played a significant role. *The Sunday Times* revealed in May 1982, 'How High Street Horror is Invading Our Home' while for *The Express* it was 'This Poison Being Peddled as Home Entertainment'. *The Mail* launched a campaign to 'Ban The Sadist Videos' while an editorial in the same paper worried about 'the Rape Of Our Children's Minds'.[10] In December 1982, Labour MP Graham Wardell took the opportunity to describe the humble video recorder as 'a potential weapon that may be used to attack the emotions of our children and young persons' (in Petley 2012). The aforementioned Holbrook article is significant as he takes aim at targets above and beyond video horror, although he does find time to suggest that 'children are actually deliberately being shown films of buggery, rape and mutilation' before going on to link this to other related actions by feckless parents which include family visits to the London Dungeon and exposure to sex education books (ibid.). Video Nasties are seen as a symptom of a larger social malaise, another element in a process of social decline.

Enter Mary Whitehouse, a tireless campaigner for her own particular brand of right-wing morality who with her National Viewers and Listeners Association had been fighting the good fight against the likes of the BBC, Dennis Potter and Chuck Berry's My Ding-a-Ling since 1963. She had recently scored a victory against the magazine Gay News, launching a private prosecution on a charge of Blasphemous Libel over an erotic poem about Christ which appeared in the magazine. She led the charge against the Nasties and sought to enlist the help of sympathetic MPs. Their first weapon was the Obscene Publications Act, which sought to identify material that would 'tend to deprave and corrupt persons' and the Director of Public Prosecutions began collecting evidence against video distributors who may fall foul of the law. Although a good deal of concern was expressed about access to uncertificated films, a BBFC certificate offered little protection as far as the DPP was concerned as Palace Video found out when copies of The Evil Dead (1981) – the most popular video of 1983 – were seized. Of course, sending police officers off to raid video shops and warehouses led to some unintentional hilarity – both Sam Fuller's war movie The Big Red One (1980) and the Stallone/Dolly Parton vehicle The Best Little Whorehouse in Texas (1982) were among the films seized due to their possibly-corrupting titles.

Not only was prosecuting films on a case-by-case basis time consuming but it quickly became unworkable, as juries in different parts of the country couldn't agree on the obscenity – or not – of any given film. The increasingly concerned trade body the Video Retailers Association asked for guidelines and this led to the creation of a list of the most problematic films. 72 films appeared on the list at one time or another, 39 of which were declared obscene, the rest either found not guilty or not prosecuted. And all this was taking place against a backdrop of hysteria, with new shocking statistics appearing with startling regularity. One frequently reprinted story suggested that 40% of five and six year-olds had seen a Video Nasty. This arose from a study undertaken by the grandly-titled Parliamentary Group Video Enquiry – a misleading title given that they lacked any official status – based on questionnaires sendt to schools. The resulting claims have been demolished by Barker, who discovered that this research was not only based on ill-gotten documentation (it was stolen in a break-in) but the eye-opening figure was arrived at by studying just 47 replies in which 3 children claimed to have seen a total of 17 films (see West's Video Nasties and Barker 1984). The whole sorry saga – a case of theft, lies and videotape – would be laughable if not for the fact that laws were drawn up and people fined and even jailed as a consequence of this kind of pseudoscience.

In 1983, the Conservative Graham Bright, who had seen the light on the Nasties courtesy of Mrs. Whitehouse, introduced a Private Member's Bill to the House of Commons aimed at curbing their malign influence. The Conservatives, the self-styled party of law and order who seemed to be losing the struggle against the forces of anarchy and permissiveness as riots raged and unemployment increased promised action if they were re-elected. They were and this led to the Video Recordings Act of 1984, which required every film released on video to be certificated by the BBFC, thus replacing the existing voluntary opt-in set-up and bringing statutory censorship to the UK. With Orwellian irony, 1984 was also the year that the BBFC changed its name, replacing Censors with Classification.

Interestingly, for such a very British witchhunt, only one of the Nasties was British, James Kenelm Clark's *Expose*. The vast majority of proscribed films were Italian or American, cannibal, zombie and slasher films but with the odd monster movie and psychological thriller thrown in. They represented a real mixed bag, the only thing uniting them being a lurid ad campaign, box cover or title. While some were very strong – and had either been refused a cinema certificate or almost certainly would've been if they'd been submitted – including *The Last House on the Left* and *Cannibal Holocaust*, others were just unlucky, such as the offbeat (and hardly nasty) *The Witch who Came from the Sea* (1979) and *The Slayer* (1982). Tobe Hooper's innocuous *The Funhouse* (1981), certificated AA on its cinema release seems to have ended up on the list by mistake because it shared a title with one of the many aliases of the notoriously grim *The Last House on Dead End Street* (1977).

There was certainly an issue with the tone of many of the films. Unlike the moral certainties provided by the horror of an earlier era, many of the Nasties were defiantly grim and nihilistic. A number of them, while being unquestionably violent are also struggling to say something. Both *The House at the Edge of the Park* (1981) and *(Don't Travel on) Late Night Trains* (1975) deal explicitly with social class and should be regarded as products of Italy's turbulent 'years of lead', *Fight For Your Life* (1977) deals with racism and the notorious *I Spit on Your Grave* (1978) offers up a kind of savage Old Testament Feminism along with the lengthy scenes of gang rape. They may be defiantly ugly – gory and gruelling but also obviously cheap, sometimes amateurish and frequently populated with deeply unappealing characters and hideous fashions – but it is a mistake to dismiss them out of hand. They may be squalid and objectionable, but then so are any number of critically lauded films such as *Bring Me the Head of Alfredo Garcia, Taxi Driver* (1976) and *Salo* (1975). In much the same way, the Nazisploitation films on the list such as *Last Orgy of the Third Reich* (1977) and *Love Camp 7* (1969) are undeniably tasteless, but surely no more tasteless than a vaguely controversial arthouse film such as *The Night Porter* (1974), just star-less, cheaper and tackier. Ian Conrich's comment about the lack of attention paid to the more excessive forms of British cinema can also be applied here. With a few exceptions (such as Stephen Thrower's fulsome celebration of *Don't Go in the House* [1980; see Thrower 2007] or Carol Clover's incisive analysis of *I Spit on Your Grave* [1992]), the majority of these films have received little critical attention outside of fan circles. In the late 1990s, I saw a 35mm print of one of the most notorious of the nasties,

Romano Scavolini's *Nightmares in a Damaged Brain* (1981) at (of all places) the Institute of Contemporary Art in London. Seeing the film not on grainy video cassette but as a handsome print was a strange experience. Under such conditions, the film could be seen for what it was – a not-wildly original but stylish enough bloody psycho thriller set in a convincingly seedy NYC. It emphasised just how the illicit nature of the pre-VRA Nasties was both part of the thrill – bad quality tapes hired from the backroom of a grocers and watched after school – and also one of the reasons behind the panic. Given a cinema release, it would've more than likely been just another generic slasher.

DON'T BELIEVE THE HYPE

The main thing however that doomed the Nasties was their eye-catching box-covers. Unable to rely on the usual audience hooks of star names and renowned directors, distributors fell over themselves to aggressively market their products as uniquely astonishing, graphic and…well, nasty. *SS Experiment Camp* (1976) was advertised with an image of a near-nude woman hanging from a large swastika and *Driller Killer* featured the titular power tool entering someone's head (the cover image was undoubtedly the most violent shot in the film, a downbeat tale of an artist coming undone in a scuzzy *Taxi Driver*-ish New York). *Snuff* (1976) attempted to reinforce its (clearly completely false to anybody who has seen it) claim to contain real murder footage with the censor-baiting tagline 'the film that could only be made in South America…where life is CHEAP!' The latter had form as far as controversy was concerned, with the distributor hiring protesters to draw attention to the film on its original New York run. The distributor of *Nightmares in a Damaged Brain*, David Hamilton Grant, a porn producer (*Snow White and the Seven Perverts* [1973]) came up with a novel gimmick to market *Nightmares in a Damaged Brain*, asking punters to guess the weight of 'a real damaged brain' floating in a tank.

This all meant that distributors who sought to market their product through notoriety ended up with more than they bargained for, often being hoisted by their own (hyperbolic, blood-spattered) petard. Grant was sentenced to 18 months in prison under the OPA (and later died in mysterious circumstances, possibly the victim of a contract killing after being accused by a tabloid newspaper of being a child pornographer and drug dealer). After all, many of those campaigning against these films hadn't actually taken the time to watch them – although the enterprising Whitehouse and her trusty sidekick Bright did arrange for a screening of 'highlights' at the House of Commons, the goriest scenes from a number of films screened completely out of context one after the other. When there was similar controversy over a series of films in the 1970s, many of the film-makers concerned – Peckinpah, Kubrick, Russell, Pasolini – had some high-profile defenders. But outside of genre fanzines, there were few willing to stand up and defend the likes of *Love Camp 7* or *Night of the Demon* (1980; no, not that one but rather a low-budget Bigfoot opus where a biker is castrated by the the beast as he pisses in the woods). Some of the directors whose work was banned have accrued considerable cult followings in the intervening years including Jess Franco, Paul Morrissey, Andy Milligan and Lucio Fulci while a couple – Abel Ferrara and Dario Argento – have attained a kind of semi-respectable auteur status. But many of their would-be defenders were too young and devoid of any real influence.

Taking potshots at the likes of Mary Whitehouse can be a bit like shooting fish in a barrel. So many of her comments seem like unintentional self-parody, her description of Richard Dimbleby's coverage of the liberation of Belsen as 'filth' and 'off-putting' (in Pearson 1994), her thoughts on children's entertainers – 'If only they could all be like that nice Mr. Savile' [Bourke 2012]) – and her bizarre belief that homosexuality was caused by parents having what she called 'abnormal' sex during pregnancy or just after (see Whitehouse 1977). But even so her blithely expressed concern in an interview for the documentary *Empire of the Censors* (1995) about 'a young man having a good watch of what he might call good violence and deciding to try it out' is telling. So much censorship is predicated on the fear of the Other, usually younger, maler and of a lower social status. Her words echo the concerns of the Victorian Prison Chaplain who suggested his charges were inflamed by lurid Penny Bloods.

The Video Nasties campaign was the moment when all the distaste for and loathing of horror bubbled up to the surface, newspapers awash with references to films 'raping minds', seducing the innocnent, drug terminology such as 'hooked' and 'fix' and the eternal, depressing correlation between sex and violence. Graham Bright summed up this vehemently-held belief in the almost occult power of horror when interviewed in 2010 for the documentary *Video Nasties*, stating that 'there was no need for them. They were unnecessary. They were evil'. James Ferman, who had been the secretary of the BBFC since 1975 – and had lobbied successfully to get the OPA to cover cinema films – appeared to relish his new role. Ferman was, in some ways an improvement on Trevelyan;he didn't even speak like a liberal. The new climate also encouraged Ferman to act on some of his more idiosyncratic ideas such as refusing to license *The Exorcist* for home video due to 'the potential use of the film in terrifying children as a part of satanic abuse' (in Barker 2002). He also went as far as to edit scenes in *Henry: Portrait of a Serial Killer* to alter their meaning entirely (see Kermode 2002).

In the years since, there have been sporadic outbreaks of tabloid-fuelled hysteria about video. While it's become harder for would-be moralists to condemn cinema releases (although that hasn't stopped campaigns against films including Cronenberg's *Crash* [2004] and Von Trier's *Antichrist*), there are still concerns about material viewed in the home. So after a gun rampage in the Berkshire village of Hungerford, the Rambo films were duly apportioned some of the blame, despite there being no evidence that the killer, Michael Ryan even owned a video recorder. Ferman didn't just raise the certificate to 18 for the cinema release of *Rambo III* (1988) – the two previous films had both been rated 15   he also made more than a minute's worth of cuts. In February 1994, the grainy video images of horror that inspired a revival of the Nasties panic were anything but fictional. As Richard Stanley put it:

> The ultimate British horror movie turned out to be a simple thing. Just one static wide-angle shot and one location – a shopping centre on the edge of Liverpool – and a cast of three, their backs turned towards the camera; two children leading a toddler by the hand, the crowd flowing by obliviously, unwitting extras in an unnoticed drama. (2002:190)

The horrific murder of two year-old James Bulger by two ten year-old boys caused horror, horror which gave way to a desire to explain the seemingly inexplicable (although by no means unique) case of children killing children. While some looked to the chaotic home lives of the young killers, others sought to pin the blame on that perennial folk devil, violent imagery. *Child's Play 3* (1991) was singled out, although there was no evidence that either child had seen it but the predictable and opportunistic tabloid hysteria generated by the crime led to a number of 'problematic' films being held back from home viewing (the list was a disparate one which included *Reservoir Dogs* [1992], *Beyond Bedlam* [1993] and – in a serious case of bad timing – *The Good Son* [1993], an update of *The Bad Seed* with Macaulay Culkin as a murderous moppet).

The fact that these campaigns about violent home entertainment have become less frequent in recent years is suggestive not of a liberalisation of attitudes but rather a displacement of fears from horror to internet porn. The targets may change but the moral panic, it seems, will always be with us. Martin Barker has observed, 'how little historical memory we have. The next time there's a panic we won't remember just how stupid the last one is' (in West, *Video Nasties*).

Aside from their folk devil status, the influence of the Nasties as films was limited, although there are a couple of exceptions. One of these is the defiantly sleazy slasher *Don't Open 'Til Christmas* (1984), which attempted to cash in on the notoriety of video horror. The story of a maniac running around London killing Santa Clauses, this was a troubled production. The star and credited director Edward Purdom was fired, as was his replacement, Derek Ford, who had co-written the script with Alan Birkinshaw, director of *Killer's Moon*. *Don't Open…* is notable for its oddball cast; Purdom was a one-time matinee idol (he played the lead in the Michael Curtiz epic *The Egyptian* [1954]) and Donald Wolfit-lookalike who ended up in a string of fantasy and horror pictures while Belinda Mayne was the daughter of Ferdy, who had played Count Krolock in *Dance of the Vampires*. Bug-eyed, big-haired Alan Lake was a familiar face from 1970s TV and British softcore films and this was his last film. In 1984, his wife Diana Dors died of cancer and Lake shot himself. (Another member of the cast, Gerry Sundquist also killed himself, jumping in front of a train in 1994.) Kevin Lloyd would become well-known through his role as 'Tosh' Lines in the popular cop show *The Bill* (1984–2010) but also achieved a degree of tabloid notoriety due to various alcohol-related incidents. One-time Hammer icon Caroline Munro has a brief cameo, singing an awful pop song which is interrupted by a dead Santa appearing on stage via a trap door. The gore level is fairly high, with Santas impaled, burned on chestnut braziers and in one hard-to-forget sequence, castrated in a public toilet with a straight razor but it's all too amateurish to be effective. The BBFC didn't think so though, cutting the film heavily prior to its release on home video. The main pleasure to be had is the awful dialogue. After 3 Santa have been gruesomely murdered, one cop asks 'Do you think we might be dealing with a psychopath?', following this up with 'the moment anyone puts on a Santa Claus costume, they become a sort of semi-holy figure'. This last line may be intended as irony, given that almost all of the Santas we see are drunks, lechers and weirdos. This would also prove to be Derek Ford's last screenwriting gig, although he would continue to direct films. He died of a heart attack in the Bromley branch of WH Smiths in 1995. Although he is best-known as a purveyor of sexploitation, Ford's lurid, exciting scripts for the likes of Robert Hartford-Davis and Jose Larraz make him a noteworthy figure in British horror.

1984 can only be seen as the Annus Horribilis of the British horror film, a year which may not quite have seen the predicted outbreak of Orwellian totalitarianism but did see the passing of the Video Recordings Act and a fat Santa emasculated at a urinal.

The 80s and early 90s were the dog days for British horror. Ian Conrich may disagree with Andrew Higson's observation that 'this was the end of the low-budget British horror film' (in Conrich 2009:102) but he goes on to acknowledge that 'many of these "Lost Continent" films are submerged at a depth at which critics have assumed nothing can exist' (ibid.). He does identify a group of very low-budget exploitation films, although most if not all of them are pretty terrible – *I Bought a Vampire Motorcycle* (1989) which features a talking turd, the necrophilia-themed *Living Doll* (1989), *The Revenge of Billy the Kid* (1992), about the mutant offspring of a goat-shagging farmer and *Rawhead Rex* (1986), a Clive Barker adaptation, the highlight of which is the titular beast pissing on a priest. After watching a couple of these pictures, it's hard to argue with Conrich's description of the 1980s as a 'dark decade' (2009).

There were high hopes for Nik Powell and Steve Woolley's Palace Productions, a company that Pirie has dubbed 'the nearest thing Britain ever had to a successor to Hammer' (2007: 205). Powell and Woolley certainly had impeccable cult credentials, having managed the Scala cinema in King's Cross before leaving to start Palace Video and releasing a series of cult items (films by Lynch and Herzog) along with *The Evil Dead*, just in time to attract the attention of the forces of law and order. They went into production with *The Company of Wolves* (1984), Neil Jordan's muddled but beautiful adult fairy tale based on stories by Angela Carter. The fact that Palace went on to specialise in glossy thrillers (such as *Scandal* [1989]) alongside their string of Neil Jordan films, making just a few arty horrors (such as the effective *Paperhouse* [1988]) is yet another sign that the genre had a great future behind it. Palace went bust in 1992 and Woolley went on to produce Jordan's adaptation of *Interview with a Vampire* (1994) a big-budget costume gothic, albeit with American money and stars, and a beautiful dud. Woolley and Jordan returned to the genre in 1997 with *The Butcher Boy*, a pleasingly weird low-budget Irish psychodrama which is the director's best film to date.

Ken Russell, the elderly enfant terrible of British cinema who had come down in the world after a string of characteristically dazzling flops contributed a couple of odd films. *Gothic* (1986) based on a script by Stephen Volk was a wild enough trip as it was, dealing with Lord Byron and the Shelleys' infamous high times in Switzerland, a period that would spawn, among other literary works, Frankenstein. Giving the project to Russell was like throwing petrol on the fire and the whole thing gets incoherent very quickly. Strangely, the director's follow-up film, *The Lair of the White Worm* (1988) although even more of a mess, seems to work better. Based on Bram Stoker's 1911 novel, it's the story of Lady Sylvia (Amanda Donohoe), a leather-clad vamp who is in reality an immortal priestess to a snake god which lives in the cellar of her country home. There are some terrible songs, amateurish gore and great dashes of semi-parodic Russellian excess (raped nuns, Donohoe biting a boy scout's dick and spitting venom over a crucifix) with a cast which includes a confused Hugh Grant (and who could blame him?). The film comes over as a kind of Carry On Hammer, a blackly comic tribute to a kind of cinema fast disappearing. Russell, undaunted carried on making films, some of which – *The Fall of the Louse of Usher* (2002), for example – he shot on video in his own garden. He died in 2011.

Although there were a handful of interesting films made in this period, the solid infrastructure provided by companies such as Hammer had been ripped away. This meant that the talent that did emerge, such as the novelist-turned-filmmaker Clive Barker and the South African Richard Stanley found it difficult to keep working. Barker's debut film was *Hellraiser* (1987), an S&M-tinged story about a murdered lover, a magic box and a bunch of leather-clad demons set in a rambling old house in Cricklewood. It's a wild and imaginative film, passionate, violent and energetic, although the special effects are slipshod. It also created a new genre icon in the form of lead Cenobite, Pinhead (Doug Bradley). But the fact that Barker's film was dubbed with native accents for its US release is surely significant, something that would've been unthinkable with Hammer's output. Pirie has lamented the lack of a viable post-Hammer horror franchise (see Pirie 2007) and *Hellraiser* certainly spawned one, alebit an American one - all of the *Hellraiser* sequels (eight to date) have been US productions and it's likely that the long-gestating remake will be too.

Barker went on to make two features in the US, the warped monster movie *Nightbreed* (1990) and the disappointing *Lord of Illusions* (1995), both of which suffered post-production tinkering. Not surprisingly, he went back to the (comparatively) saner world of publishing. Richard Stanley has had an even more frustrating time of it. He made the futuristic sci-fi horror *Hardware* (1990), an unsatisfactory film filled with odd and memorable images before going to Namibia to shoot the exciting Spaghetti Western-ish desert slasher *Dust Devil* (1992). An odd, intoxicating blend of genres with what may be the screen's greatest exploding head, the film was re-edited by Miramax and Stanley's hope of creating a European cut were dashed when Palace collapsed. Both of Stanley's features were produced by Jo-Anne Sellar, who had taken over the management of the Scala after Powell and Woolley left and she has gone on to produce a number of films for the gifted Paul Thomas Anderson.

Since then, Stanley has been fired from a long-cherished remake of *The Island of Dr. Moreau* (1996), written scripts for other directors and worked on a variety of documentaries and shorts, all the while trying to develop a number of intriguing projects including an old Donald Cammell script *Bones of the Earth*. Whatever problems a company like Hammer had with wayward visionaries, it's hard to imagine them letting the careers of Barker and Stanley fizzle out as spectacularly as they have done. Stanley has written an appropriately mournful essay about this period, 'Dying light: an obituary for the great British horror movie' (2002).

Perhaps the emblematic British horror movie of the second half of the 1980s is *Dream Demon* (1988). Produced for Palace, director Harvey Cokeliss assembled a heavyweight screenwriting team which included Wicking, Pirie and the talented American writer/director Aaron Lipstadt but after a lot of script drafts and a fair few funding problems, the end result is a murkily-shot muddled variant on *A Nightmare on Elm Street* (1984) with cameos from Jimmy Nail and Timothy Spall, best-known at the time for the TV comedy *Auf Wiedersehen, Pet*.

One sure sign of the poor state of the film industry during this period is the fact that the most notable genre offering was a prime-time BBC production, which has been described in a British Medical Journal article as 'the only TV programme to have caused Post-Traumatic Stress Disorder' (see O'Keeffe 2012). *Ghostwatch*, a mockumentary about a haunted house in the London suburbs was written by Stephen Volk and screened on Halloween night 1992. While the idea, clearly borrowed from Orson Welles and his *War of the Worlds* radio adaptation, to present the show in real time with a cast of well-known TV personalities including Michael Parkinson is extremely effective, the furore that followed has ensured that there have been no such Halloween TV treats since. The British horror film was effectively dead. But as any horror fan knows, things that are dead don't always stay that way...

The new millennium saw a notable resurgence in British horror. As well as openly referring back to this celebrated heritage of horror, it's noteworthy how many recent genre films have explored/exploited a number of social trends, in much the same way as Herman Cohen featured teen leads in the likes of *Horrors of the Black Museum* or the hippiesploitation which featured in many a 60s genre film.

DOG SOLDIERS (2002)

Neil Marshall's first feature is a real magpie of a film, borrowing heavily from a number of sources and referencing many more. The claustrophobic set-up comes from *Night of the Living Dead,* which itself was indebted to *The Birds*, while the relentlessness of the action evokes *Assault on Precinct 13* (1976), another Romero imitation. The look of the monsters owes much to *The Howling* (1981), there is a twist straight out of *Alien* and the whole war film/monster mash-up seems inspired by that film's sequel. Marshall also pinches ideas from *Southern Comfort*, a guess-the-monster plot thread from *The Thing* (1982) and explicitly acknowledges its debt to *Zulu*. There are also passing nods to *Straw Dogs* (the boiling pans of water), *Rear Window* (flash bulb employed as a weapon), *Wolfen* (the wolf-cam p-o-v), *Jaws* (a Quint-esque story about Kuwait), *The Searchers* (1956; a restaging of the iconic last shot) and even *Goldilocks and the Three Bears*. In addition, there is a Sergeant H.G. Wells (!) and even a *Zabriskie Point* (1969) joke in there (one of the film's best lines). But despite all the lifts from those disparate texts, *Dog Soldiers* works as a stripped-down monster movie, largely due to Marshall's efficient direction.

Spoon versus Werewolf: *Dog Soldiers*

Set in the Scottish Highlands (although shot in Luxembourg), this is the story of a platoon of soldiers playing war games who are set upon by a pack of werewolves. They encounter the sinister Captain Ryan, the sole survivor of a slaughtered Special Ops platoon and lose one of their number before being rescued by Megan, a young zoologist, who takes them to a deserted farmhouse. The wolves lay siege to the property, killing off the soldiers one by one until Megan is outed as a werewolf herself. As is standard in the war film, the soldiers (who are all out of necessity dressed the same) have to be clearly delineated. So Cooper is Scottish, Wells is a Londoner and there are a couple of Geordies, one of whom is obsessed with football. The character's repeatedly profane dialogue, while understandable given the situation along with the footballing references (the England v. Germany game the platoon are missing, Cooper quipping 'they think it's all over, it is now' before killing a monster) suggests the film's target audience may well be 'new lads', the offspring of a media-driven mid-90s backlash against the (fictional?) 'new man'. New laddism involved a celebration of traditionally masculine interests – football, photos of naked women in the pages of 'lads mags' like *Loaded* – with a veneer of irony, along with the fetishisation of certain aspects of 70s culture, that decade being seen as the last time men were men. In Marshall's film, Ryan's villainy is confirmed by his dismissal of football as 'crap' and the mention of *Zulu* serves more than a narrative function: it also invokes Michael Caine, rediscovered by the new lads and elevated into an icon, as evidenced by the awful remakes of some good films (*Alfie*, *The Italian Job*) and the Brit gangster stuff that offered increasingly paler imitations of *Get Carter*. *Dog Soldiers* is the most accomplished example from a group of films which set out to target this newly-defined audience seeking to reassert their unrepentant machismo. Jake West's *Doghouse* (2009) is unusual in that it appears to all intents and purposes to belong to this cycle, offering Danny Dyer and pals attempting to escape from a pack of female zombies who have been transformed by a toxic agent disguised as washing powder which only affects women! However, West set out to satirise lad culture (see Meadows 2009), a fact which missed a great many of the film's detractors.

The flip tone of *Dog Soldiers*, while often amusing does on occasion serve to dilute the horror, as in the moment where Cooper saves one of the platoon who is being strangled by cutting off the offending hand. 'Cheers, mate', his comrade replies, the severed hand still clutching his neck. The 'gross-out' scenes – a soldier being puked on, a dog gnawing on a wounded man's exposed intestine resulting in a grotesque tug-of-war – may also be a nod in a laddish direction, although the blend of blood, gore and black humour points to *The Evil Dead*, another low-budget cabin in the woods movie. This impression is further reinforced by a couple of other references to Raimi's film including the presence of a soldier called Bruce Campbell, named after the actor who played the sole survivor in the earlier film. Here, Campbell is not only the first to die but also impaled on a branch (the aforementioned malevolent trees being one of the many horrors in *The Evil Dead*). Marshall's film may be low-budget but he is able to afford some Hollywood-style destruction, blowing up a couple of cars, a barn and finally the cottage. There is also a considerable amount of grue, with a severed head tossed onto a car bonnet and the memorable image of a car door being opened allowing rivers of gore to flow forth. The best of these action scenes takes place after one of the platoon, Spoon is trapped in the kitchen with no ammo as one of the werewolves smashes down the door. The soldier spars with the creature, pelts it with crockery, pots and pans, batters it with a frying pan and subjects it to a very visceral stabbing, which leaves him splattered in its blood. Eventually disarmed, he is defiant to the end, shouting 'I hope I give you the shits, you fucking wimp' and spitting in the creature's face. The inscrutable pet dog who watches as the werewolves devour Spoon (off-screen) is another nice touch.

As is traditional in the siege sub-genre, frenetic action alternates with longueurs and the most effective scene is one of the quieter ones, as Megan's halting version of Debussey's Clair De Lune blends in with a chorus of howls.

The magpie tendencies at play in *Dog Soldiers* are almost a trademark of the new wave of British horror and this trend for substantial borrowing stands out, even in a genre which is traditionally so self-referential. *Creep* (2004) by Christopher Smith borrows the 'monsters on the underground' idea from *Death Line*, his spooky *Triangle* (2009) lifts its narrative structure from *Dead of Night* (a debt openly acknowledged by the director) and his ambitious *Black Death* (2010) owes something to *Witchfinder General* and the witch-cult cycle of the early 70s, while the Danny Boyle zombie romp *28 Days Later* (2002) is essentially a George Romero film set in London. However Edgar Wright's *Sean of the Dead* (2004) is, like *Dance of the Vampires* and *An American Werewolf in London*, a parody with a real feeling for the genre. Unlike the many witless horror spoofs that sprung up in its wake, *Sean* does more than recycle images from Romero films for laughs, although it's often very funny. It belongs to a very British tradition of 'cosy catastrophes' to use the term Brian Aldiss coined to describe the work of John Wyndham where characters sit out all manner of terrifying events in the pub (Fisher's *The Earth Dies Screaming* [1964] or *Quatermass and the Pit*) and offers a refreshingly unsentimental view of London as the capital of a certain shambling chaos, a place where it'd take a while to notice that the zombie apocalypse had actually begun.

Marshall's next film would be a huge leap forward. Set in the Appalachians (but filmed in Buckinghamshire), *The Descent* (2005) is the story of a bunch of female cavers who come face to face with a clan of carnivorous cave-dwelling creatures. Marshall again uses the *Dog Soldiers* idea of a single-sex group confronted by a band of monsters in an inhospitable world but here, the relationships in the group are brittle and easily broken. The terrifying claustrophobic world beneath the earth is depicted so well, it may well be the case, as David Pirie has suggested that the first half of the film before the monsters appear is even more exciting (see Pirie 2007). Again there are a lot of echoes, particularly of *Deliverance*, *The Thing* and a touch of *Apocalypse Now* (1980) but *The Descent* is gripping stuff, right down to that downer ending (an ending softened for its initial US release).

If the laddish protagonists of *Dog Soldiers* and the like were spawned by a passing fad inspired by the unholy trinity of Brit-pop, *Fantasy Football* and *Loaded* magazine, the hoodie-wearing ASBO monsters of *The Disappeared* (2008), *Summer Scars* (2007) and *Eden Lake* were of a much darker hue, the spawn of lurid tabloid news reports about anti-social, even murderous teenagers. The hoodie as a figure of fear wasn't only found in the horror film, with violent anti-social working class kids in sportswear turning up in thrillers such as *Harry Brown* (2009) and even the urban sci-fi film *Attack the Block* (2011). Not all of these so-called 'hoodie horrors' dealt with the mob terrorising innocents – although this was a recurring theme. Johnny Kevorkian's *The Disappeared* (2008) is an atmospheric ghost story set on a council estate with the pleasingly 1970s twist that the kids are the victims and the murderer is revealed to be a middle-aged priest.

EDEN LAKE (2008)

This is the directorial debut of screenwriter James Watkins, who was a writer on a couple of interesting British horror projects, Marc Evans' *My Little Eye* (2002), a creepy and cold generic spin on the then-voguish reality TV phenomenon and the outback horror

Gone (2007), which was overshadowed by the similarly-themed *Wolf Creek*. *Eden Lake* represents a recent – and one of the more troubling – manifestation of the generation gap theme which has so fascinated genre film-makers. It also updates the extremely influential *Deliverance/Straw Dogs* template primarily concerned with the clash between ostensibly civilised urbanites and rural savages, exploiting fears, not only of the malformed, brutal Other but also of our own capacity for destruction. And just like those films, which all came about during a time of escalating social division and civil strife, *Eden Lake* is the product of a deeply divided country, a film which undoubtedly works as a deeply disturbing, excessively intense horror film and yet for many, leave a sour aftertaste.

Steve (Michael Fassbender) and Jenny (Kelly Reilly) leave Islington for a weekend away in the Midlands, during which, unbeknownst to her, he plans to propose. Their destination is Slapton Quarry, an isolated beauty spot due to be developed into a gated community called Eden Lake. A row over loud music with a bunch of local kids escalates, with Steve's (borrowed) car being stolen. He retaliates by killing the dog which belongs to the gang's ringleader, the demonic Brett (Jack McConnell). Things rapidly get out of control, with Steve captured, tortured and eventually murdered by the gang and Jenny having to flee for her life. After narrowly escaping being burned alive, getting a nail through her foot and having to hide in a skip full of slurry, she fights back, stabbing one of the kids and running another down in a stolen car. In an extremely unpleasant ending, the wounded woman ends up taking refuge in a house which turns out to be Brett's family home.

Eden Lake fits comfortably into a number of cycles and sub-genres. It's in a tradition of hyperbolic, often hysterical films which warn of antisocial youth, especially when grouped into gangs. As well as a series of 1950s US 'social problem' films (*The Wild One* [1953], banned in the UK for 14 years and *The Blackboard Jungle* [1955]), there were a handful of British genre films which exploited similar fears: Oliver Reed played thuggish types in *The Damned* and *The Shuttered Room*. By 1971, *A Clockwork Orange* cast a typically inscrutable Kubrickian eye on the issue of youth violence and it's not such a leap to see O'Connell's vicious yet charismatic Brett as kin to Alex, charismatic, baby-faced and deeply nasty. The main difference between Kubrick and Watkins' films is the role played by the parents. While Alex's parents are well-meaning but completely ineffectual, the parents of Brett and his cohorts manage to outdo their offspring in brutality and callousness. *Eden Lake*'s depiction of the warring generations has something in common with earlier generation gap genre films but it's a world away from the anarchic, anti-establishment sleaze of Walker and Balch.

The film also portrays naïve city-dwellers out of their depth in a savage rural enclave. Indeed, their plan – to visit a spot of natural beauty before it's redeveloped in the spurious name of progress – seems to consciously reference *Deliverance*. Steve's comment to Jenny, that this is 'the last chance to see it before the developers build all over it', conveys the same sentiment expressed in the opening scene of John Boorman's film, as the protagonists head out to the valley which is about to be flooded by a dam:

'They're going to rape this whole landscape, they're going to rape it.' Urbanoia is the term coined by Carol Clover for this much-revisited sub-genre where terrible things befall those who are rash or stupid enough to leave the city behind and head out into the sticks, a journey which is 'very much like going from village to deep, dark forest in traditional fairy tales' (Clover 1992: 124). The fact that the film is actually shot in Black Park, which so often stood in for monster-inhabited European forests in numerous Hammer films is a nice touch. But there is little else nice about Watkins' film.

He certainly piles on the horror with some nasty knife wounds and very gruelling, prolonged cruelty. Steve is cut – with varying degrees of ferocity – by every member of the gang in turn, and Jenny is lashed to the same tree as her dead boyfriend and set alight, as Brett leaps up and down, gurning like an evil ape and yelling, 'Is it warm? Is it fucking warm?'

The horror genre has always been self-referential, while at the same time soaking up imagery and themes from a wide variety of sources; the postmodern hi-jinks of *Scream* (1996) led to a short-lived revival of the slasher movie which was followed by a rash of Japanese 'lank-haired ghost girl' remakes in the wake of *The Ring* [2002]). So it should come as no surprise that disparate factors such as the proliferation of PG-rated, kid-friendly scares of the likes of *Darkness Falls* (2003) and a sense of rising social anxiety (terrorism, war, global warming) have led film-makers to look to the 1970s for inspiration. Just as the auteur-friendly New Hollywood of the first half of that decade looks all the more like the last golden age, so the ferocious, nihilistic horror of Romero, Craven and Hooper still dwarfs most, if not all that came after. This twenty-first century 70s revival has led to a bewildering number of remakes, prequels and sequels to most of the best-known films from that decade and this process of reviving the dead is by no means over, despite a consistently lukewarm critical reception. At the time of writing, there are plans to revive such second string, albeit fondly remembered, titles such as *Children Shouldn't Play with Dead Things* (1972) and *The Town That Dreaded Sundown* (1976) while there are plans in the UK to produce contemporary versions of *The Asphyx* (with Danny Dyer!) and *Blood on Satan's Claw*.

But a number of films have tried to resurrect the stripped-down, low-fi brutality of 70s horror. In the US, there have been retro-gorefests from Eli Roth (*Hostel* [2005]) and Rob Zombie (*The Devil's Rejects* [2005]), as well as the fetishistic recreation of the 70s exploitation experience *Grindhouse* (2007) complete with scratches, missing reels and fake trailers. A similar kind of new brutality is particularly evident in a number of recent French films – *Haute Tension/Switchblade Romance* and *À l'intérieur/Inside* (2007). Watkins' film fits easily into this strand of retro horror and it's no surprise that the director has acknowledged a desire to look back to the likes of 'Wes Craven, *The Last House on the Left*, *Deliverance*, *Straw Dogs*, etc. The sense of queasiness and moral awkwardness you have with those films, where you're not sure what to think, what to feel or what is right' (in Risley 2009) and expressed his admiration for 'tough French horror' (ibid.). *Eden Lake's* opening, for example, the bleached-out flashes of barely-glimpsed suffering is reminiscent of the first images of Hooper's film and the scene where Steve is repeatedly, ritualistically stabbed and slashed has something of the cruel intensity of Craven's *Last House*.

It's impossible to talk about modern graphic horror without mention of that vaguely meaningless term 'torture porn', a phrase coined by David Edelstein in a 2006 *New York* magazine article discussing the likes of *Hostel* and *Wolf Creek*. While Edelstein's original bit is more searching than purely condemnatory (he is a self-confessed horror fan), the term has increasingly come to be used as a stick to beat 'any horror I don't like'. It certainly suggests a lack of generic knowledge. While Edelstein acknowledges the 'genre's inherent sadism' (2006), he underestimates the visceral savagery of early 70s horror (referring instead to the old seventies and eighties 'hack-em-ups' [2006]). But does anyone really regard *The Devil's Rejects* as more disturbing than the drawn-out sex killings of the luckless teenage victims of *The Last House on the Left* or that excruciatingly sadistic dinner sequence in *The Texas Chainsaw Massacre*, the repeated hammer blows, the screaming, the gibbering? The catch-all nature of the phrase also functions as a disturbing bit of misdirection. Edelstein does mention the fallout from 9/11, which has seen torture make a big comeback, whether in Abu Graib and Guantanomo or as practiced by the crypto-fascist CIA agent Jack Bauer in the popular 24 and its sequels. But he fails to acknowledge how his description of a scene in *Hostel* – 'the poor sap screams, weeps, pleads: He doesn't understand why he's in that place' (2006) – is precisely the situation that a great many people have found themselves in as a result of the War on Terror, whether it's 'poor saps' imprisoned indefinitely without trail in a Cuban prison camp, prisoners being piled up naked by American soldiers in an Iraqi jail or contractors in that same country being beheaded on camera. The very iconography of the 'torture porn' sub-genre – hoods, shackles and cells – is that of the military prison, 'rendition' and 'enhanced interrogation'. The whole issue is reminiscent of the gifted director Robert Aldrich's observation, 'I don't think violence in film breeds violence in life. Violence in life breeds violence in films' (undated).

Eden Lake's intensity is heightened by the nightmare logic of the whole thing. Jenny struggles to get away but her jacket gets snagged, she sets off a car alarm, her phone goes off and she is led into a trap by her very own gentle Judas, a bookish Asian kid who is corralled into the gang. She also gets her foot stuck on a spike and the scene where she tries to remove it, realises she can't so resorts to pushing it all the way through and out the other side is truly squirm-inducing.

Social class is an issue lurking beneath the surface of so much rural horror (perhaps most dramatically in the white collar city boys vs. toothless mountain men of *Deliverance*) but Watkins foregrounds this theme. *Eden Lake* explicitly references a number of social concerns which came to the fore during the premiership of Tony Blair (1997–2007). A perception that a significant minority of people were behaving 'anti-socially', if not actually criminally led to a series of initiatives, the introduction of the Anti-Social Behaviour Order

(ASBO) in 1998 which was followed by Parenting and Family Intervention Orders as part of what was dubbed the Respect agenda (2005). Not coincidentally, during the same period the terms Chav – an insulting term for young working class people – and hoodie – a hooded top which would, in theory, prevent the wearer being identified on CCTV – entered public discourse, e.g. website Chavtowns and David Cameron's much-derided 'Hug a Hoody' speech. There was also a proliferation of these heavily-tattooed, bejewelled frequently anti-social characters on TV, whether real (on the confrontational *Jeremy Kyle Show* [2005–present]) or fictional (Vicky Pollard on the sketch show *Little Britain* [2003-6]). As Jenny and Steve drive north, we even hear a snatch of a radio phone-in about the Respect agenda.

Jenny, being a middle-class North London kindergarten teacher, is stereotypically empathetic. When the couple make an evening stop at a pub, their reactions to some rowdy kids are telling.

Steve: (irritated) Isn't it past their bed time time?

Jenny: Yeah. Poor things.

Certainly, it's made clear that the real problem here isn't the sociopathic Brett (well, not just him) but his sullen, dead-eyed footsoldiers. They appear to have banded together, partly out of boredom and partly out of fear (fear of someone like their leader, perhaps). But they don't let their obvious discomfort with the situation stop them from stalking and slashing. Watkins doesn't shy away from provocative images which seem to be designed to provoke either a chill of recognition or a shudder of dismay, depending on your politics. The white van driven by Brett's dad, beer bottles floating in a half-full sink, the ants swarming over the picnic food, Brett's mocking greeting of Jenny with a perfectly-enunciated 'how now brown cow'.

The reponse to *Eden Lake* proved equally polarising. The reaction of Christoper Tookey in the *Daily Mail* is interesting, especially in the light of his frequent condemnations of screen violence (he was a key figure in the campaign against *Crash* and after seeing *Antichrist* suggested that Lars Von Trier 'almost certainly needs psychiatric help' [2009]). But he was fulsome in his praise for Watkins' film:

At last! Here's a first-rate British horror film that taps into our deepest fears and offers a thought-provoking insight into such topical subjects as knife crime and gang culture… Though nightmarish and visceral, it's the most intelligent horror film to have been made by a British director since Jack Clayton's *The Innocents* in 1960. And it fulfils the two purposes of horror: it involves you emotionally and it's frightening. (Tookey 2008)

Tellingly, he describes Jenny's dismayed reaction to the proposed gated community as demonstrating 'the blitheness of someone probably recruited for her job through the pages of *The Guardian*' before going on to suggest the couple meet their fate, in part through 'a tragically unrequited sense of kindness and social responsibility'. For Tookey,

Eden Lake is not simply exciting but it has an important social message, a film which is

willing to say what other films have been too scared or politically correct to mention: the true horrors we fear day to day are not supernatural bogeymen or monsters created by scientists. They're our own youth. This film will doubtless be accused of class hatred and demonising chavs, especially by those who accuse newspapers such as the *Daily Mail* of whipping up public concern over innocent victims of street gangs. (ibid.)

Tookey cites a couple of well-known knife murders – the killings of Phillip Lawrence and Steven Lawrence – and acknowledges the film's kinship with *Straw Dogs* before concluding that it is 'not only bleaker but also more truthful than virtually every other movie in this genre, which all too often is over-populated and under-humanised'.

Conversely, for Owen Jones, the author of *Chavs: The Demonization of the Working Class* (2012) Watkins' film was 'the most disturbing example of "chav-bashing" on our movie screens' (Jones 2012). He summarises the film, adding how Jenny and Steve 'find out the hard way why the middle-classes have every reason to fear the lower orders.' Jones is by no means alone, quoting a review from *The Sun* condemning the film's 'nasty suggestion that all working-class people are thugs' and the Telegraph's suggestion that 'this ugly witless film expresses fear and loathing of ordinary English people' (ibid.). Josh Saco has questioned 'whether *Eden Lake* is strictly a horror film, as it runs more like a nightmarish documentary' (2008).[11]

But while the film can certainly be read as offering a cautionary tale about life outside London, a grim, dystopian social commentary or a cruel attack on the vulnerable (the filmic equivalent of the so-called Bedroom Tax brought in by the coalition government in 2013) it is more nuanced than that. The director has acknowledged the influence of *Straw Dogs* (see Risley 2009) and Peckinpah's film has cast a long shadow over the British horror genre.

There is a strange ambiguity to *Straw Dogs*, an odd, uneasy chill which is often overlooked, given both the furore over the treatment of sexual violence (which boils down to 'is she or isn't she enjoying it?') and the director's defiant posturing. For one thing, although it's often described as a rape revenge film (Gaspar Noe has described his *Irreversible* [2002] as '*Straw Dogs* told backwards' [in Kermode 2004] while Mark Kermode in the documentary about the making of Peckinpah's film, *Man Trap: Straw Dogs Uncut* also uses the phrase), it's worth remembering that David Sumner (Dustin Hoffman) doesn't actually find out about the rape of his wife. Most intriguing of all is the way the characters, notably Sumner's seemingly-meek mathematician, play a role in escalating the events of the film. Rather than a put-upon victim, he is often crass (the painful bit where he blasts out bagpipe music for the local vicar) and finally murderous. Peckinpah clearly intended this, as Marshall Fine relates:

John Bryson after seeing the film, said to Peckinpah 'Where'd you get the heavies. They were incredible' referring to the beefy British actors. Peckinpah narrowed his eyes, gave

Bryson one of his reptilian smiles and said 'They weren't the heavies. The husband and wife were the heavies.' (qtd. in Fine 2005: 208)

While *Eden Lake*'s Jenny and Steve aren't by any measure heavies, he in particular has plenty of opportunities to stop the dreadful escalation of events but doesn't. As Peckinpah said of David Sumner, 'There are eighteen different places in that film, if you look at it, where he could have stopped the whole thing. He didn't' (in Weddle 1994: 399). *Straw Dogs* actor Michael Mundell has noted how Sumner 'takes on the values of the villagers' (in the documentary *Man Trap*) and there is a similar sense of doubling going on between Steve and Brett. In a ghastly kind of social aspiration, Brett tries to become the older man, wearing his sunglasses, driving his car, ogling his girlfriend. And this process works in reverse, as Steve goes from this geeky metrosexual (wearing some ridiculous cut-off trousers, admiring the Kylie-voiced sat nav) to a foul-mouthed, knife wielding dog killer. But while there is a vague sense of triumph for David Sumner as he surveys the bodies of his victims ('I got 'em all!') there is nothing like victory for Steve, as he tries to apologise for knifing Brett's dog or Jenny, who reacts to one of the kids (the sad-faced Thomas Turgoose) attempting to make amends by sticking him in the neck with a shard of glass.

Peckinpah's film also seems to have been one of the inspirations for Shane Meadow's *Dead Man's Shoes* (2004), another recent rural nightmare with Paddy Considine (who wrote the script with the director) as an ex-soldier seeking revenge on the druggy layabouts who caused his brother's suicide. As well as a startling twist (which was recently reused in the 6th season of the TV show *Dexter*), Meadows' film is notable for the very generic, very British juxtaposition of extreme brutality (one dismembered victim is packed neatly in a suitcase) with a picturesque rural landscape (the Peak District). Considine would go on to star in a much less interesting Peckinpah rip-off, the Spanish *Bosque de Sombras/Backwoods* (2006) which simply imitates aspects of *Straw Dogs* – costume, the basic outline – rather than reworking them, as both Watkins and Meadows manage to do.

The enigmatic and unusual title of Peckinpah's film has its origins in a passage from a book by the Chinese philosopher Lao Tzu:

Heaven and earth are ruthless and treat the myriad of creatures as straw dogs, the sage is ruthless and treats the people as straw dogs. (in Weddle 1994: 402)

This notion of people as being at the mercy of forces beyond their control is reinforced stylistically with the high-angles looking down, the slow dissolves, which serve to render individuals tiny, blurry, indistinct and Watkins borrows this idea with a series of helicopter shots which reduce his characters to the size of insects running around in a beautiful yet hostile space.

Eden Lake's final point, that savages breed savages would also have been familiar to Peckinpah. *Straw Dogs* opens with the sound of children playing and the narrative was supposed to be circular, with the offspring of the violent rural folk turning up to finish what their elders began. Not unusually for Peckinpah (who made a habit of winging it as the mood – or the booze – took him), the chaotic circumstances of shooting and his mercurial personality led to an altogether more ambiguous, if no less powerful ending. But *Eden Lake* appears to give new life to his original concept when Jenny crashes her car and staggers into a party where beefy couples cavort in a hot tub to the sound of 80s pop duo Mel 'n' Kim singing 'Respectable', a choice of song – with its chorus of 'we ain't never gonna be respectable' – which ladles on the irony pretty thick. The partygoers are attentive and supportive until they discover the identity of this uninvited guest. Any relief on the part of the viewer is short-lived. It is clear that it's that kind of film and these are those kind of people. As one of the women says as she tries to reassure Jenny, 'you're safe now, lots of big ugly men around', big ugly men who, make no mistake, are also monsters. And Jenny's heroic stint as the generic Final Girl comes to a peculiarly nasty end as she is bundled into the bathroom, the door slamming shut in a grim Walkeresque finale.

Some of the most disturbing scenes in the film are in the beginning, the little signs that something is rotten in these beer gardens and housing estates, the parking space stolen by a boorish fat bloke, the ignorant shaven-headed barman, the foul-mouthed mother who whacks her son in the face, the angry shouts of 'You want beef?' that can be heard at chucking out time or the holes punched in the walls of the house Steve wanders into. *Eden Lake* conflates a number of thematic strands in British horror, from the fear of the young to urbanoia. In its intensity, as well as its brand of social realist gothic, it would make a good – if gruelling – double bill with *Mum and Dad* (2008), a grim low-budget ordeal from first-time director Steven Sheil. It's the story of Lena, a Polish cleaner working nights at Heathrow Airport who is 'adopted' into a bizarre family of thieving, torturing sociopaths who live beneath the flight path. Mum (Dido Miles) likes torture, Dad (Perry Benson) is a cross-dressing sexual deviant and there are a couple of warped 'kids', one of whom lies in the attic, brain damaged, drooling and twitching. In interviews for the DVD extras, Sheil is open about his debt to both the ur-text of bad family sagas, *The Texas Chainsaw Massacre* and 70s British films like *Frightmare* and *Mumsy, Sonny, Nanny and Girly*. Indeed, the film feels like an even nastier update of the Walker template, with hideous characters doing foul things in cramped spaces, the domestic environment turned nightmarish torture chamber, all ripped wallpaper and bloody pillows. There is a touch of Mike Leigh or the TV show *The Royle Family* (1988–2012) in the arguments over breakfast and a squirm-inducing tipsy Xmas dinner but the film is clearly inspired by the case of the Gloucester duo, Fred and Rose West. The Wests were a seemingly normal couple who between 1967 and 1987 abducted women and girls to rape, torture and kill while subjecting their many children to years of sexual and physical abuse, even going so far as to kill one daughter and bury her in the back garden. As well as understandable revulsion, the case was also shocking in the way it revealed that predators could operate undetected, with many of their victims, young transients from bedsit land not even being reported missing. Just as in the West case, *Mum and Dad* features a prolonged, sexualised nightmare going on not in a gothic manor but a nondescript house on a street like any other. There are some nice touches – the constant roar of the planes taking off, the ghastly country and western version of 'God Rest Ye Merry Gentlemen' that plays during the climactic massacre – and some really very nasty images – such as Dad having sex with an unspecified organ, then placing it on the side where it sits next to a cracked cup emblazoned with 'Dad's Mug'.

Indeed, both films feel like a new spin on the hoary old 'wild family' cycle – or as Sheil calls in in one of the DVD interviews 'the fucked-up-family film' – which goes back at least as far as the Sawney Beane legend (explicitly referenced in *Mum and Dad*, the family rifling through stolen suitcases just as the Beanes recycled the clothing and possessions of the travellers they waylaid). Except that these murderous monsters are found not in a Highland wilderness, a foggy island or Appalachian cave. They're even closer than the mutant cannibals of *Death Line*. They're actually walking amongst us, on housing estates, sleepy streets, working nights in airports and watching porn at the breakfast table, slapping their kids in the face and setting fire to bookish boys, abducting East European cleaners and shackling them to the bed in the spare room. They're riding mountain bikes around quiet country lanes and beheading workmates. Like the luckless protagonists in *House of Whipcord* or *Frightmare*, Jenny, Steve and Lena only have to travel a little way out of London to encounter these monsters. The fact that they are not antiquated relics of Olde England, be it troglodytes or fascist Judges but the lower orders, bloodthirsty, rapacious and savage suggests that class rather than the generation gap, is now the wellspring of anxiety.

FROM *DOWN TERRACE* (2009) TO *HIGH-RISE* (2015)

Perhaps the most acclaimed of the 'magpie directors' is Ben Wheatley who has made his name with a string of low-budget, often blackly funny genre films which rework, mix and match a number of existing elements, twists and stylistic tics. His work is referential, elliptical and for many, infuriating but his four features to date suggest a singular talent.

Wheatley started off making viral videos before working on a number of TV comedy shows such as *Modern Toss* (2005–8) and *Time Trumpet* (2006). His first feature was the low-budget gangster film *Down Terrace* (2009). It's a striking debut, shot in eight days, part blood-soaked crime movie, part black comic family drama. The visual style is more the aforementioned *The Royle Family* than *The Long Good Friday* (1980), the performances are excellent and the whole thing can be seen as a mocking riposte to the twin traditions of British gangster film and miserabilist social realism. The moment when a friendly fellow chats to an old woman at a bus stop before pushing her in front of a car is the first example of what has become a Wheatley trademark, a shock moment which is as absurd as it is horrifying.

He followed this with the witchy hitman tale, *Kill List*, discussed below, which garnered an enormous amount of critical attention. His next film was *Sightseers* (2012), a kind of psychotic take on Mike Leigh's TV play *Nuts in May* (1976), as a misfit couple (Alice Lowe and Steve Oram) travel the backroads of rural England, taking in sights such as the National Tramway Museum and Keswick Pencil Museum and murdering anyone who annoys them (litterbugs, *Daily Mail* readers).

Wheatley's comedic roots are evident in all of his films, not least in the fact that they're often very funny. He is also fond of casting actors best-known for their work in TV comedies – Julian Barratt from *The Mighty Boosh*, *The League of Gentlemen*'s Reece Shearsmith and Irish actor Michael Smiley who graduated from *Spaced* to become a charismatic fixture of Wheatley's films. *Sightseers'* grim, vaguely depressing settings (what Peter Bradshaw calls 'an exquisitely horrible Readers Wives aesthetic' [2012]) and the cruel humour is reminiscent of some of the bleaker TV comedy offerings of recent years such as *Human Remains* and *Psychoville*. The screenplay, co-written by Lowe, Oram and Amy Jump (the director's wife who has worked on all of his films as a writer and/or editor since *Kill List*) owes something to *Withnail and I* as well as the Folk Horror tradition. A term which is frequently bandied about these days, Folk Horror is a loosely-defined horror sub-genre which often has a pronounced British flavour. The 'canonical' Folk Horror texts – *Witchfinder General*, *Blood on Satan's Claw*, *The Wicker Man* – and practitioners – Arthur Machen, MR James, Nigel Kneale – are all British, although the term is malleable enough to include the likes of *The Blair Witch Project* (1999), US Southern Gothic literature and the surreal Czechoslovakian film, *Valerie and her Week of Wonders* (1970).

This folk horror influence is even stronger in Wheatley's next film, *A Field in England* (2013). Described by the director as 'like a 60s Corman trip film which actually turned out quite like a cowboy film' (Robinson 2012) it also owes a considerable debt to *Witchfinder General*, being an English Civil War genre film with a pronounced emphasis on the rural landscape. There are also nods to off-beat British period pieces as *Winstanley* (1976) and *Culloden* (1964) as well as hints of Jodorowsky, Beckett and Richard Lester's *The Bed-Sitting Room* (1969), another apocalyptic English oddity. It's the story of a motley band of deserters searching for an alehouse who fall under the spell of a mysterious stranger (Smiley) who encourages them to search for the treasure he claims is hidden in the titular location. Filmed in stark black and white, the film has an oppressive, ominous feel to it, a feeling starkly underlined by the unsettling mix of rumbles, drones and crashes which make up Jim Williams' score. Things only get freakier when the characters consume psychedelic mushrooms, leading to a prolonged trip sequence complete with flash-cuts, mirroring and extreme close-ups. Some of the imagery is haunting – the sun going black, the jarring *tableaux vivants* and one character's terrifying slow motion meltdown – and the mood is convincingly apocalyptic (as one character notes, 'I think I have worked out what God is punishing us for. Everything'). The film doesn't entirely work – it feels overlong even at 91 minutes – and it's a defiantly sketchy and elliptical piece of work which comes across as eerily dream-like or maddeningly half-formed, depending on how you look at it. Truth be told, it's a blend of both, although it's undeniably original. The difficulty in selling such an off-beat project may have been one of the reasons for its innovative multi-platform release (it was simultaneously available theatrically, on DVD, TV and VOD). Martin Scorsese is a fan and his description of the film as 'audacious and wildly brilliant – a stunning cinematic experience' is unsurprisingly used in the trailer.

At the time of writing, Wheatley is about to release *High-Rise*, an adaptation of the JG Ballard novel which producer Jeremy Thomas has been trying to get off the ground for more than three decades (Bruce Robinson wrote a version of the screenplay as far back as 1979, and directors such as Nic Roeg, Richard Stanley and Vincenzo Natali have all been attached). Ballard's apocalyptic sci-fi may appear to be a (relatively) straightforward proposition for Wheatley, especially when compared to the social realist hit-man occult gothic of *Kill List* or the psychedelic Civil War psychological horror of *A Field in England* and he may struggle to escape the spectre of David Cronenberg's very similar *Shivers* (1975), another nightmare fantasy set in a tower block. According to the director, *High-Rise* will be 'not as dark as *Kill List*' (Singer 2013), which brings us to Wheatley's grimmest – and arguably best – film to date.

KILL LIST (2011)

Torchlight cult activity from the end of *Kill List*

To read some of the negative reviews and the more unfavourable bits of on-line debate, one could end up approaching *Kill List* as a kind of joyless English take on *From Dusk Till Dawn* (1996), a crime film which switches genre mid-way into lurid horror territory.

Certainly, the tonal shifts of the film seem to have taken many by surprise but they are there from the outset. The first thing we see is an occult symbol being scratched onto the screen while the soundtrack rumbles and drones with a smattering of Black Sabbath-ish clanking bells and eerie whistles. From this vaguely hokey gothic horror opening, we plunge into what appears to be another film entirely, with a couple, Jay (Neil Maskell) and Shel (MyAnna Buring) having a row – there's no money, he hasn't worked in a while, he forgot to buy toilet rolls. As in *Down Terrace* and the later *Sightseers*, Wheatley blends *Grand Guignol* with the conventions of social realism and this has the effect of grounding the excess in a recognisable everyday setting.

While the changes in his debut film, from mundane slice of working class life to a series of increasingly bloody murders, come as a shock, the full-blown gothic excesses of the latter half of *Kill List* are prefigured in a number of ways, some of them seemingly inconsequential (a slow motion sword fight between Jay, Shel and their young son Sam, Jay trying to understand Shel speaking Swedish on the phone), others more overt. The creepiest scene occurs during a dinner party, when Jay's pal Gal (Smiley again) brings a spookily sexy date, Fiona (Emma Fryer), accurately described by Jay as 'a glarey-eyed phantom'. We see her in the bathroom matter of factly taking the mirror off the wall and carving the same symbol we saw earlier into the back then stealing a wad of toilet paper with Jay's blood on it, the result of an earlier shaving cut. Jay — violent, impulsive and pill-popping and Gal — genial and deceptively gentle — are ex-soldiers turned hit-men with a very murky past - there are numerous references to a disastrous mission in Kiev. Over dinner, Jay offers a wine-fuelled — and judging by the reaction, all-too-familiar — speech about how he wished he'd fought the Nazis, longing for a world of black and white moral certainties. But the references to Northern Ireland, the Middle East and the aforementioned Ukraine suggest a much murkier, morally compromised world. Similarly Fiona is in 'human resources', described by Gal as a 'hatchetman' and she talks about seeing 'the bigger picture' and explaining how 'a lot of dirty work needs to be done'.

Jay and Gal agree to do another job for a mysterious Client who insists on marking the contract in blood (and after this scene, can there really be anyone in the audience who doesn't realise this is not your standard *Get Carter*-style gangland outing?). They set out to kill three men — The Priest, The Librarian and The MP as they are identified in stark white capitals on a black screen. But after finding extreme pornography — which remains unseen by the viewer although Jay's reaction to it, tears followed by homicidal rage suggests it involves children, violence or a combination of both — they go off-mssion. Jay tortures the librarian with fists, lit cigarettes and a hammer to find out who filmed the footage before beating him to death (very graphically) before going to the address he's been given and killing the occupants (including the dog).

The vaguely creepy imagery of the first part of the film — a black cat eating the leftovers at the dinner party, a ripped-up rabbit on the family lawn — is replaced by outright weirdness — the priest and the librarian thank Jay for killing them, witchy Fiona turns up outside his hotel and he has a spooky encounter with a sinister GP. The ending, when the men venture out into the country to kill a politician and stumble on what appears to be cult activity — straw masks, nudity, flaming torches and a hanging — shifts the film into more familiar (and therefore less unnerving) territory but it still carries a considerable charge. The men are pursued by the naked and masked cultists through a network of tunnels and Gal is disembowelled. In a nice bit of ambiguity, he thanks Jay for killing him moments before he is shot. In the final scene, Jay is encouraged by the masked cultists to fight someone identified as The Hunchback, a masked figure with a knife. After stabbing his opponent multiple times, Jay discovers he's been fighting Shel — who is severely wounded and appears to be laughing – and Sam, who is dead. The cultists remove their masks and it comes as little surprise to see Fiona, the Client, the GP. They crown the dazed Jay with a straw crown and the film ends. The ambiguity of this scene has provoked debate, perhaps predictably on IMDb (for commenter Suso-Pedrosa it's an 'engaging movie…until it treats you like a moron'). Similarly, some critics were not convinced, with Joe Neumaier of the *New York Daily News* suggesting that:

> It would be easy to say that the final minutes of this mixed-up thriller make everything before it meaningless but that would indicate the odd conclusion has meaning too. (2012)

A number of commentators have also noted the similarities between the ending of Wheatley's film and the notorious political allegory/exploitative shockfest (delete as applicable) *A Serbian Film* (2010), while there are numerous attempts to explain the climax on the net (some of which have been favourably noted by the director on his Twitter feed).

Wheatley may have unwittingly encouraged speculation he was making it up as he went along when he admitted to being a

> Believer in the Kubrick thing about the non-submersible unit, where you look for the main images for the movie before writing the script and work backwards from that. I think that you then guarantee that your film has moments in it instead of just plot. (Smith 2012)

Certainly, there are plenty of things thrown into the mix, some of which seem to be there largely to muddy the waters (the repeated refrain of 'Wake up', which suggests the whole thing is Jay's dream) or simply because they're effective (Fiona appearing at the hotel). But the ending clearly isn't plucked out of nowhere as a kind of last minute nod to *The Wicker Man* (an influence most critics picked up on). As with the shifts from crime to horror, the ending is telegraphed in a number of ways. There are numerous references to faith and specifically Christianity (including the film's funniest exchange when a happy clapper in a restaurant tells an angry Jay that 'God's love can be hard to swallow' and gets the reply, 'Not as hard as a dinner plate'), with all its associations of sacrifice. There are also repeated references to Arthurian legends – Jay's son wants a bedtime story about knights but instead gets one about the Middle East, the unfortunate cat is called Arthur and Jay suggests calling a dog Gwynny, which bring to mind the story of the Fisher King (and some of the more fanciful on-line 'explanations' posit that Gal might be short for Galahad).

The climactic knife fight isn't even just hinted at in the way that other events in the film are (for example, the cult's hanging of a woman echoing the killing of the cat). It's explicitly foreshadowed in the swordfight in the garden, where Jay fights Shel who carries Sam on her back. Jay wins and Shel lies on the ground, dying a dramatic death. It's also suggested that the disastrous Kiev outing resulted in the death of a child, as the Catholic

Gal rationalises killing a priest with 'At least it's not a toddler'. The comparisons to *The Wicker Man* are understandable, both films dealing with characters who are unwittingly manipulated from the outset by sinister forces but while Robin Hardy's film starts out as a seemingly innocent folky fantasy, Wheatley's film is pretty dark throughout. It just gets darker.

Kill List is an eerie and unsettling experience with an atmosphere of dread throughout. The performances are excellent and the improvised dialogue and scenes of domestic disharmony owe more to Ken Loach and Cassavetes than they do to the twin genres of the crime and the horror film. It's also rooted in a very recognisable twenty-first-century Britain – recession, money worries, foreign policy disasters. Oddly enough, this paranoid tale of diabolical cults has become even more topical in the years since, what with newspaper stories of paedophile rings involving the great and the (not so) good, the outing of celebrities as sex offenders and a revival of the 'Satanic Panic' of the 1980s (and all three stories were combined in a Daily Express story which alleged 'Jimmy Savile was part of satanic ring' [Fielding 2013]). Truth may not be stranger than fiction but it is often nastier…

CONCLUSION

The majority of the Nasties may be available on DVD, uncut, remastered and lovingly packaged. A couple of them – *Last House on the Left* and *I Spit on Your Grave* – have been glossily remade while others, such as *The Funhouse* and *Don't Go in the Woods Alone*, now sport 15 certificates. But as noted earlier, in much the same way as cinema releases were allowed more leeway as video became the new bête noire, so horror films have been deposed as folk devil and internet porn taken its place. It's instructive to see the campaign against unregulated web content gathering momentum, especially in the wake of a terrible crime such as the murder of Jane Longhurst by Graham Coutts, a regular visitor to violent porn sites. In August 2006, the Labour government announced plans to bring in a bill outlawing what they termed 'Extreme Pornography' on the net. Although this wouldn't apply to films with a BBFC certificate, possession of screen shots from certificated films – *Frenzy* or *The Fiend,* for example - may be an offence (see the proposed Criminal Justice and Immigration Act 2008 and the campaign against the bill led by the pressure group Backlash).

Similarly, concerns about sexualisation often apportion some blame to the web. Dr. Helen Wright of the Girls School Association declared in a November 2011 speech about the 'moral abyss' girls were growing up in (in Richardson 2011). In January 2013, the Labour MP Diane Abbott warned against the 'pornification of society' and the risk this posed to children (in Mason 2013). After a long period of post-Ferman liberalisation, the BBFC made cuts to the remake of *I Spit on Your Grave* (2010) and heavily cut *A Serbian Film*. It also refused a certificate to *The Human Centipede 2* (2011) on the grounds that it may fall foul of the OPA (see BBFC 2011). In December 2012, they announced that they plan to adjust their policy on 'sexual and sadistic violence' due to particular concerns about the effect on who else but 'young men' (BBFC 2012). Worryingly, this research appears to have been conducted after showing a total of 35 people in 3 cities a series of clips (including some from *Eden Lake*) from a number of films (significantly without contextualisation) and asking for their responses (see Flint 2012).

Elsewhere, there has been a revival of the Victorian crime genre. *Whitechapel* (2009–13) is a crime show with a contemporary setting where mismatched cops – and a geeky crime buff, played somewhat significantly by Steve Pemberton of the ghoulish comedy troupe *The League of Gentlemen* – try to solve new versions of old crimes, including the Ripper murders, the mob killings of the Kray Twins and the Ratcliffe Highway Murders. *Ripper Street* (2012–) is essentially 'CSI Victorian Whitechapel', a police procedural with an emphasis on forensics taking place in a lovingly-recreated late eighteenth-century London (actually Dublin).

It's almost certainly true that, as Chibnall and Petley suggest, 'the genre in Britain may never again benefit from another Hammer studio (or even another Amicus)' (2002: 8) but there are still remnants of this heritage of horror. The corpse is still twitching.

In the beautiful Hollywood mess of *The Wolf Man* (2010) and the English Civil War monochrome freakout, *A Field in England*. In the serial killer TV drama *The Fall* ('the most repulsive drama ever broadcast on British TV' [Stevens 2013]). In the glossy blood-boltered Victoriana of US shows *Dracula* (2013–14) and *Penny Dreadful* (2014–). In the creaky gothic of the Harry Potter films, the proliferation of Z grade, digitally-shot zombie films and the on-line campaigns to Save Bray Studios or Bring Classic Horror Back to TV. True, the days when every schoolboy had a copy of Gifford's *A Pictorial History of Horror Movies* and every newsagent stocked *House of Hammer* and a couple of shelves of luridly-boxed gorefests are long gone. But horror has simply stole away back into those dark places, where it belongs, lurking, ready to spring out when you're not expecting it. To paraphrase *Crimewatch*, the TV equivalent of the Newgate Calendar, providing a social service while also offering the vicarious thrills of violence and murder, *do* have nightmares, *don't* sleep well…

FOOTNOTES

1. Nilsen makes it into the Chamber of Horrors, although the Yorkshire Ripper and Moors Murderers don't. It's depressing to think this may be because Nilsen's victims, most of whom were transients, homeless or drug addicted are marginalised even in death.

2. Chapman uses the term shocker for a wide range of thrillers but I've used it exclusively for thrillers with morbid or horrific content.

3. All of original cast of the bucolic sit-com *Last of the Summer Wine* appeared in British horror films. Wilde in *Night of the Demon*, Peter Sallis in *Taste the Blood of Dracula* and Bill Owen in Pete Walker's *The Comeback*.

4. See Pirie (2007) for more on the split with Warner Bros., especially Hammer's shock when they read the small print on the contract they had signed.

5. Hodel would go on to make a much less convincing case for his father also being The Zodiac.

6. This apocalyptic view of the 1970s deserves some qualification. As Alex Cox has written of the early the decade:
   > I was a teenager then, and can assure the promoters of this depressing vision that, despite strikes and IRA atrocities, Albion was a long way from skid row. When I went to college, the government paid for it. I incurred no debt. The state owned the water pipes, the reservoirs, the airline, the lecky, the telephone system and the railways, which ran on time and were reasonably cheap. We weren't engaged in two wars of colonial aggression. Muslims weren't our enemies. And the weather was great! (Cox 2007)

7. Michael Feast used to share a house with the future writer/director Bruce Robinson and his hippy dealer in *I Start Counting* has an uncanny resemblance to Danny the Dealer in Robinson's *Withnail and I* (1987).

8. Hitchcock didn't forgive the snub. During the making of his last film, *Family Plot* (1976), star Bruce Dern suggested a garage door would look better covered in graffiti but he didn't know what it could say. Hitchcock suggested 'Fuck MCA'(see Jeffries 1999).

9. Hunt goes on to describe the Moors Murders as 'a central British horror mythology, a story to be told again and again' while also suggesting that 'the cinema won't touch it with a bargepole' (ibid.). In fact, there have been a couple of proposed Moors Murderers films, notably *Murder on the Moors*, a William Friedkin project from the late 60s. In the 1990s, the *News of the World* reported that Gary Oldman and Meryl Streep would be playing Brady and Hindley – but this seems to have been tabloid hysteria. There have been a couple of TV movies which feature the crimes: *See No Evil: The Moors Murders* (2006) with Sean Harris as Brady and Maxine Peake as Hindley, while Andy Serkis and Samantha Morton took on the roles for the mini-series *Longford* (2005). There are also thinly-disguised echoes of the case in a number of films: as well as the aforementioned *The Fiend* and *Straight on Till Morning*, the crime biopic *McVicar* (1980) features a child killer called Cody (who inspires the memorable chant 'sex case, sex case, hang him, hang him, hang him'), clearly a Brady surrogate. At the time of writing, another TV film about the murders is in production.

10. An enormous wealth of newspaper articles related to the Video Nasties phenomenon can be found at the Book of the Dead site (http://www.bookofthedead.ws/website/features_video_nasties.html)

11. A couple of recent productions can be seen as offering a riposte to the 'monstrous chav' narrative. The video for Money and Run by UNKLE featuring Nick Cave depicts some truly repulsive braying toffs who terrorise some hoodie-wearing kids while Kim Newman has described the film *Riot Club* – about Oxford's silly, vaguely sinister Bullingdon Club – as '*Eden Lake* for socialists' (Newman 2014).

BIBLIOGRAPHY

Aldrich, R. (undated) 'They Shoot Pictures, Don´t They? http://www.theyshootpictures.com/aldrichrobert.htm

Anon a (undated) *The Newgate Calendar* Part 1. Sawney Beane. http://www.mysteriousbritain.co.uk/scotland/dumfriesshire/legends/the-newgate-calendar-part-1-sawney-bean.html

Anon b (undated) *The Newgate Calendar*. William York. http://www.exclassics.com/newgate/ng221.htm

Anon c (1971/2) 'How do you like your screen lovelies, a-lively or dead?' in Cinema X 4:11.

Bakhtin, M. (1965) *Rabelais and his World*. London: John Wiley and Sons.

Barker, D. (2002) James Ferman Obituary, in The Guardian. http://www.guardian.co.uk/news/2002/dec/27/guardianobituaries.filmcensorship

Barker, M. (1984) *The Video Nasties: Freedom and Censorship in the Media*. London: Pluto.

Barr, C. (1972) 'Straw Dogs, A Clockwork Orange and the Critics', in Screen. Summer 17-31.

--- (1997) *Ealing Studios*. University of California Press.

BBFC (2012) Annual Report. http://www.bbfc.co.uk/about-bbfc/media-centre/bbfc-annual-report-2012

Benshoff, H. (1997) *Monsters in the Closet: Homosexuality and the Horror Film*. Manchester and New York: Manchester University Press.

Biodrowski, S. (2007) *Masque of the Red Death*, a retrospective on Cinefantastique Online. http://www.hollywoodgothique.com/masqueofreddeath1964.html

Boot, A. (1999) *Fragments of Fear*. London and San Francisco: Creation Books.

Bourke, F. (2012) '"If only they were all like that nice Mr. Savile"- Mary Whitehouse on disgraced paedophile', in Birmingham Mail. http://www.birminghammail.co.uk/news/local-news/mary-whitehouse-gives-her-verdict-on-jimmy-333674

Bygraves, J. (2012) *Haunted Mirrors: The Dark Side of Robert Hamer*. http://serenevelocity.com/2012/10/26/haunted-mirrors-the-dark-side-of-robert-hamer/

Caputi, J. (1988) *The Age of Sex Crime*. London: The Women´s Press.

Cawelti, J.G. (2003) 'Chinatown and Generic Transformations in Recent American Films', in *Mystery, Violence and Popular Culture*. New York: Popular Press.

Chapman, J. (2001) ´Celluloid Shockers`, in Richards, J. (ed.) *The Unknown 1930s*. London: Macmillan.

Chibnall, S. (1998) *Making Mischief*. Surrey: Fab Press.

Chibnall, S. and J. Petley (eds) (2002) *British Horror Cinema*. London and New York: Routledge.

Chollet, L. (1994) 'The Man Who Wouldn't Go Out : For 20 Years, Gerard Brach Has Occupied a World Scarcely Larger Than His Room--the Prolific Center of a Screenwriter's Universe', in Los Angeles Times. http://articles.latimes.com/1994-12-18/magazine/tm-10438_1_gerard-brach

Ciment, M., M. Perez, R. Tailleur (2005) Interview with Roman Polanski in Cronin, P. (ed.) Roman Polanski Interviews. Jackson: University of Mississipi.

Clarens, C. (1971) *Horror Movies, an Illustrated Survey*. London: Panther.

Clover, C. (1992) *Men, Women and Chainsaws*. Princeton: Princeton University Press.

Coniam, M. (2009) "I needed to earn a living" – Kevin Francis, Tyburn and The Ghoul http://carfaxabbey.blogspot.de/2009/08/i-needed-to-earn-living-kevin-francis.html

Conrich, I. (2007) ´Horrific Films and 1930s British thrillers` in Chibnall, S. and Petley, J (eds) *British Horror Cinema*. London and New York: Routledge.

--- (2009) 'Traditions of the British Horror Film` in Murphy, R (ed.) *The British Cinema Book*. London: Palgrave Macmillan.

Cooper, I. (2011) *Witchfinder General* (Devil's Advocates). Leighton Buzzard: Auteur Press.

--- (2013) 'Manson, Drugs and Black Power: The Counter-Culture Vampire' in *Screening the Undead. Vampires and Zombies in Film and Television*. London: IB Tauris.

Cousins, M. (2005) 'Roman Polanski: The Insider', in Sight and Sound 15:10.

Cowie, S. (2007) Review of The Mummy in *Little Shoppe of Horrors* #19.

Creed, B. (1993) *The Monstrous Feminine: Film, Feminine and Psychoanalysis*. London and New York: Routledge.

Cox, A. (2007) 'A very British cop-out', in The Guardian http://www.guardian.co.uk/film/2007/aug/15/1

Dansby, A. (2002) 'Reed Taps Bowie For Raven', Rolling Stone. http://www.rollingstone.com/music/news/reed-taps-bowie-for-raven-20021108

Delahaye, M., J. Narboni (2005) Interview with Roman Polanski in Cronin, P. (ed.) *Roman Polanski Interviews*. Jackson: University of Mississipi.

Del Valle, D. (2010) "Isabelle, let down your hair!" Yvonne Furneaux interview in *Little Shoppe of Horrors* #24

Del Valle, D., C. Dietrich (undated) 'The Masque of the Red Death', *DVD Drive-In* http://www.dvddrive-in.com/reviews/i-m/masquepremature626465.htm

De Quincey, T. (1827) *On Murder Considered as one of the Fine Arts*. http://supervert.com/elibrary/thomas_de_quincey/on_murder_considered_as_one_of_the_fine_arts

Duguid, M. L. Freeman, K.M. Johnston, K.M. (2012) *Ealing Studios*. London: BFI.

Dyer, R. (1997) 'To Kill and Kill Again', in Sight and Sound. 7:9.

Dyson, J (2004) 'Shadows and Fog', The Guardian. http://www.guardian.co.uk/film/2004/jan/30/2

Earnshaw, T. (2010) *Beating the Devil: The Making of Night of the Demon*. London: Tomahawk Press.

Edelstein, D. (2006) 'Now Playing at your Local Multiplex: Torture Porn', in New York Magazine. http://nymag.com/movies/features/15622/

Fine, M. (2005) *Bloody Sam. The Life and Films of Sam Peckinpah*. New York: Hyperion.

Flanders, J. (2011) *The Invention of Murder: How the Victorians Revelled in Death and Detection and Created Modern Crime*. London: Harper Press.

Flint, D. (2012) 'BBFC REACT TO SELF-SERVING REPORT ON SEX AND VIOLENCE', in *Strange Things Are Happening* http://www.strangethingsarehappening.com/news-bbfc.html

Floyd, N (2005) Review of Wolf Creek, *Time Out*. http://www.timeout.com/london/film/wolf-creek-2005

Gaiman, N. (2004) 'Some Strangeness in the Proportion, The Exquisite Beauties of Edgar Allan Poe' in *Edgar Allan Poe Selected Poems and Tales*. New York: Barnes and Noble.

Gifford, D. (1973) *A Pictorial History of Horror Movies*. London and New York: Hamlyn.

Goodman, J (1995) Introduction, *The Giant Book of Murder*. London: Parragon.

Gritten, D (2010) 'Michael Powell's 'Peeping Tom': the film that killed a career`, in The Telegraph. http://www.telegraph.co.uk/culture/film/7967407/Michael-Powells-Peeping-Tom-the-film-that-killed-a-career.html

Haining, P (1976) *Terror! A History of Horror Illustrations from the Pulp Magazines*. London: Sphere Books.

Hallenbeck, B (2009) 'The Making of Dracula AD 1972 and The Satanic Rites of Dracula', in *Little Shoppe of Horrors* #22

Halliday and Brown (2013) 'Stuart Hall and BBC face compensation claims after sexual abuse case,' The Guardian http://www.guardian.co.uk/uk/2013/may/03/stuart-hall-bbc-compensation-claims

Hardy, P. (ed.) (1985) *The Aurum Encyclopedia of Horror*. London: Aurum.

Hill, D. (1958/9) 'The Face of Horror', in Sight and Sound. V28.n1.

Hitchcock, A. (1974) Address to the Film Society of Lincoln Center. http://www.hitchcockwiki.com/wiki/Film_Comment_(1974)_-_Hitchcock

Hobson Quinn, A. (1941) *Edgar Allan Poe. A Critical Biography*. Baltimore and London: The Johns Hopkins University Press.

Hodel, S (2006) *Black Dahlia Avenger. The True Story*. New York: Harper Collins.

Hodgkinson, W. (2005) 'God, what a terrible film`, in The Guardian http://www.guardian.co.uk/film/2005/mar/11/2

Hunt, L. (1996) Frightmare in Black, A. (ed.) *Necronomicon Volume 1*. London: Creation Books.

--- (1998) British Low Culture, From Safari Suits to Sexploitation. London and New York: Routledge.

--- (2002) 'Necromancy in the UK: witchcraft and the occult in British horror', in Chibnall, S. and Petley, J (eds) *British Horror Cinema*. London and New York: Routledge.

Hutchings, P. (1993) *Hammer and Beyond: The British Horror Film*. Manchester and New York: Manchester University Press.

--- (2002) 'The Amicus House of Horrors', in Chibnall, S. and Petley, J (eds) *British Horror Cinema*. London and New York: Routledge.

--- (2009) '"I'm the Girl He Wants to Kill": The "Women in Peril" Thriller in 1970s British Film and Television', in *Visual Culture in Britain*. 10:1

Jackson, K. (2004) 'Ealing Tragedy', in The Observer. http://www.guardian.co.uk/books/2004/dec/18/featuresreviews.guardianreview7

Jacobson, H. (2008) 'Contest with Nature', in The Guardian http://www.guardian.co.uk/books/2008/jun/14/saturdayreviewsfeatres.guardianreview33

Jeffries, S. (1999) 'The Killer is Too Ugly`, in The Guardian http://www.guardian.co.uk/film/1999/mar/05/features2

Jensen, P. (2008 [1974]) 'Terence Fisher in Conversation` in *Little Shoppe of Horrors* # 21.

Jones, J. (1999), 'The Body in the River`, in The Guardian. http://www.guardian.co.uk/books/1999/aug/14/books.guardianreview8

Jones, N (2012) 'My Favourite Hitchcock: Frenzy', in The Guardian. http://www.guardian.co.uk/film/1999/mar/05/features2

Jones, O (2012) *Chavs: The Demonization of the Working Class*. Verso.

Kermode, M. (2002) 'The British censors and horror cinema`, in Chibnall, S. and Petley, J (eds) *British Horror Cinema*. London and New York: Routledge.

--- (2004) 'Bloody-minded? Dead right', in The Observer. http://www.guardian.co.uk/film/2004/aug/15/features.review1

Kracauer, S. (1947) *From Caligari to Hitler: A Psychological History of the German Horror Film*. Princeton NJ: Princeton University Press.

La Bern, A. (1972) 'Letters to the Editor: Hitchcock´s Frenzy' in The Times. http://www.hitchcockwiki.com/wiki/The_Times_(29/May/1972)_-_Letters_to_the_Editor:_Hitchcock's_%22Frenzy%22n

Leaming, B. (1982) *Polanski. His Life and his Films*. London: Hamish Hamilton.

Leggett, J. (2002) Terence Fisher: Horror, Myth and Religion. New York: Macfarland and Co.

Lewis, P. (2011) 'The Death Junkies: Victorians who lived for murder', in The Daily Mail. http://www.dailymail.co.uk/home/books/article-1346870/The-death-junkies-Victorians-lived-murder-THE-INVENTION-OF-MURDER-BY-JUDITH-FLANDERS.html

Marriner, B. (1992) *A New Century of Sex Killers*. London: True Crime Library.

Mason, R. (2013) 'Children Damaged by "Pornification" of British Society says Diane Abbott', in The Telegraph. http://www.telegraph.co.uk/women/sex/9817376/Children-damaged-by-pornification-of-British-society-says-Diane-Abbott.html

McGilligan, P. (2003) Alfred Hitchcock: A Life in Darkness and Light. Chichester: John Wiley.

McGillivray, D. (2000) Afterword, in English Gothic. London: Reynolds and Hearn.

Meadows, J. (2009) West and Schaffer are in the Doghouse, Io9 http://io9.com/5399399/west-and-schaffer-are-in-the-doghouse

Meikle, D. (2008) 'Raising Hell: Some notes on Night of the Demon', in Little Shoppe of Horrors #21.

Mordern, E. (1990) Medium Cool. The Movies of the 60s. New York: Knopf.

Murphy, R. (1997) They Drive by Night in Time Out Film Guide: Thrillers. London and New York: Penguin.

Naha, E. (1992) The Films of Roger Corman. New York: Arco Publishing.

Newman, K. (1988) Nightmare Movies. New York: Harmony Books.

--- (2002) 'Psycho Thriller, qu´est-ce que cést?' in in Chibnall, S. and Petley, J. (eds) in British Horror Cinema. London and New York: Routledge.

Nutman, P. (2008) 'Scream and Scream Again: The Uncensored History of Amicus Productions', in Little Shoppe of Horrors #20.

O´Keffee, C. (2011) 'Looking Back: the ghost in the living room', in The Psychologist http://www.thepsychologist.org.uk/archive/archive_home.cfm?volumeID=25&editionID=219&ArticleID=2176

Orr, J. (2005) Hitchcock and 20th Century Cinema. London: Wallflower Press.

Orwell, G. (1946) The Decline of the English Murder. http://www.netcharles.com/orwell/essays/decline-of-the-english-murder.htm

Pearson, A. (1994) 'Mary, Mary, Quite Contrary', in The Independent. http://www.independent.co.uk/arts-entertainment/television--mary-mary-quite-contrary-1439331.html

Perks, M. (1995) 'Night of the Living Fred', in The Dark Side #51.

--- (2002) 'A Descent into the Underworld: Death Line', in Chibnall, S. and Petley, J. (eds.) British Horror Cinema. London and New York: Routledge.

Petley, J. (1986) 'The Lost Continent', in Barr, C. (ed.) All Our Yesterdays, 90 Years of British Cinema. London: BFI.

--- (2002) '"A crude source of entertainment for a crude sort of audience"' the British critics and horror cinema', in Chibnall, S. and Petley, J. (eds) British Horror Cinema. London and New York: Routledge.

--- (2012) '"Are we insane?" The Video Nasties Moral Panic,' Recherches sociologiques et anthropologiques http://rsa.revues.org/839

Pidd, H. (2013) 'Ian Brady: What we have learned about the Moors murderer,' in The Guardian. http://www.guardian.co.uk/uk/2013/jun/28/ian-brady-learned-moors-murderer

Pirie, D. (1977) The Vampire Cinema. London: Galley Press.

--- (2007) A New Heritage of Horror. London and New York: IB Tauris

Poe, E.A. (2004) 'Masque of the Red Death', in Edgar Allan Poe Selected Poems and Tales. New York: Barnes and Noble.

Powell, M. (2011 [1992]) Michael Powell on 'Peeping Tom', booklet accompanying Region 2 DVD.

Prince, S. (1998) Sam Peckinpah and the Rise of Ultraviolent Movies. Austin: University of Texas Press.

Rayns, T. (2006) 'What might have been' in Time Out: 1,000 Films to change your life. London: Time Out Guides.

Refn, N.W. (2012) Foreword, booklet accompanying 'Nightbirds' DVD. BFI.

Richards, J (2001) 'Tod Slaughter and the Cinema of Excess', in Richards (ed.) *The Unknown 30s*. London: Macmillan.

Richardson, H. (2012) 'Girls' School Association head condemns "moral abyss"'"in BBC news http://www.bbc.co.uk/news/education-15819369

Rigby, J. (2000) *English Gothic*. London: Reynolds and Hearn.

Risley, M. (2009) James Watkins Interview: Eden Lake. On the Box. http://blog.onthebox.com/2009/01/16/interview-horror-director-james-watkins-talks-about-eden-lake/

Robertson, J.C. (1993) *The Hidden Cinema: British Film Censorship in Action 1913 – 75*. London: Routledge.

Rosen, B (2007) Penny Gaffs. http://vichist.blogspot.de/2007/12/penny-gaffs_03.html accessed April 2013

Saco. J. (2008) 'Revenge of the ASBO: Eden Lake Reviewed', in The Quietus. http://thequietus.com/articles/00416-eden-lake

Sandford, C. (2007) *Roman Polanski*. London: Century.

Sarris, A. (1968) *The American Cinema: Directors and Directions 1929–1968*. New York: Da Capo Press.

Sharp, D. (2004) 'The Strange Case of Dr. Jekyll and Saucy Jack.' http://www.casebook.org/dissertations/rip-alansharp.html

Shelley, M. (1998 [1818]) *Frankenstein*. New York: Oxford University Press.

Silver, A., J. Ursini (2000) 'Terence Fisher: "Horror is my Business"', in *The Horror Film Reader*. New York: Limelight.

Spoto, D. (1983) *The Dark Side of Genius: the Life of Alfred Hitchcock*. London: Frederick Muller.

Stanley, R. (2002) 'Dyling Light: an obituary for the great British horror movie in Chibnall,' in S. and Petley, J. (eds) *British Horror Cinema*. London and New York: Routledge.

Steel, J (2011) Witchfinder General book review, The British Fantasy Society. http://www.britishfantasysociety.co.uk/reviews/witchfinder-general-book-review/

Stevens, C (2013) 'Why does the BBC think violence against women is sexy?' in The Daily Mail http://www.dailymail.co.uk/tvshowbiz/article-2338648/CHRISTOPHER-STEVENS-Why-does-BBC-think-violence-women-sexy.html

Stoker, B (1897) *Dracula*. London and New York: Penguin.

Sweet, M. (2005) *Shepperton Babylon*. London: Faber and Faber.

Thomson, D. (2002) *A Biographical Dictionary of Film: 4th Edition*. London: Little Brown.

Thrower, S. (2007) *Nightmare USA*. London: Fab Press.

--- (2012) Milligan in London, booklet accompanying 'Nightbirds' DVD. BFI.

Tickner, L. (2000) 'Walter Sickert: The Camden Town Murder and Tabloid Crime.'

http://www.tate.org.uk/art/research-publications/camden-town-group/lisa-tickner-walter-sickert-the-camden-town-murder-and-tabloid-crime-r1104355 (accessed June 2013)

Tookey, C. (2008) 'Eden Lake: A great movie (if you can stomach it)', in The Daily Mail http://www.dailymail.co.uk/tvshowbiz/article-1054787/Eden-Lake-A-great-movie-stomach-it.html

--- (2009) 'Antichrist: The man who made this horrible, misogynistic film needs to see a shrink', in The Daily Mail

http://www.dailymail.co.uk/tvshowbiz/reviews/article-1201803/ANTICHRIST-The-man-horrible-misogynistic-film-needs-shrink.html

Török, J-P. (2002 [1961]) 'Horror Pictures' in Ciment, M. and Kardish, L. (eds) *Positif 50 Years*. New York: The Museum of Modern Art.

Trevelyan, J. (1973) *What the Censor Saw*. London: Michael Joseph.

Umland, R. and S. (2006) *Donald Cammell. A Life on the Wild Side*. London: Fab Press.

Weddle, D. (1994) *"If they move, kill 'em!" The Life and Times of Sam Peckinpah*. New York: Grove Press.

Weldon, M.J. (1983) *A Psychotronic Encyclopedia of Film*. London: Plexus.

Whitehouse, M. (1977) *Whatever Happened to Sex?* London: Wayland.

Wilson, C. (1985) *A Criminal History of Mankind*. London: Grafton Books.

INDEX

ALSO AVAILABLE

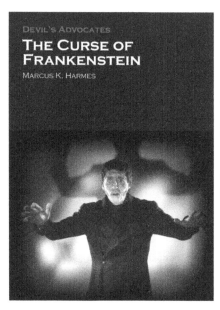

THE CURSE OF FRANKENSTEIN – MARCUS K. HARMES

"Definitively establishes the decades-long impact of The Curse of Frankenstein *on the gothic horror film genre."* Sydney Morning Herald

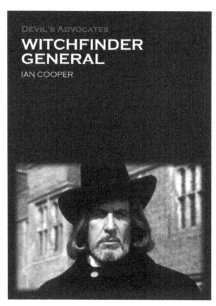

WITCHFINDER GENERAL – IAN COOPER

"I enjoyed it very much; it sets out all the various influences, both before and after the film, and indeed the essence of the film itself, very well indeed." Jonathan Rigby, author of *English Gothic*

Lightning Source UK Ltd.
Milton Keynes UK
UKOW06f0015250316

270865UK00001B/54/P

9 780993 071737